The Progress of the Protestant

The Candle of Reformation is Lighted

We cannot

An eighteenth-century artist, eager to show the the origins of early Protestantism, entitled this imaginary scene "The Candle of Reformation Is Lighted." In it he savagely caricatured the basic split between early Protestantism and medieval Catholicism by showing in the foreground a puffing pope, a water-laving friar, and a devil disguised as a dog, all frantically trying to extinguish the flaming candle which was intended to symbolize the light of Protestant Reformation inquiry. "We cannot blow it out," the three admit. But the artist also revealed at least one great historic split within the ranks of early Protestantism itself: At the center of the long table he showed a sober-faced John Calvin [15] with his face turned away from smiling Martin Luther [16], thus emphasizing the basic disagreement between early Calvinists and Lutherans. It was to one or the other of these two Protestant creeds that most of the early reformers shown here belonged, though a few earlier men were also pictured because of their influence on these two creeds.

The other figures in the engraving, as identified by the engraver's numbers, are [1] sixteenth-century English Calvinist William Perkins, who defended the theology of the early Church of England against orthodox Catholicism; [2] fifteenth-century Bohemian martyr Jerome of Prague, who, together with John Hus of Bohemia [21] and the English theologian John Wycliffe [13], helped to lay the groundwork for the Reformation by

protesting against medieval Roman Catholic excesses; [3] Alsatian reformer Martin Bucer, who tried valiantly during the sixteenth century to make peace among the dissident Protestant groups; [4] the Italian-born Protestant Peter Martyr, who fled first to England, then to Switzerland, in order to escape persecution; [5] Swiss theologian Huldreich Zwingli, one of the chief forerunners of Calvin in Switzerland; [6] John Knox, who founded the Presbyterian Church of Scotland in the Calvinist tradition; [7], [8], [9], [10], and [11] sixteenth-century theologians Zanchius, Bullinger, Occolampadius, Buxtorf, and Bolton, each of whom helped to define the early creeds of Protestantism and to promote their acceptance in one or another country of northern Europe; [12] Dutch reformer Jacobus Arminius, who broke with Calvin over the doctrine of predestination and whose tradition has, at least partly, influenced the Methodists; [14] the co-leader of the Calvinist city of Geneva, Théodore de Bèze; [17] German Lutheran leader Philip Melanchthon, who wrote the great Augsburg Confession that first established the religious and political freedom of early Lutherans; [18] the thirteenth-century Catholic theologian Thomas Aquinas, who, in his concept of God, combined elements of Greek Aristotelianism and of Neoplatonism; [19] the minor German reformer Heinrich Möller; and [20] the sixteenth-century Dutch Protestant theologian Hugo Grotius, who became the "father of international law" through his efforts to make peace among Protestant and Catholic nations.

This little figure of a Protestant, carrying his shield of faith, first appeared in an early edition of John Bunyan's famous seventeenth-century Calvinist tract, the full and trusting title of which was The Pilgrim's Progress from This World to the World Which Is to Come.

The Progress of the Protestant

A Pictorial History from the Early
Reformers to Present-Day Ecumenism

By John Haverstick

Design by Al Corchia, Jr.

Holt, Rinehart and Winston
New York / Chicago / San Francisco

Library of Congress Catalog Card Number: 66-22065 ✓

Translations from the original German of Martin Luther appearing throughout this book are from *Here I Stand,* by Roland Bainton, published by Abingdon Press, and reprinted by permission of the publisher. Much of the basic material appearing on pages 164–165 first appeared under the title *The King and Us* in *Horizon* Magazine, Vol. VII, No. 1, © 1964 by American Heritage Publishing Co., Inc., and appears here by kind permission of Martin W. Robertson, executor of Archie Robertson, author of *The King and Us.* The quotations from Arnold J. Toynbee on pages 244–245 are reprinted with the permission of Charles Scribner's Sons from *Christianity Among the Religions of the World,* by Arnold J. Toynbee; copyright © 1957 The Trustees Under the Will of Waterman T. Hewett. The original version of Dr. Martin Luther King Jr.'s *Letter from a Birmingham Jail* is reprinted by kind permission of the author. The quotations from *He Sent Leanness,* by David Head, are reprinted by permission of The Macmillan Company, New York, and the Epworth Press, London; © The Epworth Press 1959. The quotations from ''They're in a golden world, Jesus'' are from *Are You Running With Me, Jesus?* by Malcolm Boyd. Copyright © 1965 by Malcolm Boyd. Reprinted by permission of Holt, Rinehart and Winston, Inc.
The photograph of Mrs. Mary Baker Eddy's room in Lynn, Mass., appearing on page 192 is reprinted by permission © 1952 The Christian Science Publishing Society; all rights reserved.

First Edition

Designer: Al Corchia, Jr.

8602757

Printed in the United States of America

In the long history of religious thought, men have tried in countless ways to prove the existence of a Spirit of Good, i.e., a God. It is part of the Protestant genius that, always, each of these ways has been— and still remains—open to profound questioning, perhaps most of all by the Protestants themselves. Much of the history of Protestantism is, in fact, largely the history of these questionings and disagreements.

This book is a history of the major actions and beliefs—and the changing concepts— of Protestantism, which, it should be pointed out, is one and only one branch of Christianity. In the following pages the history of Protestantism with all its ups and downs (and with all its limitations) is recorded to the present day, beginning at the time of the Middle Ages and of the dawn of the Renaissance. In an age when the future of man may depend on working together in a common struggle, this history, unvarnished by myth, has perhaps never deserved closer scrutiny.

It is, of course, quite possible that whatever God there may be is laughing at the long Protestant search for him. For, as any thoughtful Protestant would be the first to admit, there have been all too many times in history when, in spite of lip service to basic creeds, the Protestant has wandered so far from the basic precepts of Christianity that he has magnificently deserved a host of uncomplimentary epithets that have often been heaped upon him by followers of other religions.

But it is also possible that God is not laughing, but weeping. For the beliefs and actions of the Protestant have influenced much of the course of Western history and, in fact, of the entire world in many ways wrongly, as well as rightly, as good Protestants would be the first to admit.

Table of Contents

The Progress of the Protestant

The Medieval God

In the mind of medieval man, God often seemed very much like a great medieval emperor. He was a stern, frightening, and frequently merciless divinity who dwelt in a high and very physical heaven, magnificently removed from man. Like many a less ethereal emperor of the time, he was constantly waging war—in his case, against evil as personified by the devil. Like most medieval rulers, too, God seemingly favored pomp and elaborate ceremony—and, sometimes, an almost mathematical theology.

The medieval church taught that God was majestic, eternal, all-powerful, all-knowing. He was both spiritual and physical. He dwelt in a heaven peopled by a multitude of angels. The angels, said the church, served as intermediaries between God and man. So, too, did the souls of departed saints—especially the Virgin Mary, who was venerated because she might intercede with her son on behalf of man. It was the medieval Catholic theologian Thomas Aquinas who best explained the teachings of the church. There were times when Aquinas' thought, which borrowed heavily from Aristotle, could seem overly tortuous in its distinctions, and it inevitably reflected many of the prejudices of the time as well as its limited understanding of science. Nevertheless, his readiness to learn from non-Christian thinking and his fundamentally intellectual approach made him a guide for later Protestants as well as Catholics; and by emphasizing the supremacy of conscience, he gave impetus toward the more personal search for salvation which led to the six-teenth-century Reformation. "The object of the intellect," said Aquinas, "is truth; the object of the will is God."

But the ordinary man of his time knew little of such theology and still less of Thomas Aquinas. He was more impressed by artists who envisioned a medieval hell so physical and so tortuous (left) that before the dawn of the Renaissance, few men cared to challenge the medieval church's claim that it really knew its medieval God as well as it said it did. In the fourteenth and fifteenth centuries, however, there were devout and loyal Catholics who made serious charges against the church. In the fourteenth century, Thomas à Kempis pleaded for spiritual renewal of inner life, and the poet Dante urged a separation of religious and civil powers, thereby hoping to remove the pope from political affairs. Furthermore, the center of economic activity was shifting from the Mediterranean city-states, like Florence and Venice, to the western European nations. Now at the geographic heart of Europe stood the Holy Roman Empire. The four dominating political personalities of the early years of the sixteenth century were Henry VIII of England, Francis I of France, Charles V, who was the Holy Roman Emperor, and Suleiman the Magnificent, who ruled the Turkish Empire and threatened to conquer eastern Europe, including the Germans, Slavs, Italians, and Netherlanders who comprised the Holy Roman Empire. To the north were the three Scandinavian countries—Denmark, Norway, and Sweden—whose economic and cultural ties with Germany were so close that they helped to explain why the Protestant Reformation, beginning in Germany, spread so quickly and successfully to the north.

The way to hell, as pictured by the medieval church, began at the mouth of a terrifying pit where damned souls arrived by the cartload (upper left). Here fiends stripped them naked and pitched them into the two gaping tunnels at left and center. Their bloody remains were carried off for further torture by a monklike assistant (far right), after their bodies had been boiled in oil or partially devoured by a batlike monster (center).

The authority of its popes, said the medieval church, descended from the apostle Peter, here shown with the other eleven apostles in a painting inside the basilica of St. Mark's Church in Venice, in which the dove at center symbolizes the Holy Spirit descending upon them at the time of Pentecost, or the birth of the church. Of the original apostles, Peter was the acknowledged leader, and, according to Matthew 16:19, it was to him that Jesus gave the keys to heaven. To the popular mind, Peter thus became very literally the doorkeeper of heaven.

The Angelic Doctor

There are five great "justifications" or "proofs" of the existence of a God. They are: the so-called "Argument From the First Cause," or the argument that since every effect in the world has its cause (and every actuality its potentiality), the first effect (and first actuality) in the world must have had its cause and its potentiality, which in itself is both cause and effect, *i.e.*, God; the "Cosmological Argument" that since the world and all that is in it seems to have no necessary or absolute existence of its own, an independent existence—*i.e.*, a God—must be implied; the "Teleological Argument" by which, since everything in the world seems to exist according to a certain plan, a planner—God—must be postulated; the "Ontological Argument" that since the concept of God is the highest concept possible to man, and since the highest concept humanly possible must have existence as one attribute, God must exist; and the "Pragmatic Argument" that since God has, it is claimed, been perceived and felt by so many people, he must therefore exist.

To all five of these classic arguments the Protestants owe much of their theology. They also owe far more to historic Greek and Hebrew concepts. To the Greek Platonists and Neoplatonists, as opposed to the Greek Sophists who denied any such thing as "ultimate truth," the supreme ideal was the "Form of Justice," or of "Good," and evil was the complete absence of this Good. To the early Jews, God was a tribal deity who, as they needed him in their exile in Egypt, was finally conceived as a universal and unified spirit bounded by no geographical limits. The Jewish concept of a God, as recorded in the Old Testament, gained new meaning among early Christians with the life and death in the first days of first-century Palestine of a Jew named Jesus, in whose teachings the universal Jewish God was conceived as a loving father, and men, his sons, as brothers to each other. Out of the Jewish concept the Christians brought forth the concept that God is a spirit who was once personified by Jesus. As the Christian church emerged, these early concepts of God were sifted, resifted, and finally in the fourth century codified.

During the Middle Ages, the Roman Catholic Church became the inheritor of the Roman Empire and, by all odds, the most politically powerful organization in the Western world; and during the life of Thomas Aquinas *(right)*, it completed the alliance of Hellenistic logic and biblical faith. It was Aquinas' hope to hold the balance between an anthropomorphic conception of God and an exaggerated transcendence. Faith, he taught, was essential to salvation. So were good acts done under the influence of faith. But fundamental to his teaching was his sharp distinction between faith and human reasoning. Recognizing that the fundamental doctrines of Christianity could not be demonstrated by rationalism, he nevertheless insisted that they were not contrary to it. Indeed, he said, human reason can —up to a point—frequently establish the probability of these fundamental doctrines and answer objections to them. But, he said, doctrines come to men both through the revelation of the Bible and through the consistent teachings of the church. Their province is that of faith, which is based on the will instead of on the intellect.

Aquinas' thought was the perfect culmination of the medieval church's proclaimed assumptions and aspirations. For modern man, many of the most curious features of his thought are the result of his combining a strict Aristotelian logic, an emphasis on the facts of the natural world (cognition necessarily sets out from sense perception) with the traditional medieval cosmology (which, for example, located the dwelling place of the various orders of angels in the ninth and highest heaven). But even during his lifetime Aquinas became a controversial figure. And later, his successors within the medieval church failed to preserve his careful balance. In 1277, some of his writings were condemned by Etienne Tempier, Bishop of Paris. The reason: Aquinas' rationalism, said Tempier, attacked the church's articles of faith.

Thomas Aquinas was the great systematizer of the thought of the medieval church. It was Aquinas who, in his Summa Theologica, *combined Hellenistic logic with biblical faith to prove the "reasonableness" of the medieval church's teachings. Here the Greek philosopher Aristotle stands at his right and the biblical author of the Gospel of John at his left.*

The eucharist or mass of the medieval Catholic Church was based on the Last Supper of Jesus with his apostles (above). St. Thomas Aquinas maintained that the consecration of the bread and wine effected a change in their substance, and that they became the body and blood of Christ, although their outward appearance remained the same.

The doctrine of the eucharist became one of the chief points of disagreement with Rome, though the Reformers themselves held a variety of positions. It was said, however, that the words "hocus-pocus" arose as a parody by the common man on the words "Hoc est Corpus" ("This is my body"), said during celebration of the eucharist.

The Serene Face of Catholicism

To many a medieval man, as well as many a medieval monk and nun, the church, as interpreted by its scholars, left little to be desired. They believed in the church's emphasis on supernaturalism, on immediate miracles, and on a future life in which good would eventually triumph over evil. A life as a member of a religious order, accepting the vows of poverty, chastity, and obedience, was considered a more perfect way to God, and, despite the emphasis on a physical torment to be endured by unrepentant sinners, the faces of devout monks and nuns often shone with a trusting serenity. To prepare their minds and souls for heaven, medieval men gloried in the physical symbolism of the church, stained-glass windows, and colorful vestments; and they observed the church's "sacrament" of baptism, which was one of seven outward signs of inward grace through which the medieval Christian sought spiritual oneness with God.

They confessed their sins to the priest, did penance for their sins as instructed by the church, and, in keeping with the church's teaching that Jesus died so that sinners might be redeemed, they went regularly to mass in physical commemoration of the Last Supper *(above)*. Medieval Christians were taught by the church that Jesus had, by his own suffering, stored up for them in heaven a treasury of merits through which they could hope for forgiveness for their own sins. They were also taught that there was a purgatory in which they would be forced to suffer the cleansing of their souls after death. But, said the medieval church, this time of suffering could be shortened. As time went on, it was the Roman church's system of selling so-called "indulgences" for shortening such time in purgatory that was to call forth protests from men like Martin Luther.

This serene-looking fifteenth-century Augustinian monk and this Augustinian nun had taken vows of poverty, chastity, and obedience, which the medieval church considered the best way to respond to Christ's call to perfection, and whose observance was believed to free the human spirit for complete devotion to God.

The Waldensians, or Vaudois, who broke with the Roman church in 1173, became the first so-called group of "Protestants." For trying to practice pure Christianity, including absolute poverty, in defiance of the sole authority of the Roman church, they were persecuted for centuries.

The Eastern Schism

chanted as their creed, while the Roman Catholics chanted equally assuredly "... Who proceeds from the Father and the Son."

If the Roman branch of the medieval church went to the Bible for its interpretations, so did other branches of the Christian church. And each came away with its own interpretations. The first so-called Protestants were the followers of a French merchant named Peter Waldo, who in 1173 renounced his worldly goods according to his own interpretation of the Bible, and, giving his property to the poor, became the founder of the Waldensians *(previous page)*—a group formed at approximately the same time as the Albigenses who, unlike the Waldensians, believed in the Gnostic concept that Jesus had lived only in semblance, not in reality. But long before that, through seven ecumenical councils dating from A.D. 325, the Eastern Orthodox had been asserting differences which were to result in their final break from the Roman church in 1054—and after they themselves had suffered a division on the part of the Copts of Egypt in A.D. 452 because of their insistence on the humanity as well as the divinity of Jesus, while the Copts believed solely in his divinity.

The Orthodox had had minor differences with the Roman church at first. The Orthodox believed in making the sign of the cross to the right shoulder first, for example. They also believed in a slightly different method of tonsuring monks. But these minor differences had been symptomatic of far greater ones. The great basic danger in Roman Catholicism, they had argued, lay in a Roman emphasis on Jesus which, in effect, made him equal to God. Thus, they insisted, the medieval church had perverted the original teachings of Jesus himself. For this reason they insisted that, according to Jesus himself, the Holy Spirit proceeded only from God, not from Jesus. "I believe in the Holy Spirit, the Lord, the Giver of Life, Who proceeds from the Father," they

The Orthodox were, in fact, sticklers for tradition. Catholicism, they pointed out, had perverted original Christianity in other ways. There is, said the Orthodox—in a logical progression from their concept of the Holy Spirit—not just *one* holy, catholic, and apostolic church, nor did the Bible say there should be. One church, they argued, meant one body of people who are one in faith, in discipline, and in type of government, but not necessarily in one united church. After the descent of the Holy Spirit on the apostles at Pentecost, they pointed out, numerous local Christian churches had been founded by the apostles, each of whom, despite the Roman belief in Peter's preeminence, passed his authority on from Jesus to different successors. Said the Orthodox: All these successors, or bishops, were equal in power, thereby undermining one of the basic pillars of Roman theology, the authority of the pope. Authority said the Orthodox, did not rest in one person but instead in a body of bishops—all of whose opinions should carry equal weight. They also discredited the Roman concepts of indulgences and they completely excluded from their doctrines any belief in the existence of a purgatory after death. Unlike the Roman church, they did not withhold the cup from the laity during mass; and in confession the role of the Orthodox priest was as witness and counselor, rather than as judge—in denial of a right which the clergy had assumed within the Roman church. Furthermore, the Eastern Orthodox, who spread through the Slavic nations after the ninth century (including the Bohemia of the later John Hus, *pages 10-11),* conferred holy orders on married as well as unmarried men and conducted their services in the indigenous languages of the countries instead of in the Latin of the Roman church.

Early Christendom was split into two halves in 1054, when the Eastern Orthodox Church broke off officially from medieval Catholicism. In this old tableau, Michael Cerularius, the "quarrelsome Patriarch" of Constantinople, is arrested in his palace (left) and forced into exile during the split with the Roman church.

Baptism, believed the Eastern Orthodox, should be observed by immersion, because it had thus been observed in the Bible. Furthermore, contrary to Roman belief, a child was confirmed in the church immediately following baptism. Eastern Orthodox priests also make the sign of the cross from head to right shoulder first—as contrasted with the Roman left shoulder first—because, in strict interpretation of the Bible, Jesus is said to sit at the right hand of God. As a result of different concepts regarding the Trinity, there have also been factions within the Eastern church which insist that the sign of the cross is rightfully made only with two fingers, and that only two instead of three "Amens" should follow the singing of the "Gloria."

Hot-Tempered John

In England, good, puckish, white-haired John Wycliffe, a hot-tempered Oxford University don, became one of the first theologians to combat the medieval church's practice of keeping the common man ignorant of the Bible, on which the church based its beliefs. In 1379, he began to translate the New Testament into English. Give the people the Bible, he said. "Then and only then will they stir themselves on the issue of their freedom and education and act on it religiously, politically, and socially." Since there were no printing presses in his day, he circulated Bible verses in the people's own language to the peasants of the countryside through a group of itinerant "poor preachers," so-called because they were neither instructed nor ordained by the church itself.

For his pains, Wycliffe's enemies dubbed him, in the same Old English in which he had translated the Bible, "Dr. Wicked-Believe," "Mr. Lying Glutton," and "Devells Instrument." But by adroitly scurrying back and forth from Roman pope to English king for protection, he managed, unlike two of his followers (*upper right*), to escape execution as a heretic. He loudly denounced the practices of selling indulgences and of excessive veneration of saints, challenged the absolute authority of the pope, and disputed the belief that the sacrament of the bread and wine became the actual body of Christ in the celebration of the Roman Catholic mass. In short, he said, the church should care less for institutionalism and more for imitating the real humility and poverty of Jesus.

Old "Dr. Wicked-Believe" John Wycliffe lived to the white-bearded age of sixty-four. When his physician told him early in life that he was about to die from a sudden sickness, a delegation of Catholic friars called at his Oxford rooms, predicted he would surely go to hell as a heretic. He listened to them cheerfully, then disappointed the entire group by recovering his health.

Czech schoolteacher John Hus carried Wycliffe's teachings to Bohemia. When he was burned at the stake as a heretic on July 6, 1415 (upper right center), his death caused a nationwide popular rebellion against the rule of the medieval church in Bohemia, where indulgences were being granted for supporting national political causes favored by the church. In the Czech language Hus's name meant "goose." According to legend his last words were: "You are now going to burn a goose, but in a century you will have a swan which you can neither boil nor harm." Later Protestants decided the "swan" referred to Martin Luther.

Jerome of Prague was something of a coward. A noisy follower of Wycliffe and Hus, he at first recanted his "heresy" when he was tortured in the stocks (left). Later he rescinded his own recantation, died at the stake in 1416. On the paper miter which was mockingly placed on John Hus's head at his execution (above), his taunters wrote: "The Ringleader of the Heretics."

Before the days of printing, John Wycliffe sent out "poor preachers" (above right), who were also known as "Lollards," to read Bible stories to the common people throughout the English countryside. Their roadside listeners, unable to read for themselves, memorized passages, then repeated them to their neighbors.

In 1428, forty-four years after his death, John Wycliffe's bones were dug up and burned. His ashes were thrown into the River Swift in an attempt by the medieval church to stamp out his "unsavory" memory.

"Listen to Me!"

In 1482, an Italian monk named Girolamo Savonarola entered the monastery of St. Mark's in Florence. In the monastery he saw, or thought he saw, a vision of a sword hanging from heaven. He took it to mean he should reform the medieval church's ways. "Listen to me, . . . O Florence," he began to preach in the streets, ". . . you are sitting by the rivers of your sins." In 1497, he staged a public holocaust which became known as "The Burning of the Vanities." For the occasion he persuaded members of the best Florentine families to don the garb of monks and nuns and to toss clothing, books, and worldly works of art—including a few pleasantly lusty portraits—into the bonfire. Then he set up a strict, moralistic government in Florence, which he called a "City of God." But he ran afoul of Pope Alexander VI, particularly for favoring the invading King of France, Charles VIII, over Alexander's own political power. He was tortured, hanged, and his body burned, on May 23, 1498.

Girolamo Savonarola had a flair for theatrics that made him a favorite subject of the portrait painters of his time (right). Once Pope Alexander VI tried to flatter him into obedience by offering him a cardinalcy. "A red hat?" Savonarola retorted. "I want a hat of blood." He was hanged, then burned (below) in the public square of Florence as a warning to all who denied the Pope's spiritual—and political—supremacy.

The Unholy See of Leo X

Of Pope Leo X, a later Catholic historian wrote, "He was one of the most severe trials to which God ever subjected his church."

Leo X, who became pope in 1513, was a fat, sleek member of the powerful Italian Medici family. In appearance *(left)*, he resembled a well-fed Persian cat. His pet project was the refurbishing of St. Peter's Church in Rome—which showed excellent, if expensive, taste. As a statesman he was indolent. As a churchman he rarely managed to exhibit the thinnest streak of piety. To raise funds for his pet project—and for the church's perennial battle with the Turks—he openly and unscrupulously sold bishoprics and cardinalcies to the highest bidder. Some of his "appointees" could not even read their native languages, let alone the Latin texts of the church. Others never saw or cared to see the diocese they ruled. In more than one instance his "bishops" turned out to be children.

Under leaders like Leo, crime and corruption flourished among the priests, who were exempted by the church from civil law. So did fee-grabbing and a crass system of "divine bookkeeping," specifying the prices to be paid for the church's services. Many clergy administered rites of baptism, marriage, confession, extreme unction, less for their real purpose than for excuse to fill the church's coffers and their own pockets.

Like at least one of his predecessors *(opposite page)*, Leo failed to recognize the resentment he was causing, especially in the already highly taxed German states. Instead, he tried to collect more money by setting exact scales of values—both financial and spiritual—on the church's holy relics. Duke Frederick the Wise of Saxony, for example, owned a collection of 19,013 such relics. Among these were a piece of cloth said to have come from the swaddling clothes of the infant Jesus, thirteen pieces of wood from the manger, a wisp of straw from the stable, one strand of Jesus' beard, and a crumb of bread supposedly "served" at the Last Supper. According to Leo's mathematics, the value of this collection alone, when reckoned by the wages of sin, could reduce a soul's time in purgatory by exactly 1,902,202 years, plus 270 days. In 1517, Leo made his greatest mistake. He dispatched priests and monks into almost every corner of Europe, including Frederick the Wise's Saxony. Their duty was to sell indulgences at prescribed amounts of money.

The originals of these four pro-Protestant cartoons, since copied and exaggerated many times, were quite blatantly intended to inflame public opinion against the excesses of the medieval church during pre-Reformation days. At Canossa, in 1074, Henry IV of Germany was forced to bow so low to Pope Gregory VII that memory of the insult still rankled sixteenth-century Germans. During the papacy of Leo X, crude drawings of Gregory putting his foot on Henry's neck were widely circulated. The drawing at lower right, showing a monk carrying a woman in a bale of hay, was entitled "The Provisioning of the Cloister." It contained enough truth to make more than one monk wince. So did the pictures showing a fool wearing a cardinal's hat and the pope as an ass playing bagpipes (right).

15

A Benign-Looking Monk Becomes the Scapegoat

Johann Tetzel was an able salesman. He was also something of a ham actor. Armed with price lists of the exact monetary values of indulgences for the forgiveness of an entire roster of sins, he went from town to town, planting a cross in the market place and setting up his booth, then crying in bad verse:

"As soon as the coin in the coffer rings,
The soul from purgatory springs."

He became particularly adept at pretending to mimic the voices of those departed souls whose relatives happened to be present in the crowd of prospective buyers. "Have pity on us," he would whine, "for we are in most grievous pains and torments from which you may redeem us with a little alms. . . ." Tetzel's success was also his undoing. It was his misfortune to be assigned by Leo X to sell indulgences near the town of Wittenberg, where the monk Martin Luther taught a Bible course at the university. Provoked by Tetzel's sales, as well as by other excesses of the church, Luther published his "Ninety-Five Theses," thus heralding the Protestant Reformation. Convinced that the entire affair was his own personal fault, the bewildered Tetzel retired in chagrin to a nearby monastery. Two years later he died in seclusion, though Luther himself, hoping to ease the poor scapegoat's feelings, wrote him, "Don't take it too hard. You didn't start this racket. The child had another father."

Sales of indulgences sometimes suffered from cartoons like these. At left, below, the Protestant cartoonists tried to show that the possibility of forgiveness through Christ outweighs the possibility of forgiveness through papal indulgences.

The pope's arrogance in accepting obeisance from a German emperor (below center) is contrasted with Christ's humility as he washes the feet of his disciples (below right).

In his sales booth, round-faced Johann Tetzel kept an exact price list of standard fees for indulgences and a cash box (left) ready for receipts. To handle the crowds of indulgence buyers outside Wittenberg (top left), he was forced to have new coins minted on the spot (top right).

Johannes Tetzel, von Leipzig
S.S. Theol. Doctor und Professor, ein Bruder
des Dominicaner Ordens, Ketzer Meister, und

The Lutheran Revolt

A contemporary German artist was so moved by the enormity of the event when, on October 31, or the eve of All Saints' Day in 1517, Martin Luther, according to legend, posted his "Ninety-Five Theses" against medieval Christianity on the doors of Castle Church in the town of Wittenberg, Saxony, that he recorded the scene in monumental proportions (*right*). Actually, there is doubt that Luther really posted the theses. But there is no doubt that he wrote them in Latin, intending them primarily for scholars. It was Saxon printers who, impatient with the excesses of the church and hoping to publicize its defects throughout the German states, circulated German-language copies of the document and catapulted Luther —against his will—into the leadership of the Reformation.

In the theses, Luther argued against the practice of selling "indulgences." He said he doubted that the amount of time a really sincere Christian should suffer in purgatory lay within the church's judgment, and he suggested that the money paid might be put to better use in feeding the poor. Indulgences, he argued, might actually do more harm than good by lulling an unrepentant sinner into a false sense of security. Besides, he later asked —thus bringing the whole matter down to earth—who knows but that a man's present, not future, life might be the real purgatory, or testing place, of a man's soul?

The quill pen with which Martin Luther wrote his "Ninety-Five Theses" seemed so powerful to one awe-struck artist that its tip here pierces the ears of a lion symbolizing Pope Leo X, then topples the crown from the head of Holy Roman Emperor Charles V (center). At far right, the Bible symbolically sheds light on the true Jesus while two gowned scholars, one a medieval Catholic theologian, the other a humanist of the Renaissance, slink away (foreground) with the burning goose that symbolized the martyr John Hus. For the benefit of his German audience, the artist translated Luther's original Latin into German on the doors of Castle Church.

A Problem for Erasmus

The humanist scholar Erasmus summed up the Protestant Reformation from a lofty height. It had, he said, with particular reference to Luther's marriage, "started out like a tragedy, but ended as all comedies do—in a wedding." "Two crimes Luther has committed," he also announced, with a twinkle in his eye. "He has attacked the crown of the pope and the bellies of the monks."

Erasmus had written several sharp criticisms of the Roman church, exposing the need for reform. He also produced his own translation of the Bible in the hope that it would be read, as he put it, "not only by Scots and Irishmen but also by Turks and Saracens." But the little Dutch scholar was a thinker, a man of contemplation, not of action, who was exceedingly adept at straddling the fence of any intellectual argument. He was quite sure he did not want to become martyr either to Catholicism or to Protestantism. When Luther's books were burned by the church, he knew he would soon be forced to choose between exile or an unwanted martyrdom. Hastily, he took up residence in Switzerland, where he remained the rest of his life. Safely away from the action, he then sagely—and frostily—announced, "I will put up with this [Catholic] Church until I shall see a better."

The Dutch scholar Erasmus personified the spirit of the Renaissance, in which, as symbolically shown in the famous drawing at upper left, medieval man thrust his head through the stars into the universe, looking for new horizons of learning. But it was also an age symbolized by Albrecht Dürer's "Four Horsemen of the Apocalypse" (right), charging ahead but uncertain of their destiny. It was the age of Copernicus, of Galileo, Michelangelo, and Columbus—of invention, and of search for beauty as well as truth. It was equally an age of emerging nationalism, when rulers hoped to break with the political power of the Roman church—a fact which immeasurably helped Luther to achieve his ends. In turn, Luther helped the national states to centralize their own power and to turn from a feudal to a primitive capitalist economy.

Stout Martin Luther

Martin Luther was a big, powerfully built man with piercing eyes and an ample jaw. At one moment he could be frighteningly bombastic —the next, pathetically gentle and contrite. He was quick-tempered but hugely affable. He was also coarse. "The only portion of the human anatomy which the pope has had to leave uncontrolled," he once remarked, "is the hind end."

As a monk, Luther suffered from an enormous sense of guilt and inadequacy—so much so that some scholars have ascribed his fits of acute depression to attacks of epilepsy. In the monastery he fasted more than the rule required, writhed in pain during prayer, wracked his brains in confession to recollect every possible sin, recognized or unrecognized, he might have committed. A kindly confessor once admonished him, "I think [sins] are your meat and drink. . . . Look here, if you expect Christ to forgive you, come in with something to forgive—parricide, blasphemy, adultery— instead of all these peccadilloes." He fainted in awe when he officiated at his first mass. On a visit to Rome he climbed Pilate's staircase on his hands and knees, kissing each step on the way and saying a *Pater Noster* for the soul of his grandfather, all the while regretting that his father was not yet dead so that he could pray for his soul, too. But at the top step he stood up and asked desperately, "Who knows whether it is so?"

Back in the monastery he fixed his mind on the terrifying possibility that whatever God there may be is cruel and unjust. It was so frightening a thought that it changed his entire concept of religion. The devil, he now decided, is precisely man's own doubt and despair concerning the real and ultimate goodness of God. God is a paradox—a God who makes man suffer, who hides his power in weakness, his mercy in anger. In fact, he began to argue, evil men go unpunished, while God first damns—makes suffer—only those whom he most wants to save—*i.e.,* bring into unity with himself. God, he said, is even in hell. Being a sinner, mere man can trust only in the divine purpose.

Luther believed literally in gnomes and elves as well as in a personal God and a personal devil. Massively logical in his medieval way, he shattered the structures of the medieval church, gave his own name to a new creed of Protestantism, translated the Bible into a German language so clear that, like the English King James Version, it remains one of the

In his mid-fifties, a stout Martin Luther stood for this portrait. "They are," he complained grandly, "trying to make me into a fixed star. I am an irregular planet." The goose shown beside him appeared frequently in portraits of scholars of the time. It supplied the writing quill in the inkstand at left rear.

great masterpieces of literature. He also composed a score of hymns, among them "A Mighty Fortress Is Our God," one line of which cries out Luther's basic belief: "By our own strength is nothing won."

His basic doctrine lay in his belief in "justification by faith." Man, he argued, has no right to expect mercy from God; he can only have faith—or hope—in God's grace. On this premise he built the distinctively Lutheran belief that only faith, not acts of goodness or so-called "good works," saves men. Without faith, he decided, good works are "idle, damnable sins." The doctrine was, of course, molded by his own reaction against the excessive practices of indulgence-selling and ritualistic salvation as prescribed by the medieval church. But it has left its stamp on Lutheranism to this day, prompting some modern Lutherans to refuse to stand up even to sing a hymn for fear the physical act of rising might be interpreted as taking precedence over a more inactive—albeit sedentary—trust.

Luther's other basic tenets, the famous doctrines of "the open Bible" and of "the priesthood of all believers," also stemmed from his reaction against the excessive practices of the medieval church. Since the church had usurped for its clergy complete authority for interpreting Christianity, the solution to this problem, Luther decided, lay in every man's right to interpret the Bible for himself. What he actually meant was "freedom of conscience" for each individual—and to this day Lutherans emphasize this basic right by assigning an important role to laity—not solely clergy—in churchly affairs.

But Luther was still a medieval man, and on several basic theological points he remained so unyieldingly medieval that he stands in real disagreement with the subsequent trends of Protestantism. With massive medieval logic he argued, for example, that the bread and wine of the mass become the "real" body of Christ during the celebration of the mass. In the midst of the Reformation, this belief was to cause a split between the Lutherans and almost all other Protestants. Of this firm belief in "consubstantiation" he once argued bombastically, "Christ is present where he wills to be, and we are not to think of him in heaven 'like a stork in a nest.' "

His second important disagreement was equally historic. He tended to respect the power of princes more than did other rising creeds—a belief which for centuries heaped upon European Lutheranism the scorn of the more democratic Calvinists. The immediate sixteenth-century result of this tenet was that it turned many a German peasant from Lutheranism to the more democratic Calvinism and Anabaptism already springing up around them —and to revolt against the German princes who, glad for a chance to escape papal taxes, backed Luther. In the greatest mistake of his life, Luther took the side of these princes. "Let everyone who can," he counseled them against the peasants, "smite, slay, and stab, secretly or openly, remembering that nothing can be more poisonous, hurtful, or devilish than a rebel." That advice, as much as his theology (and his notable anti-Semitism), marked Luther—in spite of his open break with the Roman church—as a medieval man.

An aging Luther wrings his hands as he pleads for his fellow reformers.

The Great Reforms

To some Protestants the obvious reforms brought about by Luther seemed almost as important as the deeper, less visible ones. Monasteries were abolished. So were fast days. Vestments were no longer required for the clergy. Tonsured monks let their hair grow. Priests married, including Luther himself.

But there were far deeper reforms. No longer were clergy exempted from punishment by civil law. The buying of indulgences was banned. First in Saxony, later throughout all Protestant Germany, the mass was said in German so the communicants could understand its meaning. Not only the bread but also, breaking tradition, the wine were given to communicants—an innovation so frightening to some that more than one communicant dropped the cup.

Other than the mass itself, Luther recognized the sacrament of baptism—but only because he believed it had been instituted by Jesus. The sacrament of penance he considered perhaps admissible, but only when a sinner was truly remorseful. Lutherans also were quite willing to recognize ordination as a sacrament. The result was that the great majority of Protestants, except for the Lutherans and the Anglo-Catholics who arose in England in the nineteenth century, were never again to recognize five sacraments of the medieval church: penance, confirmation, marriage, ordination, and extreme unction.

Most important of all Luther's reforms was his defense of the laity's rights, equal to those of the clergy, to interpret for themselves their own concepts of God, based on their own interpretations of the Bible. This policy of the so-called "open" Bible became so widely practiced that it split the ranks of Protestantism throughout Europe, raising individualist belief to an unprecedented level in the wake of the Middle Ages.

"Good heavens!" exclaimed Luther. "Will our Wittenbergers give wives to monks? They won't give one to me." But at forty-one (below left), he married the former nun Katharina von Bora (right), though all his friends protested, "For heaven's sake, not this one!" Later, when he had been cartooned (left) carting a host of former priests away from their vows of chastity, he happily preached in a sermon that "there is no estate to which the devil is so opposed as to marriage."

Eyn Sermon von k̍ Wucher
D.   N̍.
L.

keßall / odder giß ßinß

Luther's seal (above) bore a white rose for faith, surmounted by a black cross for mortification. His sermon against usury was printed and published with a satirical title page (left) showing a bespectacled Scotsman. It was a Lutheran reform attempt that proved notably unsuccessful, just as it had already proved for Catholics. He hoped to combat the rising commercialism that was rapidly replacing Germany's agrarian economy. He argued that only old men and women who were no longer able to work could in good Christian conscience lend money for interest, and then at rates of no more than five per cent.

The fifteenth-century Bohemian martyr John Hus stands back to back with Luther (left) in this sixteenth-century engraving of the Lutheran reform of the Catholic mass. The scene symbolized Lutheran debt to the earlier Hussites in offering both wine and bread to the communicants. One former priest, newly turned Protestant, was so enchanted with the new ruling that vestments need not be worn by clergy that he appeared at the altar with a feather in his beret.

The Burning of the Papal Bull

To show the new emphasis on the sermon, or the "Word of God," as contrasted to the ritualism of the Roman Catholic sacraments, the pulpits in some Protestant churches were raised to the height of the altar. But, in contrast to the emerging Calvinists, the Lutheran service remained chiefly a liturgical one, based on the mass of the Roman church. Its minister still faced the altar when leading the congregation in communication with God, and faced the congregation when representing God in communication with the people. Here a youthful Luther preaches from the high pulpit of the City Church in Wittenberg.

"The whole row," Leo X first announced, "is due to the jealousy of the monks." Then he changed his mind. "Luther," he soon announced, "is a drunken German." After that, he spent almost three years futilely trying to strengthen his hold on the rebellious German princes. On June 15, 1520, he finally issued his papal "bull," or official reply, to Luther's "Ninety-Five Theses."

"Arise, O Lord . . ." he began, "a wild boar has invaded thy vineyard." As an official salutation, this seemed particularly infuriating to the emerging Lutherans, since Leo had written it at the papal hunting lodge and seemed to be envisioning the impending Reformation in terms of the sport at hand. Later in the bull, however, Leo asked himself, "As for Martin, . . . what office of paternal love have we omitted in order to recall him from his errors? . . ."

In the public squares of German cities, Lutheran writings were already being consigned to bonfires. "I rejoice to suffer in so noble a cause," Luther announced, almost cheerfully. But on December 10, 1520, shortly after the bull had been delivered to him, he and his fellow professor at Wittenberg, Philip Melanchthon, built their own bonfire. For the occasion a crowd of university students gathered at Elster Gate (*right*). As the students watched, Luther tossed various ecclesiastical papers and books into the fire, following them with a copy of the bull itself. The flames shot up; the students cheered and sang the "Te Deum." Then everybody paraded through the streets, carrying above their heads another copy of the bull and a copy of a papal indulgence, each pierced by the tip of a sword.

In short time, Leo finally issued his formal bull of excommunication against Luther.

On December 10, 1520, Luther burned the papal bull while university students watched and cheered. "Since they have burned my books, I burn theirs," he said to justify his act.

This emblem appeared on the title page of a satire written by a Lutheran against Leo X's papal bull. A tiny head of a fiend appeared on the shield beneath the papal tiara.

Luther, according to legend, once threw an inkwell at the devil when he believed he had appeared to him in person. But usually he merely announced, on such occasions, "I am baptized," convinced that the rite had the necessary power to ward off Lucifer.

"I Will Not Recant!"

Cardinal Cajetan was an honest, decent, scholarly man. It was his job to bring Luther back into the fold. On October 12, 1518, having been summoned to Augsburg by Cajetan, Luther prostrated himself before him. In a fatherly gesture, Cajetan raised him to his feet, then asked him to recant his errors.

Where, asked Luther, was he in error?

The chief one, said Cajetan, was Luther's denial of the church's belief that Christ had by his suffering and example stored up a "treasury of merits" toward forgiveness which could be distributed to repentant sinners by the sale of papal indulgences. He thumbed through the bull *Unigenitus,* issued by Pope Clement VI in 1343. Here, he pointed out, was an actual record of the church's decision that the merits of Christ had become a treasury for exactly such indulgences.

Luther disagreed.

"My son," explained Cajetan, ". . . I am ready to reconcile you with the Roman church." The authority to interpret the Bible lay, he insisted, in the popes.

"The pope," argued Luther, "abuses Scripture. I deny that he is above the Scripture." The reply angered Cajetan. "Revoca! [Recant!]" he suddenly bellowed in the Latin of the church. But Luther refused.

The Augsburg hearing was the first of three. At Leipzig in 1519, Luther faced eminent theologian Johann Eck. "Are you the only one that knows anything?" Eck taunted him. "Except for you, is all the church in error?" The question frightened Luther, since, as his one-time friend Eck knew, he often feared he was being led on by the devil.

At Worms, on April 16, 1521, Luther had to face the Holy Roman Emperor, Charles V, who had come to execute the papal order of excommunication against him. "That fellow," Charles had bragged, "will never make a heretic of me."

But Luther stood firm. According to some reports, he said, "Here I stand, I cannot do otherwise," but the words do not appear in the most reliable records of the hearing. In replying to Charles's accusations. he said, by record, "Unless I am convicted by Scripture and plain reason—I do not accept the authority of popes and councils, for they have contradicted each other—my conscience is captive to the Word of God. I cannot and I will not recant anything, for to go against conscience is neither right nor safe. God help me. Amen."

A dubious Duke George (below center), who had provided the hall for the occasion, looked on as Luther debated eminent theologian Johann Eck at Leipzig in 1519. Fat, slow-witted George, who could never be quite sure that nothing happened when "the coin in the coffer rings," finally called a halt to the proceedings after eighteen days of debate, mostly because he needed to take over the assembly hall in order to "mend political fences" with his neighboring nobility.

Frail Philip Melanchthon was publicly denounced at the Leipzig disputations by Johann Eck (below) for aiding Luther who, with tears in his eyes, then pleaded Melanchthon's sincerity.

Bland-faced John Frederick of Saxony, who was soon to cut as corpulent a figure in court regalia as did Duke George, was only sixteen years old at the time of the Leipzig disputations, but they influenced him to be one of Luther's staunchest supporters all his life.

Cardinal Cajetan (right) chuckled at one point during his inquiry into Luther's "heresies," later flew into a rage and told Luther to stay out of his sight until he could recant unconditionally.

Theologian Johann Eck (far right) had been an old friend of Luther. But he openly and craftily baited him at Leipzig, later boasted he had turned the inquiry into a personal triumph for himself.

VERA IMAGO IOHANNIS ECCII
THEOLOGIÆ   D. ÆTATIS
SVÆ   XLIII

31

"The Seven-Headed Monster"

Late in his life Luther pleaded, "I beg that my name be not mentioned and that people be called, not Lutherans but Christians. What is Luther? The doctrine is not mine, nor have I been crucified for anyone. . . . Why should I, a miserable bag of worms, give my meaningless name to Christ's children?" The name had first been used against him in scorn by Leo, and had stuck. It was to prove one of the least offensive names he and his followers were to be called.

Name-calling was a colorful part of all medieval-Renaissance disputation. It was the style of the times. A papal emissary labeled him ". . . a child of Satan, son of perdition, scrofulous sheep, and tare in the vineyard." To other critics he was a "leper with a brain of brass and a nose of iron," a "serpent," a "notorious heretic," a "son of iniquity," a "scabby sheep," and "this devil in the habit of a monk."

But Luther himself was rarely outdone. Cardinal Cajetan, he once announced, was no more fit to understand the Lutheran arguments than a "jackass to produce music on a harp." "The monks," he jovially pontificated, "are the fleas on God Almighty's fur coat." Of Leo, he gibed, "Germany is the pope's pig. That is why we have to give him so much bacon and sausages." Like his enemies, he invoked the devil: "I say," he once announced, raucously, "the pope is the . . . apostle of the devil." Leo, he argued, should stand up "like any other stinking sinner" to receive communion. Of the veneration of saints and holy relics, he was known to inquire sweetly, "And how does it happen that eighteen apostles are buried in Germany when Christ had only twelve?"

The anti-Luther cartoon at right, showing him as a monster with seven heads, appeared when he was old and cantankerous—and still equal to the occasion. "I must be invincible," he said proudly, when he saw it, "because they cannot overcome me when I have only one [head]."

The devil calls the tune for Luther in this sixteenth-century pro-Catholic cartoon.

Luther, as caricatured by his enemies, was a monster of seven heads, ridiculing him, from left to right, as a sorcerer, a winking and insincere monk in cowl, a turbaned infidel, an errant theologian, a fanatic with bees in his hair, a visiting clown, and a latter-day Barabbas.

The "Open" Bible

Luther tackled the job of translating the Bible into German in the way he went about every other job—vociferously. He moaned loudly to his students that Job kept sitting in sackcloth and ashes all the time. Of Moses he complained, *"Ach, Gott!* It is so hard to make these Hebrew prophets speak German!" The Epistle of St. James, he decided, is "a letter of straw" and the Book of Esther "a heathen naughtiness." The Book of Revelation, he announced, is untrustworthy: "A revelation," he said pompously, "should be revealing." In his translation of Revelation, he did his best to compare the "scarlet woman," or "whore," of Babylon *(above)* with the Roman popes.

He was not above translating a text to suit his own purposes. Remembering his efforts as a monk to ferret out every one of his own sins during confession, he insisted on rendering the phrase "secret sins" as "unrecognized sins." To his dying day he defended his translation of the famous line "justification by faith" in Romans 3:28 as "justification by faith *alone*." The extra word, he argued, was entirely necessary to the full meaning of the text. He translated the prayer which usually reads, "So teach us to number our days that we may apply our hearts unto wisdom," as "Teach us to reflect on death that we may be wise." It was a good thing, he explained, to keep the reader's mind on death. Though the words of Jesus could not properly appear until the New Testament, he cavalierly put them into the mouths of Old Testament prophets. His purpose, he explained, was to stress the relation-

ship between the coming Jesus and the prior prophets. By the same reasoning, he insisted on translating the Old Testament epithet, "Deliverer of Israel," as the New Testament's "Savior."

If he was arbitrary, he exhibited a boundless passion for detail. He prowled around slaughter houses, inquired of the butcher and of Jewish scholars the correct German names of the anatomy to describe the sacrificial animals in the Book of Leviticus. He consulted Frederick the Wise's collection of jewels to make sure he gave the gems mentioned in the Bible, especially in the Book of Revelation, the proper German names so his readers would recognize them. It took him the better part of his life to achieve a translation that suited him—and that, in addition, helped create the modern German language. The common people loved it.

Poor, Pale Philip

By 1530 Luther was so well thought of by German princes who had freed themselves economically as well as ecclesiastically from Catholicism that saintly pictures like this one, with a dove above his head, were sold as souvenirs, while cartoons like the one below, in which he leads a beneficent Christ (in cart at extreme right) in triumphal Protestant procession, were circulated throughout the German countryside.

Nobody tried harder to heal the breach between the Lutherans and the Catholics than Philip Melanchthon. Philip was a far better scholar than Luther, and he worried about fine points of theology involved in the Reformation. He questioned, for example, Luther's sweeping argument that faith superseded good works. Luther told him, "A cow does not get to heaven by giving milk, but that is what she is made for," thus, as far as Luther was concerned, settling the matter once and for all. Once Luther taunted him, "Sin for all you are worth [Philip]. God can forgive only a lusty sinner." But Melanchthon wanted to betray neither his friend nor Catholicism. So he worried. In 1530, his troubles came to a head. Luther had been taken to Wartburg Castle to protect him from possible violence. Now Philip found himself the temporary leader of the Reformation. Caught in a dilemma, he sat down and burst into tears. Then he drew up the Augsburg Confession, which he presented to Holy Roman Emperor Charles V *(next page)*. In it he summarized for the first time the Lutheran reforms, hoping thereby to effect a reconciliation between the two opposing faiths. Instead, he succeeded only in uniting the staunchly rebellious Lutherans against the Catholics.

Philip Melanchthon was anemic, had a nervous hitch in his shoulder, and stammered. This portrait is one of the few showing him smiling. When Luther was asked how he imagined the apostle Paul had looked, he teased Philip, "I think he was a scrawny shrimp like Melanchthon."

The Augsburg Confession

On a hot June day in 1530, Holy Roman Emperor Charles V, dressed in full regalia, approached the gates of the city of Augsburg. He came as representative of the Roman Catholic Church to meet with the rebellious German Lutheran princes. At the gate he was met by John of Saxony, who walked at the head of the procession, carrying Charles's shining sword. Behind John walked the Archbishop of Mainz, the Bishop of Cologne, King Ferdinand of Austria, finally the emperor himself. When they reached the great Augsburg cathedral, Charles knelt before the altar. The new Lutheran princes remained standing bolt upright, refusing to bow.

The next day Charles officially conferred with the princes. He insisted that the reformed clergy must not preach in Augsburg, but the princes rejected this demand. "Before I let anybody . . . ask me to deny my God, I will let him strike off my head," the white-haired Protestant margrave of Brandenburg told Charles. Then Luther's old friend Philip Melanchthon presented the Lutheran case. Reluctantly, Charles approved it because he needed German support in his war against the Turks. It had taken ten years for the Lutherans thus to solidify their position, politically as well as theologically. The Confession was the first official codification of the Lutheran reforms, and its acceptance by Charles signaled the beginning of the end of the Holy Roman Empire. There were to be later—and similar—codified records of the Protestant reforms, including the famous Heidelberg Confession of the Calvinists in 1563 and the Presbyterian Westminster Confession of 1647. But the Augsburg Confession was the first to divide the new German Protestants from the Roman Catholics.

Twenty-eight years after the Augsburg Confession, the Protestants, alarmed by Catholic denunciation of their Confession during the Augsburg Interim in 1548, published this derisive scene of Catholic friars merrily downing the contents of beer steins (center) and singing a parody of the First Psalm which went: "Blessed is the man who walketh not in the counsel of the ungodly and does not willingly enter the Interim. . . ."

Holy Roman Emperor Charles V signed the Augsburg Confession partly because he badly needed support for his wars against the French and the Turks from the nine Lutheran princes who requested his signature. The young, politically minded Philip of Hesse (fourth from right, foreground) was so anxious to make his Protestant sympathies evident that he made a public show of eating meat on a Catholic fast day in the midst of negotiations for the Confession.

Those Calvinist "Devils" Struggle Against the Bastion of Catholicism

This cartoon appeared half a century after the death of John Calvin. In it, five "spirits of Calvinism," each in the guise of a devil, rally Protestant troops storming the bastion of medieval Catholicism. At far right, to the rear of the fortress, the becrowned elector of Saxony, who at the time was so indecisive that he was shifting back and forth from Protestantism to Catholicism, extends a welcome for the moment to the Catholic ambassador from Bavaria. "Away from me with your false teachings!" he tells the Calvinists. "The Holy Roman Emperor counts far more with me." Across the roof of the fortress, which symbolized the medieval church, appears in Ger-

Hailbrun
(p 127. et. 133.)
Es haben hie bei meinembrunen
Sich biconieten lang besunnen
Biß leßlich sich der schluß that hibt
Sy solten tapfer gelt hergiber

man the scriptural motto: "The gates of hell shall not prevail against it." On the turrets on the fortress are shields of the four chief Catholic rulers of the time: the pope, the Holy Roman Emperor, the King of Spain, and the King of Bavaria.

If the cartoon had appeared much later, its seemingly impregnable fortress might well have symbolized the growing strength of Calvinism itself, which, when molded into a rigid system of logic, soon became almost as unshakable as medieval Catholicism then seemed. Calvinism, spreading through sixteenth-century northern Europe, soon im-

planted itself solidly, leaving the Lutherans largely to Germany and the Scandinavian countries. Without its strength, the Protestant Reformation might have remained relatively weak within a comparatively small section of Europe, and even Lutheranism itself might not have survived.

Protected by the Augsburg Confession—and aided by rising European nationalism that went hand in hand with the power of the newly invented printing press and the freedom of inquiry during the Renaissance—the Lutherans dominated Germany. Their ideas were also taking root in Austria and Hungary (see *right*), and in the Scandinavian countries their reforms were gaining more followers than in Germany itself. Aping the German princes, Christian II of Denmark and of Norway and Gustavus Vasa of Sweden had initiated national laws against the authority of their own medieval clergy and banned the possession of land by the Roman church. By law, Protestantism was established in Sweden in 1523, in Norway and Denmark almost simultaneously. But being basically transplantations, the Scandinavian Lutheran churches actually differed far less than in Germany from the medieval church. Sweden and Denmark, for example, retained their bishops, though the first Lutheran "bishop" of Denmark was so powerless that Luther scoffed at him as a bishop "without grease."

From Italy the small, twelfth-century pre-Lutheran group of Waldensians (*pages 6-7*) had fanned into France, Germany, and the Netherlands. In Bohemia were the followers of the fifteenth-century John Hus (*pages 10-11*). Throughout Europe appeared scattered groups of Anabaptists who had hoped to join the Lutheran cause but had been repelled by Luther's cry that "nothing can be more poisonous, hurtful or devilish than a rebel," which they took quite rightly to mean themselves.

But it was the reformed doctrines of the Calvinists (*see following pages*) that were by 1530 coming to the fore. From Switzerland where John Calvin lived, his doctrines were carried not into only Germany but also into France, where the Calvinists became known as Huguenots, perhaps from the Swiss word *"Eidgenossen,"* meaning those who "confederate" or "covenant" together in democratically governed churches. By the middle of the 1550's these same Calvinist doctrines were to reach Scotland under John Knox (*pages 52-53*). In the Netherlands, too, the Calvinists were to become the backbone of the Dutch revolt under the Protestant King William of Orange against their Spanish conquerors. The geographical limits thus drawn were to remain generally the boundaries of Protestantism until the colonization of America.

The Hungarian Reformation, as elsewhere in Europe, had been helped along by the new nationalism and humanism to which Hungarian scholars had been exposed and by political dissatisfaction with the Roman church's economic hold on the country. But it differed from that of other Reformation countries in the fact that the Turks stood in diametric opposition to the pope, who had declared war on them in the hope of preserving Hungary for Catholicism—thus prompting even the Turks to indulge the reformed ideas of the subjugated Hungarians. By the end of the sixteenth century ninety per cent of the people were Protestant, though under Gabriel Bethlen, Prince of Transylvania, all religions, including Catholic, were protected. With the retreat of the Turks in the seventeenth century, the Catholic Counter Reformation crushed the strength of Hungarian Protestantism, which remained pocketed in small regions where to this day the Hungarian Reformed Church remains the principal religion in an otherwise predominantly Catholic nation.

In Calvinist uprisings in sixteenth-century Holland and Belgium, churches were ransacked and "idols" smashed, in reaction against the rule of Philip II of Spain, who had inherited the Netherlands from his father, Holy Roman Emperor Charles V.

Patient John Calvin

Most of his life John Calvin suffered from a generally frail constitution, in addition to severe migraine headaches, ulcers, gout, kidney stones, swollen toes, fever spasms, and occasional blood-spitting. To remedy these infirmities he took short walks through the streets of Geneva, Switzerland, where, in 1536, he had fled from his native France because of his Protestant leanings. His troubles taught him patience. He also had a kindly streak in his nature, though few people recognized the fact even in his own day. In the midst of playing quoits on the greens of Geneva, he would throw off his cares and become for the moment all good will and gentleness, letting the faint trace of a smile play about his pointed lips and patting the heads of little children who had gathered to watch the game.

Calvin had been trained as a lawyer, and he sometimes envisioned his God in terms of the courtroom. God, he decided, was very like a supreme judge, all-wise, all-powerful, a strict disciplinarian—and with an infinite plan for the universe. As Calvin understood him, he was "Supreme Will"; but being a truly great judge, he was also merciful. Therefore, said Calvin, God is not only Supreme Will but also Love.

In spite of his somber appearance, John Calvin was a cheerful but exceedingly shy man who occasionally took a little wine with his egg and complained only when he was treated too exaltedly by his fellow citizens of Geneva or, as on one occasion, when dogs snapped at the hem of his academic gown as he walked about Geneva. In a day of Protestant persecution, he had his five-hundred-odd-page The Institutes of the Christian Religion, *in which he set forth his theology for French and Swiss Protestants, printed in a format so small that it could not only be easily carried but also easily hidden.*

Like Luther, Calvin intended only to purify the medieval church, not to break with it. One theological difference between Calvinism and Lutheranism lay in Calvin's belief that the celebration of the Lord's Supper was a spiritual presence. But the basic difference lay in Calvin's conviction, in direct opposition to Luther, that man must become a co-worker with God against evil—and, in dead center between the Lutherans and the Anabaptists, a co-worker *through* the state. This belief led directly to the Calvinist concept that men should democratically covenant, under God, with each other to form a civil government, thus working with God who, Calvin pointed out, had already covenanted with mankind in the New Testament through Jesus.

In spite of later interpretations of his theology, Calvin affirmed earthly, as well as eternal, pleasures. "Man's chief end," he said, "is to glorify God and to *enjoy* him forever." To Calvin this meant living by what has been called a "mortified cheerfulness"—an attitude that would bring humanity to the ultimate goal of a "oneness" with God. Man, he believed, must guide himself carefully through his mortal life between the extremes of the physical and the spiritual, enjoying physical pursuits but warily avoiding the excesses of too much frivolity or too much ostentation. Above all, he must avoid the excesses of the sin of pride. "We are," he wrote in his *Institutes of the Christian Religion,* which became the cornerstone of the later Presbyterian, Congregationalist, and Dutch and German Reformed churches, "too inclined by nature to attribute all our achievements to our own flesh. . . . The best way for God to shatter all such arrogance is to prove to us by experience not only how foolish we are, but also how weak. . . . Whatever be the kind of tribulation with which we are afflicted, we must always consider the end of it to be to accustom us to despise the present life."

Practicing what he preached, Calvin patiently lived out his life, teaching his students, studying, arguing his doctrines affably and courteously—and taking short walks through the streets to bolster his ailing health. It was later generations who, exaggerating his disciplines, unwittingly perverted his doctrines into a rigid and negative creed which might well have shocked good, patient Calvin who firmly held to his belief that God is Love, and never shirked his duty while fearlessly awaiting a new and better life that would, he confidently expected, some day unite him with the infinite wisdom, goodness—and love—of his God.

The Faces of Calvinism

ROVRGVINVS INVENTOR

A student of the aging Calvin once drew the pen-and-ink sketches shown above. In all of them, Calvin looks much the same, old but sagacious. But to succeeding generations, his face assumed a cold, commercial, and even cruel aspect, as those outside—and inside—the Calvinist fold, aided by a long line of misinterpreters, became less and less sympathetic with the stern and strict theocracy he established in Geneva.

When John Calvin became too old to walk, he had himself carried about in a high-backed chair, though he disliked the fuss it caused. Just before his death he took care to leave instructions that his grave be unmarked, in a final effort to avoid the sin of pride. What Calvin left behind him was a system of theology which became one of the major influences in the development of constitutional government throughout Europe and America. The influence stemmed directly from his concept of democratic "covenants." As he had grown increasingly disillusioned with the monarchs of his time, he had sought to attain a collaboration between churchly and temporal powers and to give minor magistrates more power to restrain the absolutism of rulers. It was, therefore, no coincidence that the new middle class and the lesser nobility appealed to the 1559 edition of his *Institutes* in their attack on the divine right of kings.

The chief criticisms of his theology lay in the seemingly rigid doctrines of "predestination" (*i.e.,* the belief that among the people themselves there were those who were the "elect of God") and of "moral obedience." Under him, Geneva had been a city of the strictest morality. Its citizens paid careful attention to their style of dress, avoiding display; they shunned frivolity, including cardplaying, dancing, and joking; and one man was banished from the city for observing, when he heard a donkey bray, "That ass chants a fine psalm." As a result, some of Calvin's opponents were tortured and executed, of whom the most famous was Michael Servetus (*right*), burned at Champel as a heretic on October 27, 1553.

Later overly systematic followers of Calvin have interpreted his doctrines to mean that men who are morally virtuous are bound to prosper materialistically, and that the idle are doomed to materialistic poverty on earth. Many of these followers interpreted the biblical parable of the talents as a sanctification of those virtues related to success in business and as a reminder that idleness is sin. From this point it has been an easy step—though Calvin himself would have disagreed—to look upon worldly prosperity as a sign of God's favor.

The rise of capitalism in sixteenth-century Europe did certainly draw on Calvinist concepts of virtue. Most of all, the Calvinists admired hard work, and they believed that the duty of earning a living was essential to morality—and thus a sign of obedience to God.

But Calvin himself would rightly have pointed out that his theology was no ally of any economic system and that it is an exaggeration that one of the chief causes of capitalism lay in his doctrines.

As interpreted by many of his followers, his doctrine of "predestination" would also have proved anathema to the real Calvin. It was not the stern doctrine of God's wrath which it tended to become in later minds. It was a doctrine formulated because of his strong sense of God as sole sovereign. God, he believed, predestined some of his creatures to salvation and others to damnation. But to him, this did not entail disquietude of soul. Election could be assured by communion with Christ. It was only self-serving later followers who would read his doctrines as a justification of their own self-righteousness, and believe that a life of virtue would be rewarded by riches. In so regarding themselves as the "elect," they would have been advised by Calvin himself to inquire into the state of their own motivations—at the basis of which, he believed, lay the true doctrine of predestination and of the "elect."

Marguerite d'Angoulême, Queen of Navarre, was one of Calvin's most powerful backers. She sheltered and protected Protestant refugees. She was also the author of some licentious tales told with the purpose of pointing a moral.

Spanish theologian Michael Servetus was ordered burned at the stake by Calvin for denying the Trinity. Before the execution, Calvin tried to ferret out and destroy copies of Servetus' books that questioned the place of Jesus in the Trinity. The Unitarians of today claim Servetus as the original ancestor of their denomination.

The Dutch theologian Jacobus Arminius accepted most of Calvinism except for the doctrine of "predestination." No human creature, he argued, could ever become entirely dispossessed of his free will.

Théodore de Bèze ranked next to Calvin in the Geneva theocracy. After Calvin died, he became the first of a long line of his interpreters.

The Radical Ones

The German-Swiss theologian Huldreich Zwingli was a radical by Luther's standards. For one thing, Zwingli was inclined to favor the spirit of Carlstadt, an overzealous Lutheran who now wore feathers in his beret during mass to show his rebellion against vestments. Contrary to Luther, Zwingli also announced that the Lord's Supper should be a commemorative and symbolic feast. He argued that only the spirit, not the real body, of Christ is present, and his belief was taken up by the Calvinists, thus forever splitting their ranks from the Lutherans.

In 1523, six years after Luther published his Ninety-five Theses, Zwingli independently published in Zurich his own theses against the practices of the medieval church. Like Luther, he argued against indulgences and the absolute authority of the pope, and demanded the use of the German language instead of Latin in the celebration of the mass. But Zwingli also believed in taking up arms in the defense of his faith, and his preaching at Zurich led to the removal of images, the smashing of the organ in the cathedral, and the development of a church service that was almost exclusively an exposition of the Bible. This was plainly a reformation more puritan than that of Luther, and to this tradition, blended with the later doctrines of Calvinism, the large German and Dutch Reformed denominations of present-day Protestantism owe much of their heritage.

By comparison with rash Thomas Münzer *(left),* even Zwingli was mild. Münzer argued for "inner experience"—an "intuitive" interpretation of the Bible which had much in common with the later Quakers. From the Anabaptists or "Rebaptizers" have sprung the present-day pietistic and peace-loving Mennonites.

The Anabaptists were the real perfectionists of the Reformation. Their interpretations of the Bible alarmed the Lutherans because they claimed the Lutherans had not gone far enough in their reforms. In direct opposition to the Lutheran emphasis on justification by faith alone, they tried to emphasize good deeds in their lives in the hope that others would imitate their ways. They emphasized the literal and imminent second coming of Christ, and, citing specific scriptural passages, insisted that it was a sign of vanity for a man to wear any but the plainest clothes, that a woman who showed even the slightest curl beneath her cap was equally immodest. Infant baptism, they argued, is unnecessary. An infant, they pointed out, is not a sinner. Baptism, they argued, has no meaning unless the believer is rebaptized as an adult so that he understands the beliefs to which he commits himself. Far worse, from the property-conscious Lutherans' point of view, the Anabaptists renounced worldly possessions. It was this cavalier attitude that really got them into trouble. The earth, they stoutly insisted, is the Lord's. When they were banished from one or another district, as sooner or later they generally were because of their disregard for law

In hope of making the Bible better understood by his German-Swiss congregations, Huldreich Zwingli translated a line of the Twenty-third Psalm as "He maketh me to lie down in an Alpine meadow." An extremist by comparison with Luther, Zwingli, like Thomas Münzer (below), believed in taking up arms against governments that persecuted Protestants. When, according to some accounts, Zwingli died, sword in hand, in battle for the early Anabaptists, Luther said his death was the proper judgment of God on a minister who dared to take up the sword against the state.

"Bible, Babel, bubble!" scoffed Thomas Münzer in contempt for what he considered the Lutherans' excessive reliance on the Bible. He called Luther "Dr. Easy Chair" and "Dr. Pussyfoot" because Luther refused to back him in the Peasants' Revolt of 1525.

48

and private property, they settled on somebody else's property, refusing to budge, no matter who the owner, and preaching a pure first-century Christianity which went woefully against the grain of the law-abiding Lutherans. Worst of all (and unforgivably, it seemed to the Lutherans), the Anabaptists had learned that a state-sanctioned church, as Lutheranism had become in the German states as a result of the Augsburg Confession, boded only misery and governmental persecution for any minority group that disagreed. They therefore advocated a complete separation of church and state, thus scandalizing good Lutherans.

Of the spiritual descendants of the Anabaptists, the Mennonites, including their conservative Amish branch, most carefully preserve today their original sixteenth-century precepts, although in short time their early predilection for waging war in the spirit of Thomas Münzer (as well as their one-time belief in community property) was to be changed through the teachings of the Dutch theologian Menno Simons (right).

These early Anabaptists were perfectionists who believed in the Sermon on the Mount as a literal code for daily life, and who disliked Luther for favoring the princes over peasants like themselves. At first, they rose up in arms against the state during the Peasants' Revolt under Thomas Münzer. Later they became pacifists and refused even to take an oath of loyalty to the government.

Menno Simons, from whom the Mennonites took their name, was a Dutch theologian who advocated an absolute pacifism. His followers were protected in seventeenth-century Holland by the Protestant William of Orange.

Poor Anabaptists!

No group of early Protestants suffered greater persecution than the Anabaptists, the forerunners of present-day Baptists, Quakers, and Mennonites. Throughout Europe they were strangled, beheaded, or burned alive by Lutherans, Calvinists, and Catholics alike. Because of their special belief in the need for adult baptism, their persecutors considered total immersion in too much water—*i.e.*, drowning—a particularly appropriate death. Those who were not killed outright were slandered, scorned, and forced to wander, homeless, about Germany, France, and Switzerland until they could find another place to settle down for a while.

In Italy, Anabaptists were forced to jump to their deaths from the tops of haystacks.

In France and Bohemia, the Anabaptists were drowned for preaching violent sermons against the government.

In Amsterdam, a dead Anabaptist hangs by his neck from a forked post before his body is dumped into the sea, while others are strung up by their heels (rear).

The Rise of Presbyterianism

One midnight in his bedroom, after praying on his knees for hours, John Knox was interrupted by his wife. Angrily he told her she had just delayed the Scottish Reformation. He had, he assured her, already won half the nation to Calvinism. By dawn he would, he informed her, have brought the other half solidly over to his side.

Knox cut a fiery figure in sixteenth-century Scotland. In a country where a corrupt Catholic clergy had kept the peasantry more ignorant than in almost any other land of the time, he was a real rabble-rouser. But he was completely sincere—and fearless. Remembering the execution of the reformer George Wishart and his own period as a galley slave and exile on the Continent, he carried a giant, two-handed sword as protection when he went out preaching. At court, he faced Mary Queen of Scots herself, arguing with her over a period of several months *(right).*

In Scotland, Calvinism became known as Presbyterianism, taking its name from the democratic Calvinist system of electing ministers and ruling "elders," or "presbyters," by majority vote of each individual congregation. Knox believed that Christians not only had the right but the duty to revolt against their rulers if they impeded what the people believed to be the will of God. Once he referred to Mary as "an unruly cow saddled by mistake." But he was as politically astute as he was crude. Uniting against Mary the anti-Catholic elements of the Scottish Parliament, together with the anti-French and pro-English elements, he managed by 1560 to persuade the Scottish government to declare Presbyterianism the official church of Scotland. Successful, he set about organizing a system of schooling throughout the country. It was the beginning of a strong Presbyterian emphasis on education, evident today in numerous Presbyterian-founded colleges—and in the Presbyterian taste for long, informative sermons (and long, edifying prayers), which stand in contrast to the more liturgically (and less intellectually) oriented service of the historically more conservative Lutherans.

To the "Lords of the Congregation," a group of nobles who covenanted together in Calvinist fashion to prove that the people could establish their own democratic church, short-tempered John Knox preached so violently against what he considered to be the "popish," "undemocratic" practice of kneeling to receive communion that to this day Presbyterians shun the practice,

preferring to sit quietly in their pews during the service. The Church of England was forced to insert hurriedly into its new Book of Common Prayer the explanation that their practice of kneeling expressed only reverence and thankfulness, not "popish" adoration of the mass. Knox cheerfully scorned this insertion as the "Black Rubric."

Mary Queen of Scots tried every trick, including bursting into tears, to coax Knox to her side when she hoped to marry the Spanish prince Don Carlos and keep Scotland Catholic. Once, during their long conversations, she shrieked, "What have ye to do ... with my marriage? Or what are ye within this Commonwealth?" Knox replied democratically, "A subject born within the same, Madam. And albeit I neither be Earl, Lord, nor Baron within it, yet has God made me (how abject that I ever be in your eyes) a profitable member within the same." So frightened was one English Anglican archbishop that Knox's democratic influence might pervade England—as it soon did—that he cried, "Keep us from such visitations as Knockes [sic] hath attempted in Scotland; the people to be the orderers of things." A democrat to his very marrow, Knox took the remark as a compliment.

Tiny William Tyndale

John Wycliffe had perhaps missed becoming the chief leader of the Reformation because his early English Bible, never printed, had to be circulated only in manuscript. The first printed English Testament was translated by tiny, ruddy-faced William Tyndale, who fled from England to the Lutheran sections of Germany where he smuggled large quantities of New Testaments back to London aboard merchant ships, hidden inside bales of cotton and flax.

Tyndale managed to smuggle at least forty editions under the nose of the Bishop of London. When the bishop learned about these shipments, he bought them up—only to have Tyndale use the profits from the sale for printing more Testaments. In 1534, Tyndale, told by the bishop's agents that Henry VIII had repealed the law against English Bibles, set out happily for London. On the way he was captured near Antwerp, imprisoned for two years (his trial lasted sixteen months), and burned at the stake.

William Tyndale (right) was burned at the stake in 1536, two years after an archenemy of Martin Luther named Johannes Cochlaeus primed Tyndale's printers with wine, then persuaded them to betray Tyndale to the Bishop of London's agents (below). But Tyndale had already completed his English translation of the entire New Testament and gotten as far as the book of Nehemiah in the Old Testament.

This bookseller, found guilty of selling Tyndale's New Testaments, was burned at the stake with two of them tied to his neck.

GVLIELMVS TINDALE MARTY

OLIM EX AVLA MAGD

Hac ut luce tuas disper
Sponte extorris ero
                                    ma tenebres
                                    Sacrificium.

ERT HÆC TABELLA QVOD SOLVM POTVIT ARS GVLIELMI TINDALÆ, HVIVS OLIM AVLÆ ALVMNI, SIM
ORNAMENTI, QVI POST FÆLICES PVRIORIS THEOLOGIÆ PRIMITIAS HIC DEPOSITAS, ANTVERPIÆ IN NOV
STAMENTO, NEC NON PENTATEVCHO IN VERNACVLAM TRANSFERENDO OPERAM NAVAVI
IGLIS SVIS EO VSQ SALVTIFERAM, VT INDE NON IMMERITO ANGLIÆ APOSTOLVS AVDIRET
ARTYRIO WILFORDÆ PROPE BRVXELLAS CORONATVS A 1536 VIR SI VEL ADVERSARIC
ROCVRATORI NEMPE IMPERATORIS GENERALI CREDAMVS PERDOCTVS PIVS ET BONVS.

The Religion of the Tudor Family

In 1533, Henry Tudor's biblical scholarship was to come in handy for him. In order to please his father, who was said to have died in remorse because of his part in the affair, Henry had married his deceased older brother Arthur's widow, the Spanish princess Cath-

Fat, talkative, power-hungry Henry VIII of England had some justification for considering himself a theologian. As a younger son of Henry VII, he had little hope of succeeding to the throne and thus had been schooled for the priesthood. He had written a treatise entitled On the Seven Sacraments, *which had attacked Lutheranism— and which had been good enough to win for him and all succeeding British monarchs the papally conferred title "Defender of the Faith."*

erine of Aragon. But after long years of marriage, Catherine had borne to him no living male heir, and if the uncertain Tudor line was to be assured in England, Henry needed a son. Now Henry therefore appealed to the pope for an annulment of his marriage to Catherine, citing—and probably sincerely—the Old Testament admonition: "To take one's brother's wife is an unclean thing. . . . They shall be childless." When the pope refused (at least partially for the understandable reason that Catherine was the aunt of Holy Roman Emperor Charles V), Henry was forced to look for another solution. Mindful of the mounting English resentment against the Roman church, he set himself up as head of a newly formed Church of England, appointing Thomas Cranmer as first Protestant Archbishop of Canterbury.

The resulting Church of England was a theological and practical mixture which once caused a contemporary to remark that only Cranmer—if even he—really knew what it stood for. During the sixteenth century it was predominantly Catholic in theology and practice, following the final pattern set by the shifting Henry. Since the bishops of the English church had originally been Catholic, it stood firm—and made a point of doing so—on the rock of Catholic apostolic succession. Its communion service remained similar to the Catholic mass, except that it was celebrated in the English language. By the time he died in 1547, Henry had, in fact, reinstated into his church even those practices which he had first considered changing, including the celibacy of priests and the denial of the cup to the laity.

After his death, the religion of the Tudor family—and of the Church of England—continued to shift back and forth from Catholicism to Protestantism, depending on the inclinations of the three children who succeeded him. Of these, Edward VI (*upper right*), who reigned from 1547 to 1553, was inclined toward a combination of Lutheranism and Calvinism. Edward's half-sister Mary (*lower left*), who succeeded him in 1554 and reigned until 1558, was a belligerent Catholic. Their half-sister Elizabeth I (*lower right*), who succeeded Mary in 1558, was, following somewhat in the footsteps of her father, a middle-of-the-roader— and for very practical reasons. As the daughter of Henry's second wife, Anne Boleyn, she was forced by practicality either to maintain Protestantism or be declared illegitimate—and thus unlawful queen.

Catholic scholar Thomas More proposed complete religious liberty in his famous Utopia. In the midst of Henry's religious intrigues, he refused to break what he considered God's law by catering to either side. He was perjured in court, sentenced to death, and beheaded at London Tower on July 6, 1535. He died saying he was the "king's good servant but God's first."

"If I had served God as diligently as I have done my king, he would not have given me over in my grey hairs," Thomas Cardinal Wolsey said when he fell from Henry's favor. He had persuaded the king that the pope would grant him an annulment from Catherine of Aragon, but his plans failed.

The Characters of Mother Gooseland

The origins of most Mother Goose rhymes are obscure. But by legend, many of them originated for the purpose of ridiculing some of the characters who took part in the English Reformation. These ranged from bishops to abbots to common clergy—and included fat Henry VIII himself as the prime target.

For gobbling up the Roman Catholic monasteries for his own Church of England, he was ridiculed in the language of the common people as:

> Robin the Bobbin, the big-bellied Ben,
> He ate more meat than three-score men;
> . . .
> He ate a church, he ate a steeple,
> He ate the priest and all the people!

When one abbot, at Henry's bidding, sent the king the deeds of twenty-four churchly estates, all of them hidden in a pie at Henry's request, his act was recorded as:

> Sing a Song of Sixpence,
> A pocket full of Rye,
> Four and twenty Blackbirds
> Bak'd in a Pye.
>
> When the pie was opened,
> The birds began to sing;
> Was not that a dainty dish,
> To set before the king?

When Abbot Whiting was on trial for his life, a king's man named Horner was on the jury that convicted Whiting. There was thus understandable local feeling about how Horner later received a large estate:

> Little Jack Horner
> Sat in a Corner,
>   Eating of Christmas Pye;
> He put in his Thumb,
> And pull'd out a Plum,
> And [said] what a good Boy was I.

It was Henry's first wife, Catherine of Aragon, who, living in England but receiving "honeyed" promises of help from her native Spain in her marital woes, gave rise to:

> The queen was in the parlor,
> Eating bread and honey.

Her successor, Anne Boleyn, appeared as:

> The maid was in the garden,
> Hanging out the clothes,
> There came a little blackbird
> And snipped off her nose.

In this case the "blackbird" was Cardinal Wolsey who, at Henry's secret command, had wrecked Anne's engagement to Lord Percy and who, next to Henry himself, suffered the most at the hands of Mother Gooseland. When Wolsey and Bishop Tarbes went off to France to seek a marriage for Henry's daughter Mary Tudor (with Wolsey thereby hoping to gain the favor of the pope), their failure was told in:

> Jack and Gill [sic]
> Went up the Hill,
>   To fetch a Pail of [Holy] Water;
> Jack fell down
> And broke his Crown,
>   And Gill came tumbling after.

And Wolsey's arrogance, despite his lowly birth, plus his unwatchfulness regarding what was going on around him, gave rise to:

> Little Boy Blue, come blow your horn,
> The cow's in the meadow, the sheep in the corn. . . .

When Wolsey fell from power and died impoverished (without any assistance from the pope), the people rhymed "Old Mother Hubbard," caricaturing Wolsey as "the poor dog."

Even the affairs in Scotland were roundly satirized in the English rhymes, including the problems of Mary Queen of Scots, who became "Little Miss Muffet"—thus making good John Knox the big "spider." But probably the most famous of all the ditties concerned Thomas Cranmer *(right)* who bequeathed more enduring literature to the Church of England in the form of his great *Book of Common Prayer*. When, after Henry's death, Cranmer, along with Bishops Latimer and Ridley *(pages 60-61)*, was burned at the stake for offending Mary Tudor by their Protestant views, the people rhymed and sang:

> Three blind mice, see how they run!
> They all ran after the farmer's wife,
> Who cut off their tails with a carving knife,
> Did you ever see such a sight in your life,
>   As three blind mice?

In the Church of England service, Catholic liturgy was formalized into the English language. "We stand to praise, kneel to pray, and sit to be instructed," one wag said. The Church of England's Book of Common Prayer was the legacy of Thomas Cranmer (above) to Henry VIII's church. One of its most beautiful lines reads: "We have left undone those things which we ought to have done; And we have done those things which we ought not to have done; And there is no health in us." In 1556, Cranmer was sent to the stake by the Catholic Bloody Mary. Ashamed of the part he had played in Henry's intrigues, he thrust his hand into the fire as he approached it, saying, "Let the hand that has offended go first."

The Burning of Latimer and Ridley

On October 16, 1555, in the reign of Henry VIII's Catholic daughter "Bloody" Mary Tudor, two bishops of the Church of England, Nicholas Ridley and Hugh Latimer, were burned together at the stake near the gates of Oxford University's Balliol College, at the direction of Mary and of Thomas Bonner, Bishop of London. Their crime was that they had preached against the Catholic beliefs in purgatory and transubstantiation.

Latimer limped as the two made their way to the stake. Then a Church of England clergyman preached a sermon against them, and Ridley's brother was allowed to tie a bag of gunpowder around each victim's neck, hoping to make their deaths less painful. As the faggots were lighted, Latimer said, "Be of good comfort, Master Ridley, and play the man; we shall this day light such a candle by God's grace in England as I trust shall never be put out."

During the reign of Bloody Mary Tudor, nearly three hundred Protestant men and women died at the stake in one of the bloodiest eras of English religious history.

Bishop Nicholas Ridley was a kindly fellow who had often entertained at dinner the mother of Thomas Bonner, Bishop of London, under whose aegis he was executed during the reign of Bloody Mary.

Bishop Hugh Latimer was a timid old man who had for years been a partial cripple because a tree had fallen on him during a thunderstorm. Never much of a theologian, he had learned some of his Protestant views only a short time before his execution—from Bishop Nicholas Ridley during their time together in prison.

As the flames shot up, Latimer (right) tried to stroke his face as if to help the flames reach the gunpowder tied around his neck.

These twenty-two Protestants were arrested in Colchester, tied together with ropes, and burned as a single group by order of Mary Tudor.

Bloody Mary's Victims

In 1554, an English cleric named John Foxe, enraged by Catholic persecution of the Protestants during the reign of Bloody Mary Tudor, published the first edition of his widely known *Book of Martyrs.* In it, he described some of the scenes shown here. Later, Foxe admitted that he should have checked his facts more carefully, for they were not completely accurate. But the damage had been done, and public opinion had—with Foxe's help—become so inflamed against Mary Tudor that the Church of England was forged into a Protestant church.

The fact was that Mary's persecution of the Protestants was in large part a reaction against the bigotry on the part of the Protestants themselves during the reign of Mary's half-brother Edward VI. That bigotry was clear in the scene at right below, where a cat dressed in monk's habit was hanged in London, so alarming the Catholics (as did an incident in 1553 when the Catholic Bishop Bourne, shown in the second row on the opposite page, barely escaped a dagger thrown at him by an enraged Protestant) that reaction was almost inescapable. In addition, Mary herself had suffered real indignities from ardent anti-Catholics who not only denied her legitimate descent from Henry VIII but also refused to allow her to worship privately in her own chapel.

With Foxe's help, Mary's severity now became an integral—if exaggerated—part of Protestant history. In the top row on the opposite page, the Protestant linen draper Thomas Watts bade good-bye to his wife and six children on his way to the stake. At top center, the dissenter Robert Samuel dies. He claimed in jail to have a vision of three ladders ascending to a Protestant heaven and a voice crying, "Samuel, Samuel . . . after this day shalt thou never be either hungry or thirsty." At top right, John Kurde refused to kiss the cross offered him by a monk—an act considered so brave by the spectators that, according to the record, they cheered him for it. In the second row, Thomas Haukes, of Essex, having promised his friends to make a sign, raised his arms above his head to show that the pains of martyrdom were bearable. At far right, two women, Mrs. Margaret Thurston and Mrs. Agnes Bongeur, both of Colchester, which was a hotbed of Protestantism during Mary's reign, die together. In the bottom row, five Protestants are executed at Canterbury; at center, faggots are piled up for the execution of Protestant Bishop Farrar, of St. David's, who finally had to be struck down with a pike before he died; and at bottom right, in a scene historically, if not artistically, accurate, the right arm of Thomas Tomkins, of Smithfield, has fallen into the flames, even though Thomas himself still stood upright—a fact that was duly exaggerated in the Protestant records of the time and helped to inflame opinion against Mary Tudor.

In the arbor of Bishop Bonner's orchard, young Thomas Hinshaw was put in the stocks, then thrashed while the bishop himself (far left) looked on.

The Massacre of St. Bartholomew's Day

On August 24, or St. Bartholomew's Day, in 1572, Catherine de Medici, mother of Charles IX of France and regent for him, ordered the greatest mass persecution in the history of Protestant-Catholic strife. Worried because her son turned for advice to the French Calvinist Admiral Gaspard de Coligny, Catherine jealously hired an assassin to murder the admiral. When her plot failed, she planned an even greater atrocity to save her face. Telling Charles that the Protestants had plans to kill him, she gained his consent for the massacre, even persuading him to join in the affair himself (*below right*).

Ten thousand Huguenots died that day in Paris; Coligny himself was murdered in his bedroom and his body tossed out the window (*below*). Seventy thousand more Protestants were killed throughout the countryside. The result was that Protestantism never again became strong in France. Until then, the Calvinists had fought to make their creed the religion of France. The enormity of the St. Bartholomew's Day Massacre forced them to change their tactics. Thereafter, they fought only for survival.

Admiral Gaspard de Coligny, the political leader of the Huguenot faction that had become inextricably involved in the French government, was the first victim of the St. Bartholomew's Day Massacre. He was murdered in his bedroom (above), his body dumped out the window.

That the cause of the St. Bartholomew's Day Massacre was by no means one-sided was apparent in the scene below in which thirty Catholics in the town of Angoulême, a stronghold of French Calvinism at the time, were deprived of all nourishment (scene marked "A"), were then dragged naked over a taut rope (scene "B"), and finally tied to stakes (C) at enough distance from the kindled flames to roast their bodies agonizingly slowly. By the 1560's, the French Huguenot community had become inextricably involved in the political battle for the throne of France, allying themselves with the Navarre family and attempting to take over the government. On August 24, 1572, ten thousand Huguenots in Paris alone died during the resulting St. Bartholomew Massacre (above).

The young king Charles IX was reported to have joined in the general slaughter on St. Bartholomew's Day.

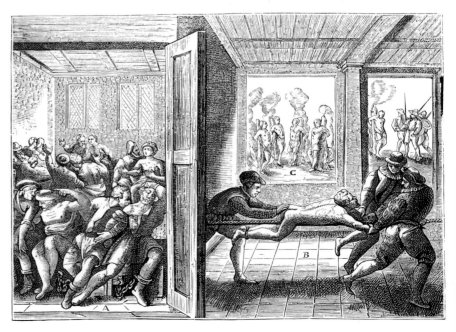

"Better a Republic Than a Huguenot King!"

The problems of the French Protestants were eased only with the reign of Henry of Navarre, and then only briefly. As the grandson of Marguerite d'Angoulême (*pages 46-47*), Henry was a Protestant. But he was also a diplomat. When the French Catholics opposed him, he obligingly turned Catholic, was crowned in 1589. With the Edict of Nantes of 1598, Henry believed he had established national unity and guaranteed a measure of freedom of worship for the Huguenots. But after his death in 1610, the Catholics ignored the Edict, forced the Huguenots to return to the Roman church or go into exile. During the century following Henry's death, nearly three hundred thousand Huguenots fled France to go to more tolerant Switzerland, Holland, England—and some of these went later to America. France was thus to remain a Catholic country to this day.

On Sunday morning, March 1, 1562, the Duke of Guise, brother of the Queen Regent of France and uncle of Mary Queen of Scots, stopped to attend mass at a church near Vassy, France. In a nearby barn (below), several hundred French Calvinists were holding Sunday services. Learning of it, Guise ordered them to disband. The congregation replied by hurling stones at him and his men. Guise commanded his soldiers to fire, and in the resulting massacre, sixty-three French Huguenots were killed, a hundred others wounded.

"Better a republic than a Huguenot king!" claimed the Catholics who were in control of France. Obliging them, Henry of Navarre, who had been raised a Protestant, agreed prior to his coronation to become a Catholic. Later he joked that Paris, which capitulated (below) because of his action, *"was well worth a mass."*

The Dutch Inquisition

In 1555, Philip II of Spain inherited the Netherlands from his father, Charles V—which included at the time not only Holland but also Belgium. Convinced, quite sincerely, that it was his divine mission to restore all Europe to the Roman church, Philip tried to impose religious unity on the entire Netherlands population. Already, Charles had established the Spanish Inquisition against Dutch Lutherans. By 1566, Philip had managed to have put to death fifty thousand Netherlands Protestants and forced thirty thousand others to flee.

Philip was the product of a Spain that had thought of itself as a special problem ever since the latter part of the fifteenth century. The reason: its population included large numbers of Moslems and Jews, and to Spanish Christian kings this fact seemed to fore-

bode possible divine displeasure on their nation. In 1478, they had therefore received from the pope the right to conduct within their own boundaries the infamous Spanish Inquisition, which, they believed, would not only please God but save the soul of many a "heretic."

It was to be the Calvinists who were to rise against Philip. The Dutch Protestant William of Orange actually did not believe that the differences among Catholicism, Lutheranism, or Calvinism were of supreme importance. Born of a Lutheran family, but reared a Catholic at the insistence of Charles V, he later turned Calvinist for political reasons. But it was exactly because Calvinism, in contrast to Catholicism and early Lutheranism, justified on theological grounds armed resistance to tyranny that it, not Lutheranism, had become the stronger Protestant creed among the subjected Dutch peoples.

Under William, the Calvinists succeeded in achieving the independence of the Dutch Republic and the establishment of the Calvinist Dutch Reformed Church. But sometimes the fanaticism of the Calvinists proved to be William's most difficult problem. At Antwerp, for example, angered by a Catholic-inspired massacre of their fellow Protestants outside the city gates, the Calvinists prepared to take vengeance against them. For the moment, William proved equal to the occasion: he simply locked the gates of the city, thereby keeping the Calvinists inside.

Under William's leadership, Holland became the only country gained for Protestantism after 1560. Belgium, which he found harder to defend, remained Catholic. As for the "divinely inspired" Philip, he went on to England, hoping to purge it, too, of Protestant "heretics." The attempt ended in disaster with the defeat of his Spanish Armada in 1588.

In the late fifteenth and early sixteenth centuries, Spain had entered the golden age of its national life. Its new spirit was infiltrated with a religious revival that emphasized deep piety and high ethical standards. But these did not preclude harsh, though sincere, attempts to rout "heretics" by means of the infamous Spanish Inquisition—attempts which Philip II (left) tried to extend to the Netherlands and to England.

The Spanish Inquisition, first imposed in Spain in 1478 and extended by Holy Roman Emperor Charles V to the Netherlands in 1521, prompted the questioning (above) and burning (below) of "heretics" under government auspices.

The Problems of the King James Bible

As the Scottish James I entered London to be crowned king at Elizabeth I's death, the Puritans handed him a petition for reforms within the Church of England. Calling a conference of the antagonistic Anglicans and Puritans at Hampton Court, he lost his temper—and the support of Puritans. Only one good resulted from the badly run conference: James agreed to back the so-called King James, or Authorized, Version of the Bible.

A "modern" language like English, it was felt by many a Bible scholar, lacked prestige. Already, Bishop Gardiner of England had objected to the style of William Tyndale's earlier New Testament. It was, he complained, too clear. Therefore, he urged the retention of more than a hundred Latin words "for the dignity of the matter in them contained." The words: *holocausta*, *panis*, *peccator*, and *zizania*, among others. In direct opposition to Gardiner stood Sir John Cheke, who began a New Testament which was to contain nothing but native English words. In his version, the word "lunatic" became "moon'd," "captivity" became "outpeopling," and "publicans" became "tollers." The word "parables" very much offended him. In its place he preferred "biwordes."

It took almost four years for the forty-seven scholars who survived the arguments to wrangle out these problems in the King James Version of 1611. They had been hired by James to revise former English Bibles. Instead, they made a complete translation from the Hebrew and Greek versions that were available to them at that time. When they had finished, the people said it "perverted the meaning of the Scriptures." Not for fifty years was it really accepted, despite its later popularity. Even the Puritans of New England were to scorn it, bringing with them to America instead the older—and what they believed to be more accurate—Geneva Bible, in the making of which a brother-in-law of John Calvin had had a hand. To James, especially, the Geneva Bible was anathema. It contained several marginal references questioning the divine right of kings. It was, as far as he was concerned, "that Calvinist Bible."

As "the wisest fool in Christendom," James I was a strange combination of shrewdness and ignorance, of piety and unscrupulousness. He promised to pay the translators of his King James Version of the Bible, but in the end gave them nothing but living expenses. In addition to the Bible, which was published in 1611, James published in 1618 a Sports Day Book *to encourage recreation and sports on Sunday, thereby infuriating the Puritans.*

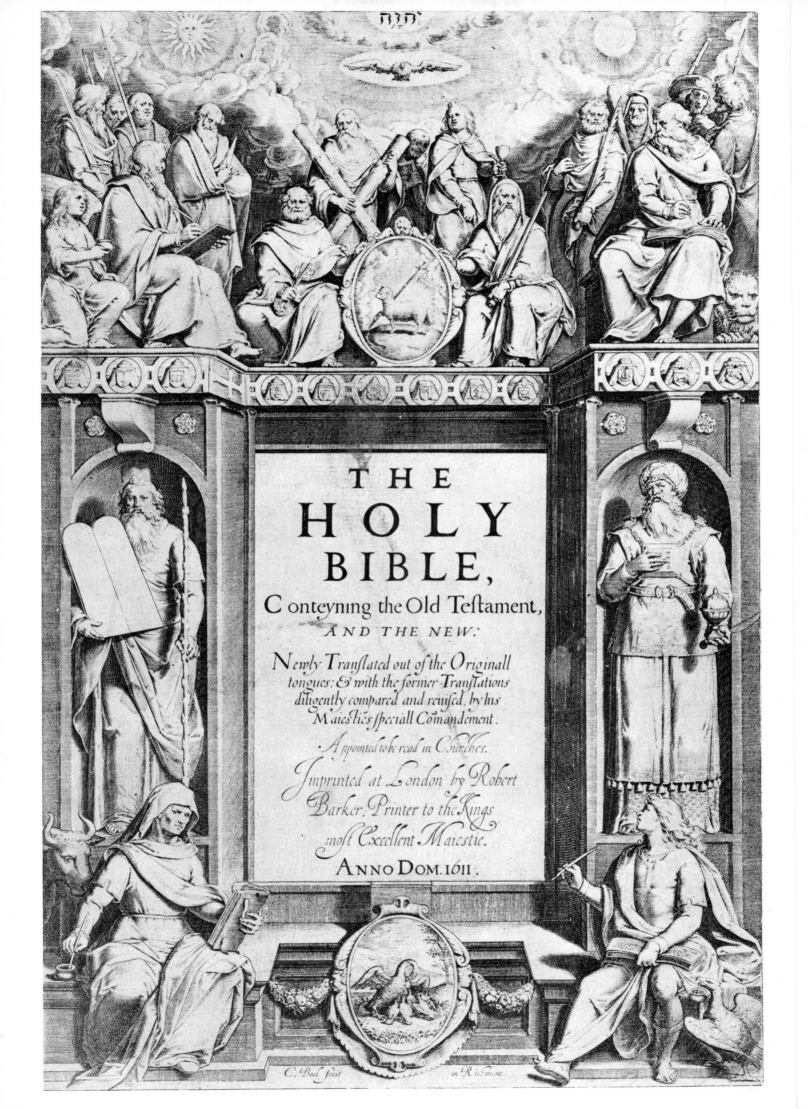

THE
HOLY
BIBLE,

Conteyning the Old Testament,
AND THE NEW:

Newly Translated out of the Originall
tongues: & with the former Translations
diligently compared and reuised, by his
Maiesties speciall Comandement.

Appointed to be read in Churches.

Imprinted at London by Robert
Barker, Printer to the Kings
most Excellent Maiestie.

ANNO DOM. 1611.

Robert Winter — Christopher Wright — John Wright — Thomas Percy — Guido Fawkes — Robert Catesby — Thomas Winter — Bates

The Anglicans and the Puritans

The two most vocal groups opposing the King James Version of the Bible in the Church of England frequently found themselves lumped together by their enemies under the name of "Presbyterians" because they were followers of John Knox as well as John Calvin. But since they actually derived from the Anglican instead of Scottish church, they were more commonly known as "Puritans" and as "Separatists." Of the two groups, the Separatists were the more radical. Having given up all hope of reforming the church from within, they decided to form their own "separate" groups outside the Church of England. The Puritans, on the other hand, stayed and worked inside the Established Church, hoping to purify it. They became the proponents of the "low-church" faction within the Church of England.

Like the Anabaptists on the Continent, both these new English groups claimed the Reformation had not gone far enough. Anglican ritualism, they said, obscured the deeper virtues of Christianity. Their first quarrels were actually minor ones. But they were violent. Both Puritans and Separatists argued that (as John Knox had said) kneeling during communion smacked of Roman ritual instead of true worship; that making the sign of the cross obscured the real importance of baptism; that clergy should wear ordinary clothes, not vestments, so that they would not be set apart from members of the congregation. They also never tired of pointing out that James I had written a *Sports Day Book* for Sundays—an act they regarded as scandalous. To make their "Presbyterian" lives more pure, they themselves plumped for an austere Sabbath in contrast to the comparatively festive day observed on the Continent.

Soon the breach deepened. The Puritans and Separatists insisted that church buildings were not the only places of Christian worship —nor were decorations or acolytes essential. So both groups began to emphasize family religion at home: a family Bible and family prayers—and the reading of the Geneva Bible instead of the King James Version. In an effort to bring religion into their everyday activities, they said that true worship services could— and frequently should—be held in "unconsecrated"—and undecorated—buildings such as their own modest homes; and in preference to formal confession, they favored what they chose to call "faithful self-examination" of their souls in the quiet of their own rooms. Most important of all, they argued like the Presbyterians in Scotland for the Calvinist right of each congregation to covenant together democratically—and without bishops—in order to rule themselves. It was this last argument that proved anathema to James I. To him it endangered belief in the divine right of kings. To less exalted Anglicans it seemed to threaten the very structure of the organized church.

To the mind of James I, the Puritan-Separatists now seemed every bit as troublesome as the Presbyterians had already proved to be before he left Scotland for England. In Scotland, his answer had been, "I will make them conform themselves, or else I will harry them out of the land—or else do worse." In England, he tried his best to keep the Puritans, if not the more radical Separatists, in line *inside* his church. Instead, he succeeded only in forcing even some Puritans out of the church and into the arms of the Separatists, with whom many of them were soon heading to America.

Archbishop Laud, here standing in the center of a triumvirate of Anglican court bishops, was the chief target of the Puritans. This cartoon accused him of dispensing superstition as well as theology.

Of God,   Of Man,   Of the Divell.

The Puritan Critics

The emerging Puritans and Separatists were scorned by Anglicans at the beginning of the seventeenth century. Although the Anglican at left is shown shaking hands with a Puritan, the amity thus hoped for did not come about. The English Civil War, or Puritan Revolution, which broke out in 1642, was far more typical of the impending rift—and so were the scenes from *Hudibras* (*right*), in which the rigid scruples of the new dissenters were roundly satirized by the Anglicans.

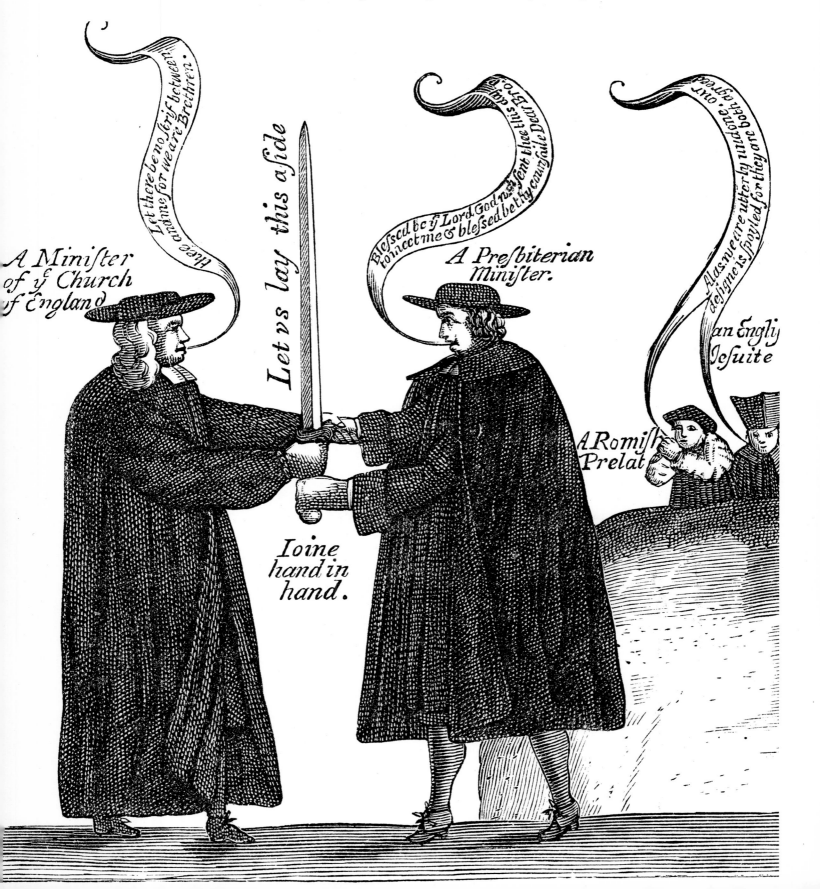

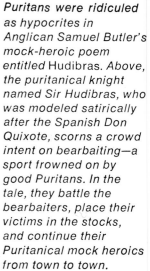

Puritans were ridiculed as hypocrites in Anglican Samuel Butler's mock-heroic poem entitled Hudibras. Above, the puritanical knight named Sir Hudibras, who was modeled satirically after the Spanish Don Quixote, scorns a crowd intent on bearbaiting—a sport frowned on by good Puritans. In the tale, they battle the bearbaiters, place their victims in the stocks, and continue their Puritanical mock heroics from town to town.

The Puritanical resemblance to the perfectionist Continental Anabaptist was lampooned by this cartoon of a Puritan who is shocked by the murder of an Anabaptist child—and to the delight of Anglican satirists carefully avows his own innocence in the affair.

"Stoope, Charles!"

By the standards of the English court of his time, Charles I was comparatively pure in character. What mattered to the Puritans was that he, like his father James, believed that a state-controlled Anglicanism, as personified by his royal self, was God's will and that the divine right (and absolute rule) of kings was unquestionable. In the Anglican-Calvinist battle within the Church of England he found theological support for these beliefs in Archbishop William Laud, a high-church—and actually high-minded—Anglican who persuaded him that true Catholic Christendom could fare better within the Church of England than in the Roman church itself.

Together, Charles and Laud steered a "high-church" Anglican course—as opposed to a democratically minded Calvinist one. They restored many traditional Catholic practices, including moving the communion table to a position at the end of the transept, where, they argued, it belonged as an altar standing

At his trial in 1649, Charles I managed to look rakish in a hat and collar which, in less elegant version, were to become the traditional garb of American Puritans.

Charles II solved his own problem regarding Anglicanism by becoming a Catholic on his deathbed. He purposely delayed his baptism until the last minute, in the belief that his prebaptismal sins might not then be held against him in purgatory.

above the Protestant pulpit. They encouraged a festive Continental Sabbath in opposition to Puritan austerity. Most important of all for those involved, they, following in the footsteps of James I, denied freedom of worship to the Puritans.

In the resulting Puritan Revolution, Charles was beheaded, almost as much for his autocratic church policies as for his royalist government methods, which included excessively high taxes. With his death in 1649, the Puritan "Roundhead" general Oliver Cromwell became England's Lord Protector, and the Puritans basked in freedom for almost a decade. When, however, Cromwell died in 1658, his son proved too weak to continue his policies. Charles II was restored to the throne in 1660, and the Church of England was returned to the Anglicanism it retains to this day.

But not even Charles (*lower left*), who became a Catholic on his deathbed, nor his successor, the seemingly pro-Catholic James II, could restore complete monopoly to the Church of England. In 1689, Parliament passed the Act of Toleration, giving freedom of worship to those creeds of Protestantism willing to join the Anglicans in subscribing to a statement against transubstantiation —which excluded the Catholics, who, even under Charles II, had hardly been tolerated except in court circles. (The "radical" Quakers were also excluded.) One provision of the Act decreed that no Roman Catholic might ever again wear the British crown.

The day of Cromwell had thus left its mark.

During his nine-year "Long Parliament," the Puritan "Roundhead" government had adopted the Westminster Confession of Faith, a seventeenth-century confession which, in formulating the creed of Calvinism in England, ranked in importance with the Augsburg Confession of the sixteenth-century Lutherans and the Heidelberg Confession of the sixteenth-century Calvinists on the Continent. In a comparatively accurate reflection of original Calvinism, the Westminster Confession asked, "What is man's chief end?" The Westminster answer, as young Calvinists throughout England and later America were to learn by memorizing their *Westminster Shorter Catechism,* was: "Man's chief end is to glorify God and to enjoy Him for ever." Though the word "enjoy" was not underscored, it conveyed an emphasis that would have pleased patient John Calvin himself.

This pro-Anglican drawing contrasted "The Orthodox true Minister" who held services in a "consecrated" building with the dissenting Calvinist Separatist whom Charles's Anglicans considered "The Seducer and false Prophet" for preaching from such unlikely spots as a tavern window (above right) to anybody who would listen.

"Stoope, Charles!" was the title of this Anglican cartoon satirizing Puritan intolerance toward Charles I, who, when finally beheaded in 1649, said before the ax fell, "I go from a corruptible to an incorruptible crown, where no disturbance can be."

Puritan Oliver Cromwell was famous for his obstinacy. He claimed God had sanctioned Charles I's execution. To emphasize the democratic processes which had brought Charles to his unhappy end, he made sure the royal beheading took place in broad daylight—at Whitehall on a scaffold set up outside the royal banquet hall.

The Thirty Years' War

Albrecht von Wallenstein, an ambitious general, was assassinated by Irish and Scottish officers. He tried to use the might of Catholic princes to his own purposes in an attempt to unite Germany and secure religious toleration between Catholics and Protestants.

These angry Bohemian Hussites, fearful of Catholic attempts to regain church lands, threw two Hapsburg agents from the windows (below) and so started the Thirty Years' War. The conflict solidified the boundary lines of Protestantism and Catholicism in western Europe.

In England, the religious policies of the Stuart kings proved the chief cause of the Protestant migration to America. On the Continent, the Thirty Years' War was to produce a similar result. The war began in May, 1618, when a group of Protestant noblemen, fearful of the land-grabbing policies of the Catholic Hapsburg dynasty, broke the Peace of Augsburg by attacking two Hapsburg agents (*below*). In reprisal, Catholic rulers throughout Europe confiscated huge tracts of Protestant property and tried to wipe out Protestantism within their realms.

Almost every country of Europe sooner or later became involved. Sometimes the issues —and the war's geographical boundaries— confused even its leaders. To the aid of the Protestants came the Lutheran king of Sweden, Gustavus Adolphus (*right*), who had fond hopes of making all Europe Protestant (and the Baltic Sea a private Swedish lake). To his aid, surprisingly enough, came Cardinal Richelieu of France, who hoped by joining forces with Gustavus Adolphus to extend French territory into Germany.

The war lasted until 1648, a conflict of almost incomparable cruelty. Most of the German Palatinate was completely devastated. Perhaps half of the German population had been killed, and nearly half a million Palatinates had been driven from their ruined homes and lands. Of these, none suffered more severely than the Mennonites. Some took refuge in Hungary. Others fled to southern Russia. Later, on three different occasions—1674, 1680, and 1688—Louis XIV of France sent his armies into the Palatinate to burn and plunder again. It was large numbers of the descendants of all these Palatinate peoples who, their lands being depleted, came to the middle colonies of America a century later.

For the Calvinists on the Continent, however, the war won equal political recognition with Lutherans and Catholics under the various governments. By the terms of the Peace of Westphalia, which ended the entire conflict, Catholic princes were required to permit not only Lutheran but also Calvinist worship in realms where Lutheran worship had existed prior to the war. Protestant princes were required to do the same for Catholics in their domains. For the first time, too, some small but unsuccessful attempts were made toward ecumenism, one of the provisions of the treaty expressly permitting Catholics and Protestants to worship in the same building, though at different hours.

The chief Protestant leader of the war was Gustavus Adolphus of Sweden (standing at left). The Swedish Lutheran church for which he fought was chiefly a political instead of religious split from Catholicism. But his attempt to gain Europe for Protestantism was idealized by later Swedish patriots in this memorial tableau identifying his expansionist ambitions with those of the later Charles XII of Sweden (right).

God in America

The early Protestants in America never tired of pointing out that Columbus had discovered the New World only a few short years before the Protestant Reformation. Therefore, they reasoned, God had reserved America for them and it should be their haven. Sometimes they also argued that North America should be reserved for Protestants only—despite the fact that Maryland had been founded at least partly as a refuge for persecuted Catholics from England. (Some Catholics, on the other hand, came to believe that South America was ordained by God for them.) And there were Protestants, too, who thought that America should remain a haven for their particular brand of Protestantism alone.

The French Huguenots, and not the English Puritans and Separatists, were the first Protestants to flee to America for religious freedom. In 1564, more than half a century before the Pilgrims arrived in Massachusetts, a small band of Huguenots arrived in what is now Florida, hoping to escape the massacres of Charles IX of France and his mother, Catherine de Medici. Within a few months their settlement was destroyed by an agent of Philip II of Spain, and not one Huguenot survived.

The next two groups of Protestants came with no particular concern for religious freedom. Though there were Presbyterians among them (and though there was some basis for claiming religion, which they did, as the "cheefe purpose of ye plantation"), the Virginia colonists at both Roanoke and Jamestown were mostly members of the Established Church of James I's England. Nor in 1632 did the Dutch Reformed of New Amsterdam, nor in 1638 the Swedish Lutherans of early Delaware, come seeking religious liberty. They simply brought their religion with them as a part of the culture of the times.

But, like the early French Huguenots, many a Protestant did come to America chiefly in search of religious liberty. In 1620, the English Separatists and Puritans began arriving in Massachusetts. A band of dissenting Separatists among them soon headed for Rhode Island with Roger Williams *(pages 88-89).* The Pilgrims were followed in 1656 by the early Quakers who, being unwelcome in New England, settled in New Jersey, then in 1682 in Pennsylvania *(pages 96-7, 100-1).* By the early eighteenth century, large groups of other Protestants seeking freedom from European intolerance began to arrive. They were the persecuted Scotch-Irish Presbyterians *(pages 108-9),* the German Lutherans, the Moravians *(pages 104-5),* the Calvinist German Reformed *(pages 108-9),* and small pietistic German sects like the Mennonites *(pages 106-7).* Together, they transformed America into colonies representing all the creeds of Reformation Europe and stamped an indelible Protestant ethos on the country—an ethos frequently quite different from the European creeds out of which they had come. In America they frequently tended to place an emphasis on morality and—especially during the nineteenth century—on a perfectionism that developed in marked contrast to their European counterparts.

According to tradition, the first American Indian converted to Protestantism was
a youth named Maneteo, who was baptized on August 1, 1587, by the settlers
of the ill-fated Roanoke colony. The conversion of the second, Pocahontas
(above), was the result of some rather questionable Protestant ethics.
The girl had endeared herself to the colonists not only by saving John Smith's
life but by her habit of turning handsprings on the colony green. In retaliation
for unchristian acts by the colonists, the Indians took several English prisoners.
In return for this unfriendly act, the English colonists seized the Indian girl, then
converted and baptized her. She was given the name Rebecca by the Anglican
colonists of Jamestown because it seemed more Christian to them than her
real name. The acting governor of the colony piously wrote back to England:
"Powhatans daughter I caused to be carefully instructed in Christian Religion,
who, after shee had made some good progresse therein, renounced publickly
her countrey Idolatry. . . ." A few years later, Pocahontas died as she was about
to return to America from a visit to England. Captain John Smith, then in England,
wrote again piously, "She made not more sorrow for her Vnsuspected death,
than joy to the beholders to heare and see her make so religious and godly
an end."

The Puritan Theocracy

The Calvinist idea of a pure theocracy in government had failed less than a century earlier in Geneva. But the Pilgrims who arrived in America in 1620 were starting from scratch in a new land. They brought with them the Calvinist zeal for democracy and for education. They also brought with them the Calvinist idea that man could work with God to improve the world. Most of all, they brought with them their own peculiar Calvinist concept of government by an *authoritarian* God. They began by covenanting together in the Calvinist manner in the Mayflower Compact. In the end, they made the church itself the political government, instituted strict laws, and set up schools.

The entire course—and final dissolution—of the Massachusetts theocracy was clear in the lives of the men shown at right. In them were

to be found both the virtues and the faults of Puritanism. Richard Mather was a dour-faced preacher. John Cotton was more sweet-natured—and less practical. Together, these two Puritans, who had fled to America from England, typified the Calvinism of the Puritan-Separatists. When, after Cotton's death, Mather married Cotton's widow, the Mather-Cotton line became inseparably linked. Sure that Puritanism was God's will, they tried to implant in America a democracy based on their congregational policy of church government, the New England town meeting, and a respect for education which almost immediately resulted not only in the founding of public schools "against ye old deluder, Satan," but also in the founding of Harvard College. They brought with them a Calvinist penchant for industry, thrift, and sternness, which, as in their Puritan England, favored strict morality and Sunday blue laws.

But they tended to conceive of God as a stern and vengeful spirit rather than a merciful one—and their brand of Calvinism turned peculiarly undemocratic. Worst of all, theologically, their emphasis on Calvinist industry and thrift caused them to ascribe virtue to the rich and successful—and sinfulness to the poor—in a manner that would have infuriated Calvin. When they had successfully established themselves both politically and economically, they emphasized the human depravity of others as opposed to their own "godliness." They became as intolerant of other faiths as had the Anglicans they had fled, persecuting and banishing from their colony all those who disagreed with their own ideas, and insisting on a rigid belief that, as a result of their growing prosperity, they themselves had miraculously become the fortunate "elect" of God.

Of genuine democracy, John Cotton was finally to write: "I do not conceyve that ever God did ordayne [it] as fitt government eyther for church or commonwealth." Richard Mather, the practical one, was forced before his death to draw up a "Half-Way Covenant" that permitted children of members to become full members, or "elect," even though they had actually had no real experience of conversion. The very fact that such a compromise was necessary indicated that their theocracy, like Calvin's original one, would fall apart at the seams. During the life of Cotton Mather, it did. Finding the idea of the "elect" had gone out of favor, he soon fell from power. He ended up writing a history of the past glories of the Puritan colony.

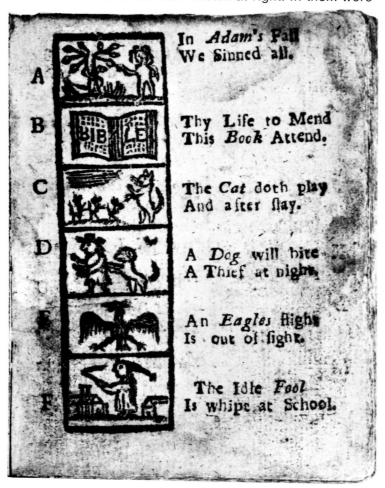

In the New England Primer *the lesson for the letter "A" began in typical fashion: "In* Adam's Fall */ We Sinned all. It also included "Samuel anoints / Whom God appoints" and "Job feels the rod / Yet blessed God."*

Richard Mather had a booming voice that helped make his sermons suitably dramatic. He made a translation into metric verse of The Whole Book of Psalms. *It was intended for pious singing in the meetinghouse. Of John Cotton (below), grandson Cotton Mather wrote: "Many believed that God would not suffer Mr. Cotton to err." As an author, grandfather Cotton included in his works an alphabetical catechism for children. Its title:* Spiritual Milk for American Babes, Drawn out of the Breasts of both Testaments for their Souls' Nourishment. *Like the New England* Primer *(opposite page), it became a standard school book for generations of New England children who learned by rote not only their alphabet but also strong little maxims pointing up their fathers' beliefs. "In his heart of hearts," wrote historian Perry Miller, "John Cotton never doubted that God was a being remarkably like John Cotton."*

"Boston," Cotton Mather once exclaimed, "thou has been lifted up to heaven!" He pompously gloried in the scholarly sobriquet "Cottonus Matherus" in the Latin style. He found it difficult to preach even that men should love their wives—without adding "all the dayes of thy vanity," since he believed human life could never achieve anything better than a "seasonable cheerfulness." "Let your Business," he wrote grandly as advice to an increasing number of Puritan merchants, "ingross the most of your time," in the belief that poverty was not a sin if it was beyond one's control, but to accept poverty voluntarily was totally reprehensible.

Cotton Mather's father, Increase Mather (below), was the son of Richard (and son-in-law of John Cotton). He was arrogant, hot-tempered, and power-hungry, though, as a contemporary Bostonian once said, he had "the face of an angel."

"The Fall of Old Adam"

Gaunt-faced Richard Baxter was a lifelong semi-invalid who stayed in England and popularized Puritanism by his writings, notably his famous The Saints' Everlasting Rest. *He thought it wrong to make the sign of the cross in baptism, but he considered kneeling in public prayer all right.*

The Puritan Michael Wigglesworth, who had become too sickly to be able to preach the typically long sermons of his time, made the best of his predicament by composing and publishing dirgelike sermons in lengthy rhymed verses. These he collectively called by the ominous title *Day of Doom.* New Englanders actually preferred it to John Milton's *Paradise Lost.*

In one particularly bleak section of these verses, Wigglesworth described the awful moment when, according to the Puritan emphasis on a literal predestination, the souls of unbaptized infants appeared before their Maker at the "Last Judgment." The first of these stanzas, gruesomely entitled "Damnation of Infants," began in a jog-trot meter:

> Then to the Bar, all they drew near
> who dy'd in Infancy. . . .

The children's souls then plead for salvation:

> O Great Creator, why was our
> Nature depraved and forlorn?
> Why so defil'd and made so vile
> Whilst we were yet unborn?

The Wigglesworthian—and Puritanical—answer to this question, based on a strict doctrine of original sin, came in the next equally doleful stanza:

> . . . what you call old Adam's Fall, and
> only his Trespass,
> You call amiss to call it his,
> both his and yours it was.

Wigglesworth thus managed to put the Puritans' too literal emphasis on John Calvin's doctrine of man's depravity and God's absolute predestination into dismal decrees that have plagued the Calvinists to the present time. The truth was that many of the Puritans dressed not in pious blacks and grays but in bright colors and that they, like many a good Englishman, often imbibed freely, had a love for field sports like hunting, fishing, and horse racing. But their attitude was strict enough to send some rebellious Puritans, tired of Calvinist rigidity, off into the woods to nearby Merry Mount with an Anglican named Thomas Morton, where they were caught by some of their stricter brethren in the act of dancing rebelliously around a Maypole. Back in England by 1637, Anglican Morton then published *New English Canaan,* in which, to the delight of Anglican Archbishop Laud and his friends, he ridiculed the "precisians" of the Puritans.

The Puritan church bell was a drummer. Seats inside were assigned on the basis of social status.

In 1646, the Puritan theocracy enacted laws making failure to attend church punishable by a fine of five shillings, and disbelief in any book of the Bible punishable by whipping or banishment, let alone the stocks. But in contrast to previous orthodoxy the Puritans emphasized the important concept that God did not fully reveal himself in the Bible and was, in fact, far bigger than the minds of human beings could envision. "This was," historian Perry Miller wrote, "the portal through which ran the highway of intellectual development." Therefore, Miller argued, Puritanism was a major expression of Western intellect and Western idealism.

"Up-Biblum God"

CATECHISMVS LUTHERI
Lingva
SVECICO-AMERICANA.

This Lutheran catechism was translated into the Algonquin language in the mid-1600's by the Swedish Lutheran pastor John Campanius, who settled in New Sweden near the site of present-day Wilmington, Delaware. Campanius was fond of pointing out similarities between the Indian language and that of the ancient Hebrews. The catechism was printed in Sweden in 1696 by command of the king—and at his own expense—because he hoped to buck up the failing Swedish Lutherans in Pennsylvania. Having been culturally absorbed by their English neighbors, the Swedish colonists were turning to the Church of England.

For a time the Puritans considered the Indian a God-given opportunity for testing the force of the Calvinist ideal of changing the world. The Indian, they decided, was actually a white man whose skin had been darkened by dyes and by weather—and whose soul had been led astray by the devil. Almost fondly, they began to call him "a child of Satan." Cautiously, they began writing back to the English Puritans of their missionary efforts with him.

One of their first reports, published in London in 1647, was uncertainly entitled *The Day-Breaking, if not the Sun-Rising, of the Gospel with the Indians in New England.* Later, more sure of themselves, they called their second report, in 1658, *Some Helps for the Indians Showing That They Improved Their Natural Reason to Know the True God and the True Christian Religion.* A few Puritans even hit upon the idea that the Indian might be descended from the Bible's ten lost tribes of Israel.

In 1663, Puritan John Eliot *(opposite page)* completed translating the first Bible into the Algonquin language. There is little evidence that his *Mamusse Wunneetupanatamwe Up-Biblum God,* or, literally, "The Whole Holy His-Bible God," was actually much more than a historical curiosity. But he tried hard. For the "dukes" of Genesis 36:30, he made the first English use of the Indian word "mugwump," a word later to become famous on the American political scene. He also made some interesting decisions. The Algonquin word for "father" failed, he decided, to convey the full meaning of Christian love. To convey its real import, he used the word for "chief," which contained within it not only the connotation of "authority" but also of "loving care for children." For the word "heaven" he decided on the Algonquin equivalent for "regions of the far west part of the skies." Like many an early Protestant missionary, he sometimes majestically dismissed the indigenous religion of his converts by insisting on the word "God" instead of the very logical Algonquin "Great Spirit."

Shipped to stay-at-home Puritans in England, its colorful language delighted Londoners of many creeds. They were moved to found the Society for the Propagation of the Gospel in New England, the first organized Protestant overseas missionary effort. The organization was the forerunner of all Protestant overseas missions.

By 1674 there were, as a result of the efforts of John Eliot on the mainland, as well as Thomas Mayhew and his sons on Nantucket Island, approximately four thousand "praying Indians," as the Puritans called them. At Natick, Massachusetts (top), a special village was built for them. Farther south, Church of England, Moravian—and Lutheran missionaries were active for a time.

The American Baptists

The rising English Baptists were not simply a split from the established Anglican church. Instead, they were formed from a split within the ranks of Puritans and of Separatists who had, in turn, split from Anglicanism.

In 1606, the Rev. John Smyth, an English Separatist clergyman, went to Amsterdam with the band of Separatist Pilgrims who were soon to come to America. In Holland, he met the Dutch Mennonite descendants of the early Anabaptists and blended his Separatist ideas with their beliefs. To him, the Anabaptist belief in adult baptism seemed both biblical and sensible, since it tested the believer's faith as an adult instead of as an infant. Soon other Separatists followed Smyth's lead, among them young Roger Williams, of the Massachusetts Bay Colony. "Williams," wrote the disapproving John Cotton, "was the most prodigious minter of exorbitant novelties in New England." Cotton Mather was equally scathing. Williams, he said, was a windmill whirling with more fervor than sense.

Soon Williams was battling John Cotton. In his pamphlet, *The Bloudy Tenent of Persecution,* he argued that God did not require uniformity of religion and that, for all he knew, the religion of the Indians could prove as acceptable to God as Christianity. Cotton replied with a pamphlet of his own, *The Bloudy Tenent Washed and Made White.* Williams fought back with *The Bloudy Tenent Yet More Bloudy,* in which he accused Cotton of putting the "church before godliness." Calvinism, he argued, is a democratic creed. Therefore, a "free church" should exist in a "free state." A man might well be mistaken in his beliefs, but if he is sincere, he should not be molested by any government, including Puritan theocracy.

Williams broke with the Massachusetts Puritans when he insisted that civil courts, in contrast to New England Calvinist efforts to merge state and church into a theocracy, should have jurisdiction over only civil, not religious, matters. A government, he said, cannot rightfully deny a man freedom of conscience by forcing him to worship in a certain manner. Furthermore, he pointed out, the Indians were the true owners of land in Massachusetts, and it might benefit the Puritans to examine their real motives in taking land from them.

He was banished from the colony in 1635, after which he was, by his own account, "sorely tossed" through fourteen weeks of

Holding a quill pen in his hand, Roger Williams looked the elegant patriarch he became in his later days. As a freethinker he originated a Rhode Island colonial law against the right of a husband to influence his wife's religion. But in Massachusetts he had refused to say grace with his wife at dinner after she disobeyed him by going to Puritan services.

bitter wind and, "sick with fever," forced to wander through the wilderness "not knowing what bread or bed did meane." By foot, by canoe, and with help from friendly Indians (who learned to greet him with "What cheare, Netop [Friend]"), he managed to arrive at Manton's Neck on the Seekonk River.

The Puritans immediately sent word to him that he was still within the boundaries of Massachusetts. Crossing the river, the harried Williams founded the town of Providence, in which freedom of conscience was to be for the first time really observed in America and church and state governments were for the first time separated. He paid the Indians for his land, giving them a fair amount in cash, although his missionary zeal prompted him to advise them, "Why do you paint yourself? Wipe off. . . . The God that made you will not know you."

In Rhode Island, there was no religious test for holding a public office as there was in Massachusetts. On the grounds that the first four commandments of the Decalogue are religious injunctions instead of simply ethical ones, magistrates were forbidden to punish citizens who broke them. Blasphemy and non-observance of the Puritan Sabbath were thus tolerated. Contrary to practice in Massachusetts, the punishment for a poor man's crime was no greater than that of a propertied man. Use of the term "goodman" was banned—only God, Williams pointed out, is truly good; and a Jew named Michael Lopez became the first of his religion in America to be allowed freedom to follow his creed in the midst of Protestants. "It hath fallen out sometimes," Williams wrote, "that both papists and protestants, Jews and Turks, may be embarked in one ship; upon which supposal I affirm, that all the liberty of conscience that I ever pleaded for, turns upon these two hinges—that none of the papists, protestants, Jews, or Turks, be forced to come to the ship's prayers or worship, nor compelled from their own particular prayers or worship, if they practice any. . . ."

Shortly after his arrival in Rhode Island the freethinking Williams was rebaptized, became for a few short months a Baptist, and thereby gave rise to the Baptist claim to him as their founder in America. Actually, he remained a Baptist for only three or four months at most, then continued his rebellion and became a "Seeker for Truth," a Christian discontented with every institutional religious

Thomas Hooker, the founder of Connecticut, was one of the judges who banished Roger Williams from Salem, Massachusetts, for his "Anabaptist" tendencies. In 1636, Hooker himself got into trouble and headed with his congregation (above) for Hartford. There he founded his government on the premise that "the foundation of authority is laid in the free consent of the people."

organization. Like Williams, but unlike the Anabaptists of Europe, the early Baptists in America, as in England, had no strict belief in immersion as the proper method of baptism. They were far more concerned with the state of mind of the believer as an adult than in the method of the actual rite. It was not until after 1640, when a group of English Calvinists came over to the Baptist side, that this Continental custom was firmly adopted by English Baptists. True to their Separatist heritage, however, they became a militant, hymn-singing lot, clinging solidly to their own individual intuitions in interpreting the Bible, and, in reaction against formal churches, expressing a distinct distrust of the need for an educated clergy. To them, democracy meant absolute freedom of the local church. It was partially this demand which made them split into more groups than almost any other denomination in Protestantism.

In addition to the "General Baptists" of Williams' day, who believed democratically that salvation is available to all men, there developed the "Particular" Baptists, often known as "Primitive," or "Hard-Shell," Baptists because they emphasized the Calvinist doctrine of the "elect"; the "Free-Will" Baptists, who stand in exact opposition to this fatalistic Calvinist concept; the "Seventh-Day Baptists," who split off from others because they observe the Sabbath on Saturday; the "Anti-Mission" Baptists, who argue that God will find his "elect" without missionary help; the "Missionary" Baptists, who rebelled in turn against the "Anti-Mission" group; and the United Baptists, who, far from uniting, claim to be the direct descendants of the original Anabaptists of Reformation Europe. They have also split into the "Two-Seed-in-the-Spirit" Baptists, who take literally the biblical injunction that every man contains two seeds in his soul—one for good, the other for evil.

In America, early Baptists included not only Williams but a short list of important colonists, among them Henry Dunster, first president of Harvard, who was forced to resign from the Puritan-founded college for espousing Baptist beliefs. In the twentieth century, such liberals as Harry Emerson Fosdick were acceptable to the individualist spirit of the Baptists, though not to the Presbyterians. But as an early American group they were not measurably to increase in numbers until the Great Awakening of the eighteenth century (*pages 114-5*) and the rise of the American frontier. Here, in complete opposition to early American Baptist principles, a literal interpretation of the Bible had enormous (and to some later liberal Protestants unfortunate) appeal, with church services full of thunderous "Amens," and a propensity for fighting reminiscent of their early Anabaptist cousins.

A half-frozen Williams sat desolately on a stump in the winter of 1635 on his way to Rhode Island.

This log building was the first church erected in Hartford, Connecticut.

Some Pitfalls for the Sinner

The best-known of all seventeenth-century English Baptists was a Calvinist Separatist named John Bunyan, who was arrested in 1660 for preaching in a farmhouse without proper license from the established Church of England. In jail, Bunyan began to write a wry allegory of the condition of English Protestantism that was to become a mirror of life itself. In *The Pilgrim's Progress from This World to the World Which Is to Come,* he managed to pin down a host of human faults and foibles, although his wit and good humor were obscured for centuries by the fact his book almost immediately became revered as a pious classic instead of the lively story he had to tell. He satirized the sheriff who had coaxed him at the time of his arrest to escape jail and make insincere obeisance to Anglicanism. The sheriff made a pompous Mr. Wordly Wiseman (lower right). In addition to the group shown here, he took aim at easy marks like "Mr. Gripe-Man" and a fellow understandably named "Ready-To-Halt," as well as a motley group named Lord Hate-Good, Mr. Money-Love, Mr. Little-Faith—and plain Pride, Prejudice, Presumption, and Ill-Will.

When the going got dull, he was not averse to sprinkling his story with aphorisms. "Every vat must stand on its own bottom," his allegorical character named Presumption mumbles. "The whole and every whit is mine," Bunyan once said testily when his authorship was questioned. His message was Calvinism at its best. He took pains to make it abundantly clear that the Calvinist belief in a divine plan—including an elaborate seventeenth-century version of that plan *(see following pages)* was not an easy one to hold. Life, his book preached, can be understood only when a man patiently bears his troubles—and trusts in God. At the end of his tale he forced his pilgrim Christian to plunge alone into the River of Death, sustained mostly by a companion named Hopeful, thus making clear the exact point of his book.

Baptist John Bunyan craftily made his elegant Atheist (left) in The Pilgrim's Progress *"fall into a very great laughter" while teetering on the brink of disaster.*

Head in hand, the Giant Despair, who had a shrewish wife named Diffidence, constantly bemoaned the hardness of his lot and recommended suicide as the best way out.

...morous met ...hristian on ...e Hill of ...fficulty, urged ...m to follow ...m down the ...rong side.

Mr. Wordly Wiseman advised Christian to forget his spiritual goal by seeking out practical Mr. Legality and a simpering fellow named Civility.

Hypocrisy was especially good at finding shortcuts, then fatuously pointing out their practical advantages.

Pliable was so weak he listened to everybody's advice, was first to give up the journey.

Mistrust refused to believe that two lions on the road ahead were harmless.

Ignorance, a mere boy, was cheerfully consigned to hell by Bunyan for not being a Calvinist.

In a long sequel to The Pilgrim's Progress, Madam Bubble cooed at a wavering Mr. Steadfast.

MOUNT CALVARY

Wall of Salvation

Here Christian looses
His Burthen

Here Simple Sloth
and Presumption lay asleep

Beelzebubs Castle

Devils
Garden Interpreters
House

Morality

Christian at
the Gate

River of God

Christian found by Evangelist
out of his way
under Mount Sinai

Hill Lucre

Silver Mine

A Strange
Monument

Christian leads
Hopeful out of the w...

PLAIN CALLED EASE

Here Christian
meets Worldly Wiseman

Christian & Hopeful
Overtake Byeends

VINE YARDS

Here Heedless &
Toobald lay asleep

Evangalist saves Christian

Help assists
Christian

Here Faithful
was burned

An Arbour called the
Slothfuls Friend

Enchanted
Ground

CELESTIAL
CITY

SLOUGH OF DESPOND

VANITY FAIR

They are Seduced
by Flatterer

Deadmans Lane
leading to Broadway Gate
here Little Faith was robbed

RIVER OF DEATH

APOSTACY

Here Greatheart
kills Giant Slaygood
& rescues Mr Feeblemind

Pliable turns back

They meet
Evangalist

Ignorance meets
them

DELECTABLE MOUNTAINS

Hill ...

Mount Marvel

Turnaway
dwelt here

Road to the Town of Carnal Policy, the residence of Worldly Wiseman

They meet
Talkative

An Oak here Old Honest
was found Asleep

Mt Charity

Hill Error

CITY OF DESTRUCTION

Christian
overtakes Faithful

Here Greatheart
Slew Giant Maul

VALLEY OF THE SHA...

Christian first meets
Evangalist

Cave of Pagan
Pope

Snares & his

94

PLAN
of the Road from
THE
City of Destruction.
TO THE
CELESTIAL CITY.
Engraved expressly for
VIRTUE'S,
Elegant Edition of
THE
PILGRIMS PROGRESS.

The Amazing Journey of a Man Named Christian

This old engraving shows some of the more harrowing obstacles bristly John Bunyan forced his struggling pilgrim to face in *The Pilgrim's Progress.* In Bunyan's mind the journey symbolized life itself. Beginning at lower left, Christian, weighted down by troubles, leaves the City of Destruction and, directed by Evangelist, heads toward his allegorical goal, the Celestial City (*center*). Deserted almost immediately by his fair-weather friend Pliable, the pilgrim falls into the Slough of Despond, from which he is rescued by Helpful. Then, in the Town of Morality, he meets Mr. Legality, who has a simpering son named Civility. Escaping this limiting environment, he arrives at the Interpreter's House, avoiding the Devil's Garden nearby. There he learns the meaning of the crucifixion, and his burden falls from his shoulders. But the course he must travel is no less rugged. Tempted to enter the Land of Vain Glory and the Plains of Ease, he is saved only by recognizing the faults of Formalist and Hypocrisy, a pair of oafs who believe in shortcuts. Then he heads up the Hill of Difficulty and soon finds himself in the Valley of Humiliation, where he must battle the ancient Greek devil Apollyon. Victorious, he must then enter the Valley of the Shadow of Death. Safe on the other side of that valley, he is able to rescue Mr. Feeblemind from despair and to help a character named Old Honest, who has fallen asleep under an oak tree. At the Town of Vanity Fair his companion Faithful is burned at the stake, but he meets Hopeful, with whose aid he skirts Doubting Castle. Avoiding the wiles of the Flatterer and other dangerous characters, he finally plunges into the River of Death. The allegory ends when poor Christian arrives at his goal, amazed as much as anybody that he has made the grade.

A Baptist Gets a Tongue-Lashing and Some Quakers Fare Worse

Watch in hand, Peter Stuyvesant tongue-lashed Baptist William Wickendam for having "dipped" a convert in the nearby river.

William Wickendam was a short, stocky Dutchman who worked in a cobbler's shop in Flushing, New York. If, like Governor Peter Stuyvesant, he had been a member of the Calvinist Dutch Reformed Church, things might have gone better for him. Stuyvesant, whose father and father-in-law had both been pastors of the Calvinist church, was so bitterly opposed to some creeds of Protestantism that he publicly tongue-lashed more than one Baptist in the early days of.New Amsterdam. When Wickendam not only preached a Baptist sermon but actually "dipped" one convert in the East River, Stuyvesant would not tolerate it. He upbraided the cobbler *(left),* fined him 12,500 guilders (approximately $5,000), and banished him from the colony.

The directors of the Dutch West India Company, who had become accustomed to putting up with Anabaptists because of William of Orange's original enlightened policies toward Mennonites, tried to stop Stuyvesant by ordering him to "allow all [believers] the free exercise of their religion within their own houses." The governor ignored the order.

Stuyvesant's intolerance was little different from that of colonial authorities up and down the Eastern Coast. In Puritan Massachusetts, things went equally badly for Baptists and for Quakers. Of necessity, the early Quakers were a stubborn and aggressive lot. They were determined to propagate their new creed in America, and they purposely tried to infiltrate the ranks of New England Puritans by dispatching missionaries to New England to convert any who would listen to them. The first two were women, Ann Austin and Mary Fisher. Their arrival in Massachusetts in 1656 sent chills up and down official spines. They were imprisoned, then deported. But no sooner was one Quaker team sent home than another equally zealous group arrived. Sometimes, as in the case of Mary Dyer *(lower right),* the same missionaries returned, refusing to give up.

These two Quakers, stripped to the waist, were tied to a cart and whipped until they had been driven out of the Massachusetts jurisdiction.

Baptist Obadiah Holmes got thirty lashes when he refused to pay a fine for attending Sunday services in a private house instead of in church.

Quaker missionary Mary Dyer insisted on returning to Massachusetts after being banished. The second time she was hanged.

Practical George Fox

George Fox was a bulky, unkempt, unschooled shoemaker's apprentice whose long, thick hair reminded the historian Macaulay of rats' tails. He had some of the radical Anabaptist spirit in him, and he would have joined the English Baptists except that he could not understand the symbolism of baptism, let alone total immersion. Such religious formalities, he believed, obscured the real meaning of what he called "right living." He was an abstemious soul. His dislike of tobacco and cardplaying caused an Anglican vicar to advise him, wholeheartedly, to "take tobacco and sing psalms," with emphasis on the former. Another Anglican cleric recommended a physic and bleeding as the only possible solution to Fox's problems. Instead of going to church, he spent his Sunday mornings reading the Bible, and his Sunday afternoons and evenings visiting the poor.

There was a practical as well as a mystical reason for everything Fox did, including his Quaker discipline of silence in meeting (*right*). He almost always kept his hat on, not only because of his own unfortunate appearance but because in class-conscious seventeenth-century England he believed Christian equality could not be served by doffing one's hat to a so-called "social superior." When he saw the thriving business of English liquor distillers had raised the price of grain so high that the lower classes were going hungry, he added liquor to his prohibitions. For practical reasons, too, he had little regard for ministers, Bibles, and church buildings (which he scorned as "steeple houses"). A good minister, he said, must be more than a scholar. He must practice what he preaches. In his rebellion against the "scholarliness" of the clergy of his time, he therefore found less need for books—including the clergy's interpretation of the Bible—than did Anglicans, Calvinists, or Lutherans. Instead, he kept Quaker meetings purposely simple to allow worshipers to commune with the spirit of God, unhampered by decoration, altar, organ—or pulpit. Because of his fight against the clergy, Quakers perform their own marriage ceremonies, without benefit of clergy. He even forbade his Quakers to pray the Lord's Prayer. Its needless repetition, he said, tended to become a formality which made it meaningless.

He was against oaths, not only because they were forbidden in the New Testament, but, on a practical basis, because they implied two standards of truth: one under oath and one when not under oath. Since a good man should always be truthful, his Quakers "affirmed" to a truth, never swore to it. Because he believed in a divine spark in every human being, he insisted on using the democratic form of address customary to his time—the singular "thou" or "thee," which, he believed, emphasized the divine spark in ordinary people. In his insistence on equality before God, he recommended a form of simple, unadorned attire for his Quakers and a familiar form of address by first name only.

The Quakers were Fox's straightforward protest against formal theology as exemplified by Anglicans—and even Puritans. In the theology around him, he saw little genuine effort to make Christian love actually work. What mattered, he believed, was the "inner light." In practical application of his beliefs, he and his fellow Quakers behaved trustingly to everybody. This included criminals and jailers. For the same reason, he gave women equal status with men in a day when most Protestants did not.

At first Fox called his followers "The Children of Light" to underscore his belief in the divinity within everyone. Soon he changed the name to "Truth's Friends," then, in characteristic simplicity, to plain "Friends"—a name which seemed to him to convey adequately his concept of universal brotherhood. They were dubbed "Quakers" when Fox told an English magistrate, "It is time for judges and magistrates to quake at the word of the Lord." Turning the phrase against him, the judge ironically branded him and his followers "Quakers." In England, a quarter century after their founding, they numbered, as a result of Fox's organizational genius, almost sixty-five thousand members.

The seventeenth-century Quakers were, according to the historian Macaulay, a motley crew who were "too much disordered for liberty and not sufficiently disordered for Bedlam." They were an odd assortment of visionary "ranters," "ravers," "shakers," and social "levelers," all of whose names pretty well described what they stood for and against—and whose actions showed a notable lack of organization. Practical George Fox organized them. He enforced a rule of silence during meeting, which, he discovered, helped any man at meeting better to search his own conscience and also had the very practical advantage of keeping the meeting in order. It was a rule that also perplexed magistrates. When a Quaker preacher was hauled off to jail for preaching outside the established Church of England—as Fox himself was six times— the congregation could continue to meet quite legally in silence, since there was no law against quiet assembly.

"The Holy Experiment"

William Penn had luxuriant hair and courtly manners which Samuel Pepys, the diarist, a friend of Penn's father, scorned as "Frenchified" when Penn was a young man. He was so eloquent a speaker that he impressed even Peter the Great of Russia with his Quaker views when the czar visited London.

William Penn had been successful in establishing a few Quaker colonies in New Jersey before he founded Pennsylvania. But his charter from Charles II gave him a chance to test his bigger hopes for a community of religious liberty based on Thomas More's *Utopia*. His first Pennsylvania Assembly democratically adopted laws far less stern than in many other colonies. Though his Quaker scruples necessitated blue laws prescribing jail terms for "profane swearing, blasphemy, adultery, intemperance, theatergoing, cardplaying," and a catalogue of other "evil sports and games" —and though the rights to vote and hold public office were limited to "such as profess faith in Jesus Christ"—murder alone was considered the only capital offense. Even to the Indian, Penn proved trustworthy. "I will consider you," he said, "as the same flesh & blood with the Christians. . . ." And he kept his word, though his agents frequently did not *(right)*.

But religious freedom proved far more a problem than he had counted on. To Pennsylvania came not only Quakers but also a host of Anglicans, persecuted Scotch-Irish Presbyterians, and, from Germany, all persuasions of Lutherans, Reformed, and pietistic Mennonites. They included even the Schwenkfelders, who had evolved a mystical explanation of "the deification of the humanity of Christ"– and a nonliturgical creed. This "Middle Way" had got them into hot water in Europe with both Lutherans and Calvinists.

Harassed by debts and by almost endless disputes among these varying groups and between his governors and the Pennsylvania Assembly which he had so democratically formed, Penn himself was finally forced to go to debtors' prison. Six years before he died in 1718, he was stricken with apoplexy, which left him helpless—and a care on his friends for the remainder of his life.

"Oh, Pennsylvania!" William Penn wrote years after he received its charter from Charles II (above), "What hast thou not cost me? About thirty thousand pounds more than I ever got by it, two hazardous and most fatiguing voyages . . . and my son's soul almost." The son to whom he referred had not only renounced his Quaker faith but deserted his wife.

Of Penn's treaties with the Indians, the French writer Voltaire said, "The only treaty in history never sworn to and never broken." Voltaire thought of the treaties as one. Actually, Penn made several, including the famous "walking purchase," in which Penn's son Thomas persuaded his agents to run, instead of walk, to encompass as much ground as possible, though the agreement had clearly stated the Penns should be entitled only to that area they could walk in a day and half's time. The exploit gave the Penn family half a million acres of Indian cornfields and hunting grounds, to the disgust of the Indians themselves.

The young Penn refused to doff his hat even to Charles II, and landed in prison for his Quaker scruples, where he was visited by his family.

A Welcome for the Salzburgers

In 1732, the elaborate procession shown here, headed by a pious burgher on a white horse, marched seventy-eight strong from city to city in Germany. They were the Salzburgers, the descendants of early Waldensians (*pages 6-7*) who had taken refuge in Salzburg in the Austrian Alps after centuries of persecution. In Salzburg, they became known as "secret Lutherans" because, in a region where religion still shifted back and forth from Catholicism to Protestantism depending on the belief of the ruler at any one time, they attended Roman Catholic services by day, then secretly sang Waldensian hymns at meetings by night.

By 1685, after the heads of some of their leaders had been literally nailed to their pulpits by angry neighbors, they had attracted the sympathy of the Protestant Frederick William I of Prussia. With his help they came to Germany. In 1732, they were invited to England by James Oglethorpe. From there they embarked for Georgia.

On their way through Germany in 1732, they arrived at Augsburg, where, in spite of the fact that the great Lutheran Augsburg Confession had been signed in that city in 1530, the gates were closed to them. They were admitted for a few days, only after Lutherans in the city prevailed upon the officials to be more lenient. Before they left Augsburg, some of the Lutherans provided the women and children with three carts, one of which is shown at extreme right in this old print. Their next stop was Leipzig, where they received a warmer reception than in Augsburg, including a friendly wave from the man at lower right.

Sub umbris alarum tuarum

Der abzug 16. u. 17. Jun.

The Pious Moravians

In 1722, having endured centuries of persecution in Moravia and Bohemia, the simple—and music-loving—seventeenth-century peasants shown here were invited to settle on the estate of Count Nikolaus Ludwig von Zinzendorf in Saxony, where they became known as "Moravian Lutherans" or "Moravians." Zinzendorf, a Lutheran, had been deeply influenced by the Pietism of his godfather, Philipp Jacob Spener, who had tried at the end of the Thirty Years' War to bring about a Lutheran return to simple piety and the everyday practice of Christian ethics at a time when Lutheranism had become more interested in intellectual theology than in practical life. The Moravians kept Spener's principles alive. They tried to set up "little churches within the church," hoping to make their own lives an example to others and thus to become a "leaven in society." With refreshing candor, they said church doctrine is of little importance. To them, it mattered little whether a man was Lutheran or Calvinist as long as he was genuinely Christian and examined himself faithfully at church sacraments. "In essentials unity," they preached, "in nonessentials liberty, in all things charity." Far from forcing any denominationalism on others, they gathered in little retreats throughout the world. But they nevertheless made their services as colorful as possible. They emphasized their love of music and developed through the centuries ceremonial customs, including foot washing and pietistic prayer (right), which they believed helped them to keep a true Christian spirit alive among themselves. Their pietistic emphasis on "little churches within the church" was also to have its influence on the founding in England shortly thereafter of the Methodists under John Wesley.

The leader of these sturdy Moravians, Count Nikolaus Ludwig von Zinzendorf, was banished from Saxony because, as Frederick William I of Prussia said in his defense, "He wished to live piously though a count."

Anxious to keep Pietism alive, the early Moravians prayed as a group, lying prostrate on the floor beneath their benches. Their love of music, including brass bands at funerals, invaded their ceremonies. To emphasize community over family, early Moravians buried their dead in plots according to age—or church choir classes—instead of by family. They purposely kept their communities small, and treasured and preserved their unique folk customs, including Christmas putze, love feasts which included the "holy kiss of peace" (below) and foot washing.

A Pietist Colony

Ephrata Cloisters was founded near Lancaster, Pennsylvania, in the 1730's by a Mennonite hermit named Johann Conrad Beissel, who had been influenced by the pietistic movement in Germany. At right, a smiling snake looks upon Eve as she eats the apple in this Ephrata Fraktur *illustrating the story of the fall in the Book of Genesis.*

The Moravians and the Lutherans were not the only ones influenced by Pietism. Among the first of those whom William Penn had welcomed to his colony were the Mennonites, who settled in Germantown in 1683, exactly one year after the founding of the colony. A second group of German-speaking Swiss Mennonites followed in 1710, settling in mid-eastern Pennsylvania. This second group belonged to the conservative, or "Amish," branch of the Mennonites, believing in a doctrinal rigidity that encouraged them to take the Bible literally in such matters as wearing plain dress, even refusing to have carpets on their floor because they connoted ostentation.

One of the sectarian groups, being influenced by the Pietism of Germany, founded a cloister near Lancaster, at Ephrata. Led by Johann Conrad Beissel, they had rebelled so thoroughly against what they considered the luxuries of the world that they sought to live in medieval asceticism. In their community buildings, narrow hallways symbolized the "strait and narrow" path of virtue, low doorways emphasized their practice of humility,

and lack of adornment stressed spiritual as opposed to material beauty. Like medieval monks and nuns they devoted their lives to labor, meditation, and worship. In their hymns they sang:

> Happy the man whose wish and care
>   A few paternal acres bound,
> Content to breathe his native aire,
>   In his own ground.

But they also sang of their basic mode of life, in which the chief "sin" to be avoided was the "original sin" of sex:

> Since each man is safe and sure;
> And should look with eyes secure
> On the snake raised up to view,
> Why should fear then weaken you?

After the American Revolution, the cloister declined rapidly. But its occupants, who had revived the medieval monastery art of illuminating manuscripts, left their German *Frakturschriften* illustrations for the Bible to remember them by *(right).*

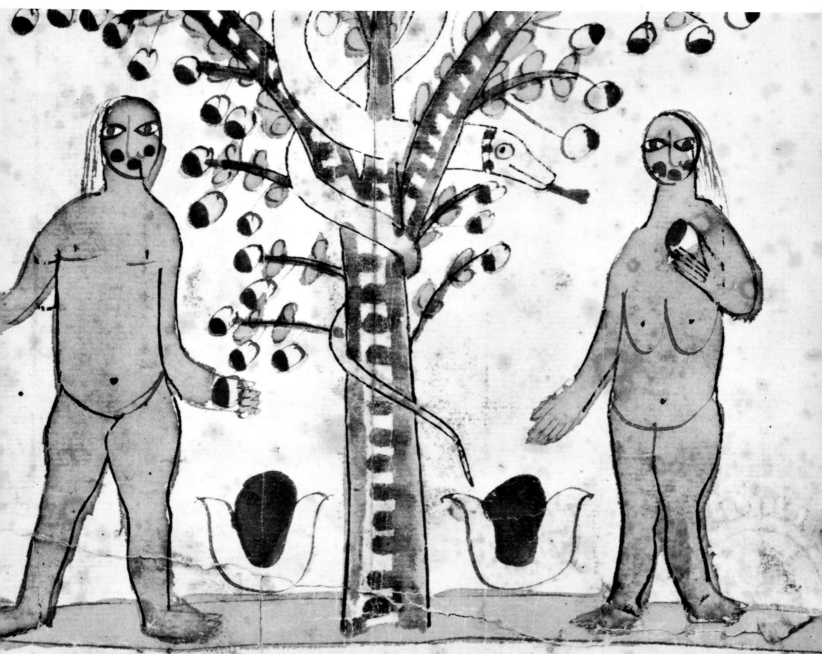

tt die Welt erschaffen, und alle Creatur, ohn
lff und Waffen, sprach er: es fehlet nur ein
r jetzt da wäre, mit Witz und gutem Sinn;
ie steht ganz leere, und ist kein Mensch darin.

HErr thät nieder kommen, auf diese schöne
wenig Erd genommen, daraus ein Mensch gestellt,
dam spazieren, im Garten hin und her, ach
iemand führen, und allzeit bey mir wär.

thät sich umsehen, und dachte hin und her,
dann hin gehen, wann nur ein Mensch da wär,
quicken könte, so könt ich ruhig seyn und alles
e, das ist was ich nur meyn.

thät nun einschlafen, ihn niemand wecken kan,
r ihn erschaffen, von ihm ein ribbe nahm, und

Schlange.

9. Die Schlang sich freundlich neiget, vom Baum
runter schaut, die schöne Frucht ihr zeiget, Komm iß, o sc
ne Braut, sie thät sie noch anschauen, nahm, gab auch
rem Mann, Adam du kanst mir trauen: er nahm, und
auch an.

10. Die Schlange sprach: mit nichten hat GOtt a
gesagt, ich will mich selbst verpflichten, eßt nur und fr
gewagt, ihr müsset selbst gestehen, seyd doch nicht so
zagt, daß ihr alles könt sehen, der Tod euch gar nicht plö

11. Als sie die Frucht gegessen, wurden sie bald gewa
daß sie nackend gewesen, schämten sich beyde gar, versteck
sich im Garten, mit Furcht bedecket gar, die Strafe zu
warten, war ihren Augen klar.

The Presbyterians and the German Reformed

Francis Mackemie, father of the Scotch-Irish Presbyterian churches in the American colonies, preached up and down the coast from Virginia to New York, was arrested by the governor of New York, Lord Cornbury, for preaching without a license in 1707. Mackemie, said Cornbury, was a "Jack of all Trades, a Preacher, a Doctor of Physick, a Merchant, an Attorney, or Counsellor at Law, and which is worst of all, a Disturber of Governments." But Mackemie was acquitted. "My license," he pleaded, "which I got in England as a dissenter is good in all Her Majesty's dominions . . . including New York." Cornbury was soon recalled to England.

The Calvinists who came to Pennsylvania were radically different in origin—and in belief—from the Puritans of New England. The German Reformed, who came from the German Palatinate, were followers of Calvin as interpreted by Germans; the Scotch-Irish Presbyterians were the followers of Calvin as interpreted by the Scottish John Knox. The two groups disagreed with each other, according to their national origins. The Presbyterians were a radical and democratic group; like the Puritans, they rarely knelt to worship. A good Presbyterian of colonial times was as strict a moralist as any Protestant in the colonies. He usually did not dance, smoke, or play cards. He neither worked nor played on Sunday, supposedly spending his day browsing through the Bible. He knew the *Westminster Shorter Catechism* by heart, having memorized it as a child. His ministers stressed the value of religious truth as equal even to the value of prayer, and he was forced to develop a taste for long sermons—as well as long prayers. A good Presbyterian was taught to scorn soft thinking and to look for the firmly thrust points. Sermons went on for three hours at a sitting; then, after a break, another three hours.

In America, the Presbyterians tended to merge with others more doctrinally than nationalistically, especially in the southern colonies. Calvinistic Huguenots, who had arrived in large numbers in Georgia through the tolerance of James Oglethorpe, were soon coming into Presbyterian churches, since to a great extent they held beliefs in common. By contrast, the early German Reformed, in keeping with their proximity to their fellow Germans, were more liturgically inclined than either their neighbor Presbyterians or the Puritans. They had many real differences with the German Lutherans, one of which lay in their acceptance of a more symbolic understanding of the Lord's Supper than that held by the Lutherans. But they frequently held their services in Lutheran churches. The Pennsylvania Germans finally said the real difference between the Lutherans and the Reformed congregations was that the Lutherans began the Lord's Prayer with "Vater unser," and the Reformed with "Unser Vater."

The Scotch-Irish Presbyterians shared with the German Reformed of the Palatinate and the Dutch Reformed of New York a common heritage. This included the Calvinist interpretation of apostolic succession as in the Swiss Calvinist ceremony for ordination of elders and deacons. The ceremony of "the laying on of hands" (above) was practically the only time a good Calvinist would kneel in formal worship. But true to their national heritage, the German Reformed, unlike the Scotch-Irish, ignored Calvinist disapproval of dancing and drinking. Many a German Reformed pastor was questioned hopefully regarding his leniency on these matters before his German-oriented congregation saw fit to call him to their church.

The seventeenth-century English "Presbyterian" shown at left was confined in a cage on London Bridge while spectators jeered at her. In Ireland, in 1641, Scotch-Irish Presbyterians were massacred on the bridge over the River Baen.

The Last Puritan

In 1734, Jonathan Edwards preached a sermon that became his most famous—and most frightening—one of all. Its title: "Sinners in the Hands of an Angry God." "The God that holds you over the pit," said Edwards, "much as anyone holds a spider, or some loathsome insect over the fire, abhors you and is dreadfully provoked; his wrath toward you burns like fire."

"Sinners in the Hands of an Angry God" electrified the country and helped to start what was to become known as "The Great Awakening." In religious hysteria, much of the nation fell into revivalistic wails and groans, shouts of joy—then physical prostration. The hysteria joined forces in the middle colonies with the sermons of two Presbyterian ministers, William and Gilbert Tennent. William Tennent had started a college in a log cabin. The Log

In 1745, David Brainerd, who became a missionary to the Indians as a result of the Great Awakening, happened upon an Indian in Pennsylvania who was dressed in bearskins and carried a rattle in his hand. The Indian, a Christian convert, had left his tribe because they scorned his advice to give up whiskey.

Jonathan Edwards, of Northampton, Massachusetts, always preached in a quiet voice, rarely making a gesture. The titles of his sermons, alone, were frightening enough to keep his listeners awake: "The Eternity of Hell Torments," "The Final Judgment," "Future Punishment of the Wicked Unavoidable and Intolerable," and "The End of the Wicked Contemplated by the Righteous."

College was later to become Princeton University.

In the South, the Baptists took up the cry. At its peak the Great Awakening resulted in such excesses that Edwards himself was shocked. He had intended to launch an intellectual, not an emotional, crusade; and there was a difference between Edwards and the Puritans. Where the Puritans had said "holiness," Edwards and his revivalists said "love." Nevertheless, he was sure he had observed in his own town of Northampton, Massachusetts, what he called a "glorious alteration" in morality. The town, he said sweetly, was "never so full of love, nor so full of joy, and yet, so full of distress as it was then, for the people were fearing for their souls."

Perhaps the more realistic results of the Great Awakening were educational. From it sprang colleges and secondary schools all over the land—"mushrooming," as one historian has said, "after a summer rain." So did asylums and societies for the care of blind, deaf and mute, the insane and the feeble-minded. Every humanitarian cause—temperance, peace, prison reform, the amelioration of poverty—became the rallying point of ardent souls inflamed by the gospel.

Another important result of the Great Awakening was the fact that religious issues became associated in men's minds with political issues. The hitherto persecuted Baptists, especially, swelled in number. They refused to pay taxes for the Established Church in the South and began to see that they were actually in harmony with the political philosophy of the rising American Revolutionary leaders. Thus, politically, the American cause was strengthened.

As for Jonathan Edwards, he was sent off to Stockbridge to preach to the Indians when his congregation tired of his exertions. There he wrote "Freedom of the Will" which set forth his Calvinist view of predestination *(following pages)*. Having been invited by Gilbert Tennent to come to the College of New Jersey (Princeton) as its second president, he died of smallpox after a very short time in office—the last of the great Puritans.

The Great Paradox

"From my childhood up," wrote Jonathan Edwards, "my mind had been full of objections against the doctrine of God's sovereignty, in choosing whom he would to eternal life, and rejecting whom he pleased; leaving them eternally to perish, and be everlastingly tormented in hell. It used to appear like a horrible doctrine to me."

The question that had worried him was that of the Calvinist doctrine of predestination, as he understood it. Did, in fact, human beings have any control over their actions? If man's actions were already preordained by God, Edwards, like many another, wondered how man was to have any hope.

Predestination was a doctrine that once again was beginning to split the Calvinists, just as the orthodox doctrine of the Trinity was also being questioned by some of them (right). But Edwards was to remain on the side of old orthodoxy, in spite of his earlier questioning. "I saw . . . ," he wrote in 1740, "and my reason apprehended the justice and reasonableness of it. . . . The doctrine has very often appeared exceedingly pleasant, bright, and sweet. Absolute sovereignty is what I love to ascribe to God."

He had found the classic Calvinist answer. Even the most idealistic behavior of man, he reasoned, is suspect. Who, he asked, is to say that human purpose even in the most seemingly altruistic behavior is not, in reality, a selfishness which merely disguises itself as altruism? Man, he pointed out, is incapable of knowing his own motives. Therefore, man's will is really dependent upon "God's" will—and man is nothing.

It was Edwards' belief that any possibility for human hope lies solely in having the *desire* to behave for the highest good. But, he argued, the attainment of that desire is not man-made but God-made. Man, as Edwards summed him up, has the power to act in accordance with the choice of his mind; but over the origin of that inclination for choice he has no power.

To the rising anti-Trinitarians, his concept of Calvinism was abhorrent. In turn, Edwards was so alarmed by the anti-Trinitarian movement—and the consequent reliance on human striving instead of divine grace—that he fought all the more intensely for his brand of Calvinism.

On the surface Robinson Crusoe, *published in 1719, told of the trials and tribulations of a shipwrecked sailor. But its author Daniel Defoe intended his story as a Calvinist tract. As a good Calvinist, the shipwrecked Crusoe reads his Bible daily to preserve his belief in God's sovereignty in the midst of spiritual doubts regarding the forces of civilization and nature. The third and final part of the book is seldom read or even printed today because Defoe preached so much in it that he ruined his story.*

The two-faced fellow in the lower left corner of this cartoon made his appearance in Europe at the beginning of the eighteenth century, proving that all was not smooth in Protestant theology at the time. He symbolized a new split: between the old orthodoxy and a rising group of anti-Trinitarians who opposed the orthodox concept of God as Father, Son, and Holy Spirit.

The Great Awakening

George Whitefield was the most rousing preacher of the early eighteenth century. He loved to preach in open fields as well as city streets. In churches where he appeared, clergymen complained that regular parishioners were crowded out by motley throngs. In Georgia, Whitefield had read one of Jonathan Edwards' treatises. "Surely this is the Lord's work," he said, and began his career as an evangelist. His open-air congregations responded by shrieking, rolling on the ground, and running generally amuck. They were tired of the well-modulated voices of Yale- and Harvard-trained preachers. He was a tear-jerking, histrionic revivalist, but he also proved that preaching to uneducated throngs is a special gift. If, as sometimes happened, a clap of thunder interrupted a sermon in midsentence, he took full advantage of the moment. Making a tragic gesture for which he had become famous, he would launch into his favorite discourse, "The Last Judgment." But his main theme, like many an evangelist, was "New Birth." Whitefield's enemies said he frequently uttered "sound without sense" and exhibited a lamentable "zeal without knowledge." In return, he labeled such criticisms "earthly-minded." When Benjamin Franklin went to hear him in Philadelphia, the rousing Whitefield had such a reputation for eloquence that Franklin left his purse at home for fear he would be tempted into giving money to the orphanage in Savannah, Georgia, which the evangelist was sponsoring. "I had in my pocket," Franklin later wrote, "a handful of copper coin, three or four silver dollars, and five pistoles in gold. As he proceeded, I began to soften and concluded to give him the copper. Another stroke of his oratory made me ashamed of that, and determined me to give him the silver; and he finished so admirably, that I emptied my pocket wholly into the collection dish, gold and all." Pragmatically, Franklin once decided to measure the range of Whitefield's voice. From the spot where the evangelist held forth on the courthouse steps on Philadelphia's Market Street, Franklin moved back toward the river. He could, he later reported, still hear the preacher's voice distinctly at Front Street. By calculating the crowd within this distance at two square feet per person, he concluded that thirty thousand people could hear Whitefield at a single time. To accommodate the crowds in Philadelphia alone, a special building was erected for his preaching; this became the first structure of the University of Pennsylvania. "The Great Awakening," in which Whitefield played a colorful part, aroused religious excitement from Maine to Georgia. Its fervor was responsible for the founding of three new colleges: Dartmouth, Princeton, and Brown. Whitefield himself was responsible for increasing the number of dissenters from the Church of England in the colonies, especially in the South, thus not only bringing large numbers into expanding Methodist and Baptist churches but also weakening colonial links with Mother England.

On the night of September 29, 1770, Whitefield preached his last sermon on the stairs of the home of the Rev. Jonathan Parsons, in Newburyport, Massachusetts. Then, because of his custom of arising at 4 A.M., he summarily sent his callers home and went to bed at ten. During the night he had an attack of asthma and died the next morning about six o'clock.

Of evangelist George Whitefield, the English actor David Garrick said, "I would give a hundred guineas if I could say 'Oh!' like Mr. Whitefield." Others said he could stir the souls of an entire crowd just by the way he pronounced the word "Mesopotamia." For his largest crowds, Whitefield repeated his key sentences four times to make sure they would be heard, turning around on the platform until he had addressed all four points of the compass.
On one occasion he cried, "Father Abraham, whom have you in heaven? Any Episcopalians? No? Any Presbyterians? No? Have you any Independents or Seceders? No? Have you any Methodists? No, no, no? Whom have you there?" The answer, as if from heaven itself, was quoted on the spot by Whitefie   "We don't know those names here," he would ⌐⌐out. "All who are here are Christians. . . ." Then he would add, contritely, "Oh, is this the case? Then God help us, God help us all, to forget party names, and to become Christians in deed and in truth."

The Battle of the Hymnals

In their music, early Protestants revealed their differences. Some sang. Some remained silent. Some also slept (*above*). The early Calvinists absolutely refused to go along with Lutheran hymn singing. Hymns, John Calvin had said, were the works of man. To praise God worthily, divinely inspired music was necessary. As a solid bloc, Calvinists therefore sang only Old Testament psalms, and often stiffly so *(opposite page)*. In each congregation, they appointed a leader, or "toner," who had the job of reading aloud one psalm line at a time for the congregation to repeat in song—sometimes

with disastrous results. An early deacon, suffering from poor eyesight, apologized aloud to his congregation for not being able to see the words in the master psalmbook. "My eyes, indeed, are very blind," he explained. The unsuspecting congregation repeated his complaint in song.

Following the example of Luther himself, it was a seventeenth-century Lutheran, not Calvinist, who wrote one of the oldest hymns in present-day Protestant hymnals, "Now Thank We All Our God." The Swedish Lutheran king Gustavus Adolphus ordered it sung in battle by his troops in the Thirty Years' War. Its second stanza contained a line that seemed to him particularly suitable to that long and confused Protestant-Catholic conflict: "And guide us when perplexed." To the horror of early

Calvinists, the Lutherans knowingly retained the Catholic tradition of liturgical responses in church. True to Luther's ideals, they included not only the choir but the entire congregation in these responses. As a result, Johann Sebastian Bach—a Lutheran—purposely made the endings of his two-hundred-odd chorales simple enough for the entire congregation to join in. Bach's chief Protestant contemporary Handel had the comparative misfortune of serving a Calvinist church as choirmaster.

The seventeenth-century Lutheran Paul Gerhardt composed hymns emphasizing Luther's doctrine of "justification by faith alone." But from the beginning the Lutherans also adapted for their own use parts of the Catholic mass, simply translating the "Te Deum," the "Gloria Patri," and the "Gloria in Excelsis" into German. They also sang of Catholicism unknowingly. Like other nineteenth-century Protestants, they were to sing "Faith of Our Fathers," unaware that the Anglican-turned-Catholic priest who had composed the hymn was referring to Catholics, not Protestants, in the line "Our fathers chained in prison cells" —and that some of the Catholic fathers had been chained there by the Protestants themselves.

By the eighteenth century only the Quakers remained silent, emphasizing their own method of worship. It was an Anglican who wrote

This "toner" gave out the lines for the congregation to sing in Calvinist churches of the eighteenth century. Many Calvinists frowned even upon the pitch pipe because of their belief against musical accompaniment. A Boston Congregational church refused a rich parishioner's offer of a pipe organ. A nearby Episcopal church promptly accepted the rejected gift.

Even toward the end of the eighteenth century these psalm-singing Calvinists (lower left) refused to go along with Lutheran hymn singing, though the father of English Calvinist hymnody, Isaac Watts, had died early in the century. The Moravians (below), being distant cousins of the Lutherans, brought Bach's music with them to Bethlehem, Pennsylvania, and hired music professors to teach them to sing properly.

117

the resounding "Doxology." Its author, Thomas Ken, had another claim to fame. He refused to allow Charles II to bring Nell Gwynne to his house as a guest, on the grounds that a mistress—even a royal one—was immoral in the eyes of the church. (Charles later made Ken a bishop.) The hymn "Rock of Ages" was written when an eighteenth-century English Calvinist had a falling-out with John Wesley, the founder of Methodism. In 1776, the Rev. Augustus Toplady, disagreeing with the democratic—and to him very dangerous—Wesleyan concept of salvation for everybody, published a long and highly emotional defense of the Calvinist doctrine of predestination in *Gospel Magazine*. To clinch his argument, he ended the assault with a few verses he had just written. Set to music, they became "Rock of Ages." Angrily, Wesley replied: "Mr. Augustus Toplady I know well; but I do not fight with chimney-sweepers. He is too dirty a writer for me to meddle with; I should only foul my fingers."

Like Toplady, other Calvinists during the eighteenth century began to give way to hymn singing over pure psalm singing. They were led by Isaac Watts, son of a deacon in a dissenting chapel of the Church of England. Watts, born in 1674, had a talent for writing verses for children. In his *Divine Songs for Children* he became the originator of the phrases: "How doth the little busy bee?" "Let dogs delight to bark and bite," and "Birds in their little nests agree." Since he was a Calvinist, many of his six hundred hymns for adults were understandably based on psalms. But they also included the great, New Testament-based "Jesus Shall Reign Where'er the Sun," as well as the more traditional "O God, Our Help in Ages Past."

It was with the rise of Methodism—and of Charles Wesley, brother of John—that hymn singing really came into its own in the English-speaking world. The brothers Wesley frequently disagreed between themselves about excessive emotion which gave vent to un-called-for singing in their meetings. Charles, impatient with John's revivalistic appeal, once

told a group at meeting to go into a corner until they could quiet down. But Charles's own rhymes, when turned into hymns, probably did as much to make Methodism the popular success it became among the common people as John's very logical—and sometimes too methodical—sermons. When Moravian Peter Böhler once told Charles he wished he had a thousand tongues to sing the praises of Jesus, the younger Wesley immediately appropriated the words as "O For a Thousand Tongues To Sing!" When a songbird, fleeing a hawk, plummeted into Charles's window and alighted in his arms, Wesley was so moved that he set down the first lines of the most famous of all eighteenth-century Methodist songs:

> Jesus, Lover of my soul,
> Let me to Thy bosom fly.

He added:

> While the nearer waters roll,
> While the tempest still is high,
> Hide me, O my Saviour, hide,
> Till the storm of life is past!
> Safe into the haven guide;
> O receive my soul at last!

The "nearer waters," the "tempest," and the "storm of life" were based on Charles's harrowing trip to America with brother John, when the two had been caught in a storm at sea with a group of Moravians, who were among the most avid of all Protestant hymn singers. In all, Charles wrote approximately sixty-five hundred hymns, including "Love Divine, All Loves Excelling," "Soldiers of Christ, Arise," and "Hark, the Herald Angels Sing," borrowing the music for his words. "Doggerel!" his critics called some of his efforts. At Charles's death, even John felt obliged to observe that his brother's "least praise was his talent for poetry." But Charles had proved as generous as he was prolific. On his deathbed, seemingly aware of his own limitations, he paid the supreme compliment to none other than a Calvinist—Isaac Watts—by singing not his own but one of Watts's hymns, thereby helping to heal Protestant musical differences. Watts himself had died half a century earlier; on his deathbed, he had sung two lines from his own "When I Survey the Wondrous Cross," which was one of the best of eighteenth-century hymnody:

> Love so amazing, so divine
> Demands my soul, my life, my all.

Later Methodist hymnal editors felt obliged to tone down Charles Wesley's overuse in his hymns of the word "worm" as an appellation for human beings. The word hardly seemed to fit the Methodist concept of salvation for everybody.

In addition to writing Calvinist hymns, Isaac Watts composed a collection of Divine Songs for Children in which he delighted in dreaming up such lines as "How doth the little busy bee?" "Let dogs delight to bark and bite," and "Birds in their little nests agree."

Augustus Toplady wrote the hymn "Rock of Ages" when he had a falling-out with Methodist John Wesley. Toplady disagreed with the democratic—and to him very dangerous— Wesleyan concept of salvation for everybody, and wanted to defend the "rock" of Calvinism. There is a legend that he wrote the hymn on the back of a playing card. At right is part of the original score for Handel's "I know that my Redeemer liveth" in The Messiah.

George Frederic Handel (above) was a Lutheran like Johann Sebastian Bach. But he had the misfortune of serving a Calvinist church as choirmaster in Germany, later went to England where he wrote secular operas.

The Deists

In 1776, historian Edward Gibbon (*below*) tipped his hat to a growing skepticism regarding orthodox Christianity. In his famous *History of the Decline and Fall of the Roman Empire*, Gibbon attributed the basic reasons for the spread of Christianity to a religious zeal it had inherited from the Jews, to the fact that it held out to its believers a hope of immortality, and to the efficient organization of the medieval church. Gibbon's analysis was considered notably superficial by many a clergyman of the day. But it helped to strengthen a growing eighteenth-century trend within Protestantism toward examining the Bible and the origins of Christianity from the point of view of historical—and scientific—investigation.

The truth was that in spite of its break with the past, the Protestant Reformation had remained remarkably medieval in many aspects and had developed its own brand of scholasticism, as was clear in the beliefs of many of its leaders. Now the eighteenth century was to become an era of rationalism in religion as well as in other fields of inquiry. One powerful spur to the development of this religious rationalism was the moral reaction against the cruelties of the past age of religious wars. But there were other equally important spurs, most notably the gathering force of scientific inquiry, stemming from as far back as Copernicus in the sixteenth century, from Galileo in the seventeenth century (who was excommunicated from the Roman church for his scientific beliefs), and from Isaac Newton's mechanistic conception of the universe. These spurs, combined with the rationalism of Descartes and Spinoza, and now with the rationalism of John Locke and David Hume, were largely responsible for the rise of the Deist movement in Protestantism—a movement of all shades of opinion (including a shade by which God, once having created the world, left it to work out its own evolution) but whose basic tenet of questioning orthodox Christianity—both Protestant and Catholic—was true to the entire movement. In England, as early as 1624, Lord Herbert of Cherbury had published *De Veritate,* in which he had attempted to formulate a "natural" religion shared by wise men of all ages and races, as contrasted with Christianity—a Christianity that had, he argued, obscured genuine truth by adding unessential doctrines to its dogmas. For old orthodoxy, John Locke's seventeenth-century approach was even more of a blow. There was, said Locke, much in traditional Christianity that is contrary to human reason. But, he argued, there is a religion which man can arrive at by the use of his unaided reason—a "natural" religion. God, he argued, has furnished man with natural senses which are a surer means of knowledge than the Bible for arriving at a knowledge of religion. Therefore, Locke set himself to examining the Bible for the purpose of discovering the essence of

Historian Edward Gibbon, here tipping his hat in an eighteenth-century sketch of himself in military uniform, was a Deist who helped give rise to the growing eighteenth-century skepticism regarding orthodox Christianity.

Christianity. Christ and his apostles, he said as a result of this examination, set forth only two conditions of salvation: the belief that Jesus is the Messiah and the belief in living a righteous life. These two conditions, he argued, are fundamental in "the new covenant to be performed by all those who would obtain eternal life." But if Locke had struck a blow against orthodoxy, the eighteenth century's David Hume struck an even harder one. In his *Essay on Miracles*, Hume argued against the apologetic value of miracles. Furthermore, he traced both God and man to concepts of human sensation itself.

Locke and Hume were progenitors of the English Deist tendency to break down orthodox religion. But their influence spread to Germany, where the eighteenth-century rationalistic tendency to make clarity of thought and reasonableness the sole criteria of truth was promoted by the Leibnitz-Wolffian school of philosophy. And in France the efforts of the Deists were applauded by, among others, Voltaire. "Every man of sense," approved Voltaire, "every good man, ought to hold the Christian sect in horror. The great name of theist, which is not sufficiently revered, is the only name one ought to take. The only gospel one ought to read is the great book of nature, written by the hand of God and sealed with his seal. The only religion that ought to be professed is the religion of worshiping God and being a good man. It is as impossible that this pure and eternal religion should produce evil as it is that the Christian fanaticism should not produce it." Later, in France, Huguenot-born Jean Jacques Rousseau's romantic belief in the goodness and worth of man was to influence American Deists. But, unlike many an early Deist, Rousseau believed not in pure reason but in the deep need of human nature for emotional insight as well. The Deists were opposed by many, including George Berkeley (*right*). In England, too, William Law became one of the foremost of these opponents. Argued Law: The assumption of the Deists that a revelation claiming to be divine must approve itself to the reason of man is a false assumption. God's character and will, he said, are unfathomable. Only by divine revelation can man know what is right and what is wrong. In so arguing, Law had hit upon one of the chief weaknesses of Deist thought. That weakness lay in the Deist tendency to gloss over the problem of human evil—and to tend to make man potentially better than poor mortals may be capable of becoming.

Philosopher John Locke believed that man, the world, and God were all properly the objects of human reason. He denied religious toleration for both Roman Catholics and atheists in England. Though he never took the final step of outright negation of the existence of a God, as Deist David Hume (below) came very near doing, he was nevertheless expelled from the Church of England in 1683 by direct order of Charles II for his rationalistic beliefs.

David Hume was a fat, amicable Scotsman whose philosophies implied a vague Deism which, like the rationalism of John Locke (above), was to influence the course of much eighteenth- and nineteenth-century Protestant thought.

Joseph Priestley was a scientist and Deist who believed that man's thought and man's soul are products of the human mind itself. But he held fast to the belief that his views could be reconciled with Christianity.

George Berkeley was a kindly, high-minded philosopher who tried to explain the argument between Deists and orthodoxy by arguing that the world has no being except as man conceives it to exist but that the object of science is to interpret God's ideas.

In his satirical Gulliver's Travels, *Jonathan Swift parodied the high-church—low-church problem in the Church of England in the Lilliputians' war over "High Heels" versus "Low Heels," and in whether eggs should be broken at the big end or the little end. Religion, argued Swift, ought never to be ridiculed. But, he said, "surely the corruptions of it may." He also pleaded satirically that he favored only nominal Christianity, "the other having been wholly laid aside by general consent."*

Little John Wesley

Little John Wesley could not accept the Calvinist concept of predestination. Good works, Wesley preached, are important to faith. It was in this way that he appealed to his followers, the common people of the time. It was an age when Deism was, in effect, preaching "Be not righteous overmuch"; when Calvinism offered little hope except for the "elect"; and when the common people had been neglected by the established Church of England. It was also a time when England was shifting from an agrarian economy to the Industrial Revolution, when the masses were being exploited, and when one of the most serious problems of the nation was the liquor problem. Every sixth house in London was said to be a saloon, and morals were at a notoriously low ebb. In the end, Wesley's Methodism adopted the Anglican *Book of Common Prayer,* the Anglican order of worship, and the Anglican beliefs regarding God and Christ. But Methodism was a new Puritanism, a counterpart of the Pietist movement on the Continent.

The real importance of Methodism lay in the fact that it brought a new standard of morality to the English lower classes. Wesley brought

On a last visit to Scotland in 1790, the aged John Wesley, who had in his day traveled a total of two hundred thousand miles to preach the gospel, needed the support of two stalwart friends in getting about the streets. At the ripe old age of eighty-seven, Wesley, who was the founder of the new Protestant group called "Methodists," had become one of the most familiar figures in all England, as well as in much of Scotland. He had preached, by his own account, a grand total of forty thousand sermons, traveling by foot, by horseback, and by carriage over gutted country roads, and, as he himself recorded, frequently as far as fifty miles a day, occasionally ninety. "I am," he once wrote late in life, "a wonder to myself."

them a manner of living by which to strive "methodically" for Christian morality—and for a perfection that he doggedly believed was possible for others, though he was not at all sure it was possible for himself. In opposition to a Calvinism which held out little hope except for the elect, he brought hope to everybody.

Wesley came by his methodicalness naturally. His mother was a systematic woman who devised a plan of teaching, by which all but one of her ten children who survived infancy (of nineteen) learned their alphabet in one day. His father was a preacher who had equally systematically devised a code for attempting to communicate with what the Wesley family decided was a private family ghost—a rapping in their garret, to which they affectionately gave the name "Old Jeffrey." As a student at Oxford, John himself habitually scheduled his intellectual activity by the clock, perhaps meditating from eleven to twelve, for example, on the Calvinist doctrine of predestination, and, from twelve to one, on perhaps the doctrine of free grace. He and his fellow students organized what other students derisively called the "Holy Club," or "Method-ists," at whose regularly scheduled meetings the members sought to achieve Christian perfection through systematic worship, study, prayer, and a day-by-day persistence on right living—all of which were properly recorded in daily journals by the entire group. All his life, John limited his haircuts to one a year in order that the money thus saved might go to churchly benevolences.

Immediately following Oxford, Wesley's career was notably unsuccessful. As an early minister from the Church of England to the colony of Georgia, he tried to impose his own discipline upon those emigrating from London debtor prisons, as if they were pious Oxford graduates. With the mothers of colonial Georgia, he was equally strict. They turned against him when he insisted on immersing their babies for baptism in cold water. So did a girl named Sophia Hopkey, whom he courted but who married another man. When, after her marriage, Wesley insisted she come to preparatory services before taking communion, Sophia refused—an occurrence that long gave credence to the story that Wesley excommunicated her from his church in a huff, more for refusing to marry him than for the actual reason.

Back in England he had a deep religious awakening. At Aldersgate Chapel, on May 24, 1738, he heard a passage read from Luther. "I felt my heart strangely warmed," he faithfully recorded in his ever-present journal. From that moment on he turned his efforts toward genuine evangelism instead of legalistic discipline. Realizing that the poorer classes were not welcomed in the Established Church, he began preaching in the fields and on city streets, taking his cue from his fellow Oxford "Holy Club" member, evangelist George Whitefield (*pages 114-5*). By contrast with Whitefield, he delivered straightforward, unemotional, and plain advice.

Wesley's genius lay in his ability to organize groups. He once told a long-winded Methodist preacher that he talked too long and too loud, thereby helping the preacher to achieve a greater popular appeal—and greater attendance at his meetings. He methodically watched the effects of his own sermons, changing them to suit the circumstances. To make sure attendance was high at meeting, he reprimanded those who did not come frequently enough. Even in the smallest gatherings, he often stood on a chair to make sure he could be seen.

In keeping with his belief in good works, he systematically explored the social evils of the day, taking a firm stand against the enclosure act, which hurt the farmers, against child labor, and against the sale of liquor, which was depriving the poor of their money. His Methodists followed his example. They concerned themselves with abolition of the English slave trade, with prison reform, and with better care of the insane—but most of all with the improvement of working conditions in the midst of the Industrial Revolution. By encouraging lay preachers, as well as ordained clergy, to speak up, the Methodists immeasurably helped their members to take active and vocal roles in the later trade unions.

In his own time Wesley was frequently misunderstood (*pages 124-5*). In keeping with his idea of methodicalness, the Methodist disciplines came into being: rules against dancing, drinking, and gambling. But these prohibitions were not formulated so much because of any inherent evil in the acts themselves as because of their danger—said Wesley—to a man's spirit. So successful was he in appealing to most of the common people that English standards of morality improved enormously—which was no small accomplishment in an age characterized even by the worldly satirist William Hogarth as the age of "Gin Lane" (*pages 124-5*).

An Anti-Methodist Cartoon

Like every other new group of Protestants, the Methodists were roundly berated in their time. In 1762, satirist William Hogarth published a cartoon *(right)* ridiculing them. In it an incredulous Turk stands outside a church window gazing upon what Hogarth called the "Credulity, Superstition, and Fanaticism" of the Methodists. From a high eighteenth-century pulpit a Methodist preacher dangles an imp from one hand, a witch from the other. The Methodist congregation is portrayed as an emotional crowd whose members rave in the pews, make love, and collapse in the aisles.

"Thank God that I am not a Methodist," Hogarth's Turk says. But his cartoon was strong on fancy, weak on fact. More truthful were his drawings showing the conditions of the poor *(left below)* which Wesley's movement helped to alleviate, and the conditions of the Anglican church, where, it was said, a tame brand of Deism that put parishioners to sleep was being preached. The effort to combat Deism was by no means among the least of the reasons for the rise of Methodism.

The Deists and the Revolution

"I have always tho't that so far as any Man is pure (let it be in a greater or less degree), he is not filthy," said a liberal Protestant of the mid-eighteenth century. Here and there throughout the country, a more liberal attitude was emerging out of English Presbyterianism, and letting in new trends. Back of it was the rise of eighteenth-century rationalism with a theology rooted in the new political and social philosophies of the Deists. Its doctrines of God and man were hostile to Calvinistic determinism of Jonathan Edwards.

Young men who had broken with the old dogmas were arising in pulpits throughout the nation. One of the most notable of these was Jonathan Mayhew, pastor of West Church in Boston from 1747 to 1766. His father, Experience Mayhew, had been liberal enough in his own day by proclaiming that "the best actions of the unregenerate are not properly called sins." Bold, frank, and radical, son Jonathan was the most free-spoken—and most popular—preacher in Boston prior to the American Revolution. In a famous sermon condoning civil disobedience—provided such disobedience was necessary for Christian purposes—he championed the Revolution. He was an early advocate of Deism in America. It was the beginning of a new liberalism, by which the Bible was freshly examined, questioned, and interpreted in the light of rational scholarship. But Mayhew's early death in 1766—and the coming of the Revolution—put a stop to popular development of the movement. Instead, a general reaction was to follow the treaty of peace and give new encouragement to orthodox Calvinism. The reaction resulted temporarily in the strengthening of the school of Jonathan Edwards—and the great fundamentalist revivals of the early nineteenth century.

"Let us all learn to be free and to be loyal," preached Jonathan Mayhew, pastor of West Church in Boston, on January 30, 1750, which happened to be an anniversary of the execution of Charles I. His sermon was intended to undermine British royal power prior to the American Revolution. "Let us not," he said, "profess ourselves vassals to the lawless pleasure of any man on earth; but let us remember, at the same time, government is sacred and not to be tampered with." It was a time when Americans like Mayhew accorded special weight to such Enlightenment writers as Locke and Rousseau, as well as the democratic values derived from the covenant theology of New England Puritanism.

A Deist Rewrites the Lord's Prayer

When Benjamin Franklin was asked to help abridge the English Book of Common Prayer, he cut the Catechism in it down to the only two questions he regarded as essential. They were: "What is your duty to God?" and "What is your duty to your neighbor?" In his middle years, independent-minded Ben, who, like many of the founding fathers of the new nation, was a Deist, sat down with the King James Version of the Bible beside him and marked out two columns on a ledger. The first column he labeled: "Old Version"; the second, "New Version, by B. Franklin." In the "New" column he rewrote the Lord's Prayer into the language of his own day, carefully annotating the reasons for his changes. One reason his version was shorter than the normal Protestant version lay in the fact that a few lines had been added in the King James Bible that never appeared in original manuscripts—lines that, incidentally, do not appear in Catholic Bibles. The lines: "For thine is the kingdom, and the power, and the glory, for ever."

But Franklin also made more drastic changes. In his ledger, he explained he preferred "Heavenly Father" to "Our Father who art in heaven." It was, he said, not only more concise but also better "modern English" than the older version. He changed the next line, "Hallowed be thy name," to "May all revere thee." The Elizabethan word "hallowed," he had decided, was obsolete in the eighteenth century. "Give us this day our daily bread," he argued, seemed to put in a claim of man's right to God's mercy and to contain too little of the grateful acknowledgment and sense of dependence that "becomes creatures, who live on the daily bounty of their Creator." Curtly, he then pointed out that the old words, "Lead us not into temptation," seemed unworthy of God. "Temptation," he wrote in this column, "so far as it is supernatural, comes from the Devil only."

As a theologian, Franklin was an amateur, and his complete revision of the Lord's Prayer brought forth protests. But nevertheless it

As the author of the Virginia Bill for Establishing Religious Freedom, Thomas Jefferson was so proud of helping to guarantee American separation of church and state that he insisted the fact be recorded on his tombstone, along with his authorship of the Declaration of Independence. The Virginia bill provided: "That no man shall be compelled to frequent or support any religious worship, place, or ministry whatsoever, nor shall be enforced, restrained, molested, or burdened in his body or goods, nor shall otherwise suffer, on account of his religious opinions or belief. . . ." Like many an eighteenth-century Deist, Jefferson was as much influenced by Newtonian philosophy as by biblical Christianity. By 1764 he had begun to lose faith in conventional religion and to test the literal accuracy of the Bible against his own knowledge of history. At sixty he finally decided to extract from the Bible—and to record for himself—only the moral sayings of Jesus and to use them alone as a moral guide. His questioning of the Bible was indicative of the widening gap in America, as well as in Europe, between traditional Protestantism and the new movement known as Deism.

made sense to many a Deist of the day, including a handful of founding fathers who, contrary to popular history, had espoused Deism over any denominational creed. The final Franklin version read:

Heavenly Father, May all revere thee, And become thy dutiful children and faithful subjects. May thy laws be obeyed on earth, as perfectly as they are in heaven. Provide for us this day, as thou has hitherto daily done. Forgive us our trespasses, and enable us to forgive those who offend us. Keep us out of temptation and deliver us from evil. Amen.

George Washington was frequently pictured in prayer, particularly at Valley Forge. But the fact is that Washington, though nominally an Episcopalian, was a Deist who became a favorite whipping boy of the Protestant clergy for accepting religious doctrines that were founded on eighteenth-century rationalism. Tom Paine was also a Deist who, more than a century later, was untruthfully called by Theodore Roosevelt "that filthy little atheist"; and so were John Adams, James Madison, and Alexander Hamilton, all of whom were also inclined to break with strict church doctrines. They questioned the inspiration of the Bible and even its importance for mankind. Their interest in religion was frequently limited to its usefulness in inculcating civic virtues.

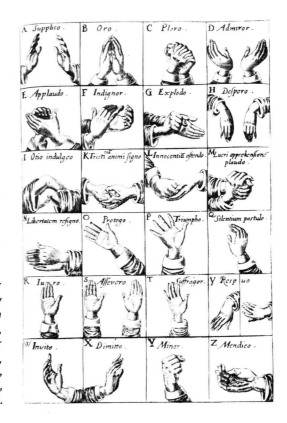

Eighteenth-century preachers, as well as other public orators, learned the formal elocutionary gestures shown in these illustrations from an old textbook. The diagrams showed, among other approved gestures, the proper sermonic ones for supplication (A), prayer (B), admiration (D), despair (H), self-indulgence (I), sorrow (K), triumph (P), requesting silence (Q), affirmation (S), and pleading (Z).

"No bishops!"

The cartoon at right, showing a frightened Anglican bishop clinging like a frog to the mast of a British frigate, was one of the first of a long line of cartoons intended to inflame American opinion against bishops—and toward insuring the separation of church and state in the new nation. It appeared in 1769 in the American *Political Gazette,* on the eve of the American Revolution. To Calvinists among the colonists—especially to Baptists, Congregationalists, and Presbyterians—a hierarchy of bishops smacked dangerously of government control of religion, a control which in their minds harked back not only to the days of the Holy Roman Empire but much more recently to the days of England's Archbishop William Laud and the stifling of individual conscience.

The clamor against bishops was only symptomatic of the general fever; the real problem lay in American fears of the entire system of the "divine right of kings" and the ecclesiastical authority of any government. Even the Deist John Adams, later to be second President of the U.S., wrote in his journal: "If [the English] Parliament can erect dioceses and appoint bishops, they [might] introduce the whole [church-state] hierarchy, establish tithes, establish religion, forbid dissenters. . . ." In short, any government-controlled church could stamp out religious freedom.

Theologically, the American Calvinists were simply standing firmly in their tradition. The Lutherans, too, who had long been accustomed to state control of the church in Europe, had come around to the conviction that bishops in the U.S. were a threat to their religious as well as their political freedom. But for the American clergy of the Church of England, the solution was not so clear-cut. They believed in apostolic succession—and the king who stood at the head of the English church was George III, who was, by church canon, "the only supreme head in earth." In Philadelphia, an unsure Jacob Duché headed

During the latter years of his life, kindly Bishop William White of the new Protestant Episcopal Church was deeply involved in promoting the new Sunday-school movement. But White had seen chaotic times. One Sunday morning in 1776, after his predecessor at Christ Church in Philadelphia had fled to England, White offered a prayer for Congress in place of the traditional liturgical prayer for the king of England, then proceeded to tone down a few other passages in the Church of England's Book of Common Prayer. After the Revolution, he set about writing plan after plan for the organization of the new Episcopal church.

for England after offering up prayers as chaplain of the first Continental Congress (*right*). The Rev. William White, who succeeded Duché as rector of Christ Church in Philadelphia, steered a middle course in the dilemma. White, the brother-in-law of Revolutionary financier Robert Morris, was a staunch patriot. Later, after tempers had cooled, he sought consecration as a bishop from the English clergy. The result was the founding of the Protestant Episcopal Church in the United States, which in almost every way resembled the Church of England except for its emphasis on complete separation from the government.

As American Calvinists pelt him with a copy of their founder's works, an unwelcome Church of England bishop, who had attempted to land in the colonies, scrambles up the rigging of a ship headed back to England, his episcopal carriage standing dismantled on the deck below him. "Lord, now lettest thou thy Servant depart in Peace," prays the harried bishop. The placard in the foreground of the cartoon refers to the fact that bishops, as state officials, were supported by taxes. In New England, the forces for separation of church and state were led by Baptist Isaac Backus. Radical patriots like Samuel Adams made the most of English attempts to install bishops in the colonies. It was, they said, in attempting to fan the flames of rebellion among American Protestants, an instance of English tyranny. One Church of England clergyman wrote that the controversy over bishops lay at the heart of the American Revolution, along with heavy taxes and political restraints imposed by George III's government.

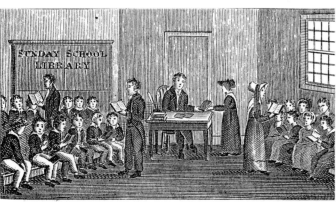

The first Sunday school was founded in England in 1780 by a philanthropist named Robert Raikes. His purpose was to provide rudimentary education—reading, writing, and arithmetic—to poverty-stricken children whom he found roaming eighteenth-century English streets on Sundays.

"I am no bigot," said archpatriot Samuel Adams. "I can hear a prayer from a man of piety and virtue, who is at the same time a friend of his country. . . . I have heard that Mr. [Jacob] Duché deserves that character. . . ." Duché was then asked to offer the prayers in the Continental Congress. "I must confess," opined John Adams, "I never heard a better prayer, or one so well pronounced." But, like all Church of England clergy, Duché was caught in conflicting loyalties to church and to nation. As soon as the British captured Philadelphia, he restored to the liturgy the prayers for the king instead of for the Congress. Then, as a self-admitted Tory, he fled the country, leaving Christ Church in Philadelphia to the Rev. William White (opposite page).

"Now, Boys, Give Them Watts!"

No churches in America had so large an influence in the American Revolution as the Congregationalists. Their clergy had been influential in public affairs from the days of the Separatists, and their radical strain of English Puritanism, frequently derived from the spirit of hot-tempered John Wycliffe's Lollards (*pages 10-11*), gave them kinship with the new doctrines of civil liberty taught by John Locke. But in later years almost every denomination —and sometimes justly so—was to claim equal credit in the American Revolution. It was the Baptists who probably stood most staunchly not only for independence but for separation of church and state. The reason: They had suffered most from Anglican intolerance. (But it was the Anglicans who, though greatly divided, sent more representatives—though many were actually Deists—to the signing of the Declaration of Independence and to the Continental Congresses.) On the whole, the Calvinist Presbyterians and Dutch and German Reformed—and the Lutherans—supported the Revolution.

Strangely enough, it was the Methodists who found themselves in a ridiculous spot. The reason: John Wesley himself. Though founder Wesley was inclined to be critical of the English government's methods toward America, he was loyal to the king, and the Methodists in America were at the time few and far between. In 1775, Wesley published a paper entitled *A Calm Address to the American Colonies,* urging them to listen to Samuel Johnson's advice that "taxation was not tyranny." Later Wesley wrote other pamphlets in the same vein and preached that American Methodists should remain free of all party. ". . . Say not one word against one or the other side," he wrote. But his advice frequently fell on deaf ears.

Of all the groups, it was the Presbyterians who could claim to have received the greatest kudos from the enemy itself. "Cousin America," said Horace Walpole in a speech in Parliament, "has run off with a Presbyterian parson." The "parson" was John Witherspoon (*left*). The Presbyterians never forgot the fact—and that his action in signing the Declaration of Independence led many another Englishman to entertain the suspicion that the "radical" early Presbyterians who had caused trouble for their Charles I more than a century earlier were really at the root of the entire problem.

In Woodstock, Virginia, Lutheran pastor John Peter Gabriel Mühlenberg stripped off his clerical robes to reveal the uniform of a Continental officer. "There is a time to preach . . . and a time to fight," he said. He enlisted some three hundred volunteers on the spot.

"Cousin America," said Horace Walpole in the English Parliament, "has run off with a Presbyterian parson." The parson was Scottish-born Presbyterian John Witherspoon (right), the only clergyman to sign the Declaration of Independence.

Patrick Henry's first great claim to oratorical talent had been as a lawyer in the "Parson's Case" over the right of Anglican ministers to be paid in money instead of tobacco when the tobacco crop was scanty. Later he defended Baptist clergy when they were thrown into jail by the Anglicans. On March 22, 1775, at the Virginia revolutionary convention in St. John's Church, Richmond (left), in a time when church buildings were often used for political meetings (right), he cried his most famous line "I know not what course others may take, but as for me, give me liberty or give me death."

In a church near the battleground in Elizabeth, New Jersey, the Rev. James Caldwell, who had become a marked man to the British because of his revolutionary tendencies, grabbed all the copies of the English Isaac Watts's hymnal he could lay his hands on, rushed them to the soldiers who had run low on wadding for their muskets. "Now, boys, give them Watts!" he cried. Then he helped them tear up the hymnals.

The American Methodists

"There is indeed a wide difference between the relationship wherein you stand to the Americans and the relation wherein I stand to all the Methodists. You are the elder brother of the American Methodists: I am under God the father of the whole family. . . . But in one point, my dear brother, I am a little afraid both the Doctor [Thomas Coke] and you differ from me. I study to be little: you study to be great. I creep: you strut along. . . . One instance of this, of your greatness, has given me great concern. How can you, how dare you suffer yourself to be called Bishop? I shudder, I start at the very thought! Men may call me a knave or a fool, a rascal, a scoundrel, and I am content; but they shall never by my consent call me Bishop! Thus, my dear Franky, I have told you all that is in my heart."

The letter, addressed to Francis Asbury in America, was the last he received from John Wesley in England. It was, Asbury said, a "bitter pill." Wesley had been exceedingly upset by Asbury's calling himself a bishop. It was an interesting reverse in the problem the Episcopalians had experienced. In England, there were no Methodist bishops. But in America, where the rapidly increasing Methodists needed organization, Asbury and Thomas Coke had felt justified in leading them under the self-styled title of "bishop." After the Revolution, these two men led Methodist strength in earnest. In 1775, membership in the colonies had been less than four thousand. By 1780, it had climbed to thirteen thousand.

Though John Wesley had approved of card games, American Methodists were more strict. In New York City, a woman named Barbara Heck, having been influenced by the Wesleyan movement, seized a deck of cards from a group of men, threw them into the fire, then ran to the nearby home of Philip Embury. ". . . You must preach to us," she said, "or we shall all go to hell. . . ." The result, according to legend, was the founding of the first Methodist society in the American colonies.

Of Thomas Coke (above), whom John Wesley finally consented to make a "bishop," or "superintendent," Wesley's brother Charles, questioning the propriety of the action wrote:

How easy now are bishops made
At man or woman's whim;
Wesley his hands on Coke hath laid,
But who laid hands on him?

Captain Thomas Webb was a tough Englishman who, while staying in the colonies for a few years, raised the money for the first Methodist meeting hall in Philadelphia.

Francis Asbury (above) was consecrated a superintendent of American Methodism on Christmas day in 1784 (below), despite John Wesley's protests. He soon began to call himself "bishop." From England Wesley wrote crossly to American Methodists, "You do not know the state of the English Methodists. They do not roll in money, like many of the American Methodists."

One reason for the great success of Methodism in America lay in the loneliness of farm life, where church buildings were few and far between. More important was a rural suspicion that Lutheran theological seminaries—or "preacher factories" as the country people called them—had been too much influenced by Deism.

Of the Germans whom William Penn had welcomed to his "Holy Experiment," an early Pennsylvania governor complained: "[They] imported with them all the religious whimsies of their country and I believe [have] subdivided since their arrival." He was absolutely right. They were a stubborn group, many of them descended from Palatinate peoples decimated by the Thirty Years' War. They were separated from their English neighbors by a lack of education as well as by language. And they were divided by their own numerous creeds: Anabaptists, Lutherans, Moravians, Schwenkfeldians, in addition to Calvinist-oriented German Reformed. It was a situation that had worried both the Moravian Count Zinzendorf and the Lutheran Henry Mühlenberg, each of whom had tried valiantly during the eighteenth century to unite not only Lutherans and Moravians but also some German Calvinists.

Now Methodism arrived, splitting them farther apart. Its outdoor meetings suited farmers, since church buildings were scarce. If the Methodists had seized the opportunity, it is possible they could have increased their own number. But not even the Methodists wanted the Germans. They spurned them on the ground that the German language would not long continue in America—and the Germans insisted on using their own language. As a result, there sprang up under the Lutheran Jacob Albright *(upper left)* the "Evangelical Association," with Lutheran leanings but Methodist organization, and, under the influence of Philip William Otterbein *(right),* the United Brethren in Christ, with German Calvinist leanings but similar Methodist propensities.

A Methodist Leaning

Jacob Albright was a German Lutheran with Methodist leanings.

Philip Otterbein was a German Calvinist with Methodist leanings.

Even in York, Pennsylvania, which was important enough to be the seat of the Continental Congress during 1777–1778, a rural atmosphere often prevailed. Here, in an early Lutheran church, where a portrait of Luther along with those of the apostles and biblical prophets framed the gallery, dogs had to be chased out by the sexton. At the time, a growing conservative party within German Lutheranism was insisting on the continued use of the German language during services and on a strict adherence to the Augsburg Confession.

of the old Lutheran Church in 1800, York, Pa

The Fundamentalist Heaven—and Hell

Although succeeding generations of more liberally minded Protestants were beginning to believe that "heaven" might be a state far more selfless—and perhaps less physical—than that envisioned so literally by many a Bible reader, and "hell," too, a far less visible condition, the artists'—and the theologians'—conceptions of heaven and hell within many a creed of early American Protestantism differed little from those of earlier days. In this old woodcut a Pennsylvania German depicted for his fellow Protestants a heaven, or the New Jerusalem, as a biblical city of gold, with darting cherubs on the wing—and hell as a holocaust of flames presided over by a devil and the biblical whore of Babylon. At lower left, a father holding his son by the hand points toward an ascending road to heaven. The boy points to those headed in the wrong direction—downward. The moral, as summed up by the artist, to make sure everybody understood it, was that those on the lower road sought splendor, luxury, and pride, in contrast to those on the "strait and thorny" upper road, who bore crosses symbolizing the burdens of Christian life. At upper right, one man in a precarious position is saying, "Foolish and vain, I went astray, ere I had felt thy scourges, Lord! I left my guide and lost my way, but now I repent and love thy word." Presumably his change of heart gave some hope for his salvation.

To save, to bless, to comfort me, like Jesus will I bear the cross; vile sinners perish in surprise, beneath thine angry rod.

O Zion tune thy voice, and raise thy hands on high; tell all the earth thy joys, and boast salvation nigh.

True
thorn
they
migh

New - Jer

Our fruits

I want to go to Zion.

But they are going thither

Here is the entrance great and wide, open to all fro
gently ahead, not a word will be said : If you seek h
sign, have travelled this road in proper line, ye that l
some in great numbers with music full of sound, a
small, in Abraham's lap hope to be taken up, yea, r

In a later version of the large drawing shown at right on these pages, the artist made his devil more ferocious than before.

138

Give us of your oil.

Many are called but few are chosen.

Where are your fruits?

As I live saith the Lord God, I have no pleasure in the death of the wicked — but that the wicked turn from his way and live.

Foolish and vain I went astray, ere had felt thy scourges. Lord! I left m guide and lost my way' but now I r pent and love thy word.

Death comes without dela All classes become its prey

The whore of Babylon.

ead at court, ain support.

ass on ye with sack and pack be unconcerned be not exact : walk hastly appear and record thy name : thousands with a similar de dor, luxury and pride, pass on, the path is fully wide : the frolic the place to which they are bound ; the rich, poor, the tall and

A Quaker Heaven

Edward Hicks was a Pennsylvania Quaker who was born during the American Revolution. Before his death in 1849, Hicks painted approximately a hundred versions of the scene shown here. In each of the paintings, all of which he named "The Peaceable Kingdom," he managed to set forth a basic Quaker emphasis that had frequently seemed more the exception than the rule in the practices of many a Protestant. As a Quaker he emphasized the ultimate peaceful reconciliation of man and nature *(right)*—and neatly ignored the eighteenth-century concept of a "hell." He based his paintings on the "Kingdom of God" described in the biblical Book of Isaiah.

To make his point clear, Hicks frequently included in the background a symbolic scene of William Penn's treaties with the Indians, then bordered the entire painting with simple verses. Being a Quaker, however, Hicks spoke of art with a typical plainness. Painting, he once said, "appears to me to be one of those trifling, insignificant arts . . . the inseparable companion of voluptuousness and vice. . . ." To make sure that his purpose would not be misunderstood, he handed out sermonlike poems along with his paintings. In the poems he explained that he intended his depictions of peaceful children and animals to symbolize the peace of soul that comes to men when they control their animal passions.

The leopard
And not on

The wolf did with the lambkin dwell in peace
His grim carnivorous nature there did cease

When the g
With indian

the harmless kid laid down

vage beast was seen to frown

The lion with the fatling on did move
A little child was leading them in love;

PENN his famous treaty made

s beneath the Elm-tree's shade.

The Swedenborgian Vision

Emanuel Swedenborg was a brilliant inventor, scientist, mathematician, and linguist who ranked in mid-eighteenth-century Europe on a par with Isaac Newton as a scientist and with Voltaire and Samuel Johnson as an intellectual. He had invented a machine gun, discovered the circulation and uses of cerebrospinal fluid, and was the first man to sketch the nebular hypothesis of the solar system. But like many an eighteenth-century scientist, Swedenborg also concerned himself with religious problems. It was, he believed, possible to reconcile religion with science, and, after his notable early career, he decided to devote his life toward this goal.

In the annals of Protestantism, Swedenborgianism has long been considered vague, spiritualistic, even theosophist. But this was not strictly true. Contrary to Luther's beliefs, said Swedenborg, man's best chance for salvation lies not in faith alone but in active service to the world. Man's task, he said, is not to combat nature but to conform to it. The theologians of the traditional church had, he argued, grossly misinterpreted the questions of God, man, and the problem of evil. Jesus alone, he believed, was and remains God.

It was not so much Swedenborg's conclusions as his way of arriving at them that startled more traditional eighteenth-century Protestants. At the age of fifty-seven, he claimed to have seen a vision of Christ and to have visited —in person—the spiritual worlds of heaven and hell. To prove his claim, he spent the rest of his life writing a total of thirty fat volumes, all of them interestingly matter-of-fact in tone. In these he set down his observations on the world beyond, together with a symbolic interpretation of the Bible which he derived from

these observations. His ultimate conclusions were that, at death, all men, being spirits clothed in bodily form, must enter the spirit world, choosing by their actions in the present world—like Jesus—the ultimate spiritual goal at which they wish to arrive.

Through his writings he hoped to bring about a union of all churches into what he believed to be the one true Christian church so that love and service to others would prevail. Fifteen years after his death a small but theologically interesting Church of the New Jerusalem was founded to perpetuate his teachings. After his death, too, his writings, though scorned by many, were to make their mark far into the nineteenth century on the transcendentalist philosophies of Thomas Carlyle and Samuel Taylor Coleridge, of Ralph Waldo Emerson, Immanuel Kant, and Johann Wolfgang von Goethe.

During the eighteenth and nineteenth centuries the European churches remained state-controlled, relatively traditional in belief and custom (above), in contrast to American Protestantism. Small splinter groups, like the Swedenborgians, who perpetuated the doctrines of philosopher Emanuel Swedenborg (left), were the exception rather than the rule in Europe. Swedenborg himself remained a member of the Swedish Lutheran Church until his death, after which his followers formed a new church.

"I Love to See Them Stamp and Grin"

I love my faithful brethren more
Than any souls I've seen before
I love to see them stamp and grin. . . .

In 1776, an illiterate, emotionally unbalanced Englishwoman who delighted in being called "Mother Ann" Lee brought a small group of "Shaking Quakers," or "Shakers," to Watervliet, New York. It was Mother Ann's conviction that the chief "sin" keeping men and women from achieving perfection is the "sin" of sexual desire. "There never was," she said, "nor can be, a child conceived and born under Christian auspices."

Before coming to America, Mother Ann had waged a personal vendetta against lust in the streets of English cities. She had been mar-

Shaker folk art, which was as delicate as their more famous skill at cabinetmaking, was often based on Mother Ann's harrowing experience in prison, where she claimed to have received her vision that she was the female Christ and where, according to the drawing below, an angel in the form of a dove guarded her from the vantage point of a weeping willow.

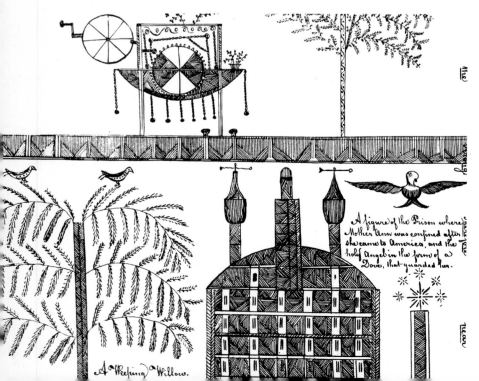

A Weeping Willow.

A figure of the Prison where Mother Ann was confined after she came to America, and the holy Angel in the form of a Dove, that guarded her.

ried to an English blacksmith, by whom she had four children, all of whom died in infancy. Christianity, she taught, had hitherto ignored an important fact—the equality of the sexes. God, she said, is both male and female.

On this basis, she refuted many traditional church doctrines, including, naturally enough, the virgin birth—and the resurrection of the body, since she believed the body, having been created through sex, is impure. Under Mother Ann's scrutiny, too, the Trinity became a "Quadruple" to include herself. Since she claimed to be the female Christ, she also refuted the forgiveness of sins through Christ —and, in fact, the authority of the Bible. But she relied on the Bible when it came to banning marriage. The Apostle Paul, she pointed out, had advised the early Corinthians not to marry.

She taught that the history of the world is divided into four major cycles. The first cycle, she said, ended when, as she understood her Bible, God revealed himself to Noah as a "Spirit" able to heal the world's ills; the second cycle ended when God revealed himself as "Jehovah" in the time of Moses; the third with the birth of Jesus, through whom God was again revealed. But, said Mother Ann, since Jesus was a male, he could reveal only the fatherhood, not the motherhood, of God. This "fact," she announced, was the reason for the final cycle, which had now reached its climax with the birth of none other than Mother Ann. Having taken the female form, she was, she argued, better able to express Christian love than was the male Jesus.

For the Shakers, the second coming of Christ had thus already taken place in the person of Mother Ann. Their dances were joyful *(right)*, their singing argumentative. "So say our blessed mother," they would chant. "Our mother paved the way."

Out of Mother Ann's sexually repressed colonies has sprung a great deal of modern theosophy and spiritualism, she herself being considered by practicing spiritualists to be one of the best possible mediums to contact. But being celibate and thus dependent on attracting only orphan children or other celibates to their colonies, the Shaker communities were soon to dwindle. Well-meaning later followers adopted a general view that salvation is freedom from all wrongdoing, not simply sex—but they nevertheless learned to hate their fathers and their mothers, as Mother Ann had taught them to do.

In their dances the Shakers acted out the songs they sang. They "shook off sin" and "trampled evil underfoot" to rid themselves of sexual desire. Sometimes a member fell into a trance and sang a song as a "gift" prophecy to help out another member.

The Great Camp Meetings

"The first jerk or so," wrote frontier preacher Peter Cartwright of early nineteenth-century American camp meetings, "you would see their fine bonnets, caps, and combs fly; and so sudden would be the jerking of the head that their long loose hair would crack almost as loud as a wagoner's whip." To gain relief from their "jerks," he then reported, the revivalists danced hysterically; they shouted, sobbed, leaped in the air, writhed on the ground, fell down like dead men, then lay insensible or in grotesque contortions on the ground. They laughed senseless "holy laughs," were seized with the barks, then jumped around like dogs on all fours and, still barking, "treed the devil" like dogs chasing a squirrel. When all else failed, they spoke in a gibberish which they believed to be the "other tongues" used by the apostles in the Bible.

The revivalist fervor had been triggered by the coldness in Deistic religion immediately following the American Revolution, by the frontiersman's need for emotional religion, by his rebellion against authority—and by the Methodist enthusiasm that harmonized beautifully with all these needs.

The "Second Awakening," as it was called, had been started by the Presbyterians. But the camp-meeting technique was soon taken over by the Methodists. It had its beginnings in 1801, in Cane Ridge, Kentucky, through the preaching of two frontier preachers named James McGready and Barton W. Stone. People camped by the thousands on the revival site, were exhorted by preachers day and night. The movement lasted at its height fully five years, and typed the religion of the "Bible Belt" for a century. Later, it spread to much of the rest of the nation. By 1833, a wag in Illinois reported that a zealous revivalist was "bellowing and blowing through the Bible, shedding no more light upon the passages quoted than the roar of artillery does upon our Declaration of Independence."

The Frontier Gospel

In Kentucky, the Second Awakening was as much Methodist and Baptist as it was Presbyterian. But it had hardly gotten really under way before a similar movement began in western Pennsylvania and Virginia under the leadership of two Scotch-Irish Presbyterians, Thomas Campbell and his son Alexander. The Campbellite movement was one crystallization of the frontier's answer to old-line denominationalism. It fought the narrow control of denominations from the older settled regions—and, with frontier straightforwardness, tried to purge Protestantism of all dividing creeds and sects. Alexander Campbell had a habit of calling old-line clergy "stall-fed" and "agents for milking schemes." His following was made up of a pragmatic frontier membership that refused to take theology very seriously. For them, a theological opinion was right only if it could be subjected to two practical tests: "Is it in harmony with the Scriptures?" and "Does it square with common sense?" "Where the Scriptures speak, we speak," they said, and "Where the Scriptures are silent, we are silent."

The Campbellites thus set up their own comparatively rugged theology. They practiced immersion like the Baptists. They observed the Lord's Supper every week in reaction against any egocentricity in the pulpit. They governed their church absolutely democratically. They admitted no element in their worship that was not explicitly authorized in the Bible—a fact that soon caused them trouble because pipe organs were not specifically authorized in the Bible. And, true to their frontier independence, they preferred for many years the title "Elder" over any such "preacher" titles as "Pastor" or "Reverend."

By 1832, true to the Campbells' ideal of unity, they reached an agreement with the revivalist Barton W. Stone in Kentucky, by which the two revival movements were united. By 1827, the new so-called "Christian Church" thus formed numbered approximately thirteen thousand communicants, chiefly in Ohio, Kentucky, Tennessee, and Indiana. But true also to the longer course of Protestantism, the new "Christian Church" soon split apart—partly because of the insistence of one group that pipe organs should not be allowed in church. Such instruments, they claimed, were not a help but a hindrance, since worshipers might falter during the hymns to admire the organist's skill. After the split, some called themselves the Disciples of Christ, some the Churches of Christ, and some simply remained the Christian Church.

"Practical men," said Alexander Campbell, one of the founders of the frontier Disciples of Christ, "have always been the most useful; and, therefore, practical principles have been more beneficial to mankind than the most ingenious and refined speculations." Though his denomination was founded in the frontier revivalistic movement (left), he based much of his interpretation of the Bible on common sense. He had been a Presbyterian minister who saw no reason for excluding members of other denominations from taking communion in his church.

Peter Cartwright was one of the shrewdest and most hard-fighting of Methodist frontier circuit riders (right). He had a kind of "knock 'em down power" that proved even more irresistible at frontier than at Eastern revivals. Cartwright was not above using his fists when necessary, so he thrived in Logan County, Kentucky, where the majority of citizens were escaped murderers, horse thieves, and counterfeiters. He perhaps provoked the frontier proverb, repeated in bad winter weather, "There's nothing out today but crows and Methodist preachers," and perhaps also the saying, "Of all the religions I profess, I much prefer the Method[e]st." On one occasion, when he tried to hold a meeting, he was attacked by a mob carrying whips. When his supporters and the magistrates fell back, he ordered a trumpet blown and the meeting site lighted up. Then he preached from the text, "The gates of hell shall not prevail." After two days, he reported two hundred frontiersmen had joined the Methodist Church, helped along by such exhibitionism as calling forth the devil (below).

The Early Ups and Downs of Spreading the Gospel

In 1735 a carpenter named John Bonike accompanied the first Moravian missionaries when they arrived on St. Thomas Island in the West Indies to work among the impoverished plantation slaves. Bonike, carried away by his remarkable revivalistic powers of persuasion, scorned more conservative Moravian methods and set up a separate station on the opposite side of the island. When his Moravian brethren tried to reason with him, he was stubborn. "Let God judge between us," he said, mounting his horse and heading back to his own station. As he rode out of sight, the Moravians heard a violent clap of thunder. A slave who had followed him returned to report that Bonike had been instantly killed by lightning *(lower left)*.

The Moravians were among the first Protestant "overseas" missionaries, half a century ahead of most others. Spurred on by the Pietism of Herrnhut in Germany *(pages 104-5)*, they had gone during the eighteenth century not only to the Caribbean but to Greenland, India, Africa—and even Russia. As early as 1732 they arrived in Greenland, where the natives tried to get rid of them by raising the price of seal meat until the missionaries almost starved.

Their situation was eased only when a native named Kayarnak became curious about the Rev. John Beck's efforts to translate the Bible into the local dialect. Kayarnak showed little interest in the biblical account of creation and the fall of Adam. But when Beck told him of the sufferings of Jesus, he sent to Beck's cabin *(right center)* twenty-one boatloads of relatives and friends to hear him tell it again.

In 1765 the Moravians received permission from Catherine the Great to enter her domain, and two missionaries were soon accompanying a group of nomadic Kalmuck Tartars of the Volga region to the Great Steppes. Though every now and then a Tartar spurned a proffered Bible *(below)*, most Kalmuck priests behaved more gently. They listened attentively to everything the Moravians said and graciously accepted Bibles from them, but after a few days they returned the Bibles, explaining that the print was "too fine for Tartar eyes" *(upper right)*.

By the late eighteenth century the English Baptists, like the Moravians, had entered the mission field and were having their troubles, too, as these pictures show. In the Friendly Islands, where he represented the London Missionary Society (and where English missionary activity brought about complete British political domination over the natives), a missionary named Veeson *(upper left)* tried to keep some English sailors who had deserted ship from land-grabbing on the island. The sailors retaliated by hiring two natives to kill him. He was saved from disaster only when the moon suddenly emerged from behind a cloud one night, and the assassins recognized him as a friend of their chief.

By 1814, however, things were beginning to look up for the missionaries. Though the Rev. Samuel Marsden, together with a colleague, was forced to spend the night with New Zealand cannibals who surrounded him with spears stuck upright in the ground *(lower right)*, he was soon able to report that the cannibals were proving remarkably receptive to his efforts and that he was able to go about his mission without any real danger.

To India—and to China

In the emotion of nineteenth-century revivalism, it seemed quite clear to Protestants that they should join in the great effort to "convert the heathen" of the entire world. Now, moved to action by the efforts of a shoe cobbler named William Carey *(below),* who had persuaded English Baptists to send him out to India in 1792, other English, German—and American—Protestants followed suit. Missionaries mushroomed from almost every denomination. Only the Antimission branch of the Baptists remained at home, convinced that it was an effrontery to God who, they as strict predestinarians believed, had already chosen his "elect." They were sure that missionary work was thus completely useless.

The first great English and American efforts were to India, then to China, as these pictures show. The first Hindu to become a Christian in the golden age of nineteenth-century Protestant missions was a carpenter named Kristno, who, having dislocated his arm, asked help from the Rev. John Thomas of the Baptist Missionary Society. So impressed was Kristno when Thomas managed to reduce the swelling in his arm that—in an act so unusual that he was the first in fifteen years to take the risk—he voluntarily renounced his caste by eating in public with the missionaries. An angry crowd dragged Kristno and his family before the Danish magistrate. But, instead of punishing them, the magistrate congratulated Kristno on his wisdom, and he was baptized by William Carey in the River Hooghly *(right).* Usually, Carey was scorned not only by Indians but also by his fellow Englishmen. He was particularly scorned by the East India Company which, for political and commercial gain, did not encourage missionary effort. It was the East India Company that had forced him to move to a Danish, instead of English, colony in India.

William Carey was a short fellow with a humble opinion of himself. In later years Carey, a Baptist, was called the "consecrated cobbler," partly because of the trade he had originally practiced back in England and partly because of his missionary work. In India, where he arrived in 1793, he worked in an indigo factory near Malda, established a church nearby. When the English East India Company forced him to move, he found haven in a Danish-governed province. He began preaching in the common dialect, learned Sanskrit and Chinese, and translated the Bible into forty-four languages and dialects. It was Carey, more than any other man, who gave rise to the missionary movement of the nineteenth century. Reports of his work among the Indians reached the Western world at a time when Americans were becoming increasingly expansionist. God, they had decided, needed to be introduced to the rest of the world.

China's doors were closed to the English, who were attempting to import opium against the government's will, when Robert Morrison, first Protestant missionary of the interdenominational London Missionary Society, arrived in 1807. As the sole Protestant missionary in all China for almost a decade, he supported himself by working as a translator for the East India Company. When the company discovered he had also translated the New Testament into Chinese, it fired him. Sixteen years after he died, the Taiping Rebellion of 1850–1864 (pages 170-1), for which the establishment of his mission was indirectly responsible, broke out in China.

At the baptism of the first Hindu convert, a carpenter named Kristno (right), William Carey preached a sermon to make clear to watching Hindus that the River Hooghly held no special mystical values, then immersed him. The Danish governor of the district was so moved by the scene that he wept, and a German woman thanked Kristno for renouncing "devils."

The Golden Age of the Missionary

The official symbol *(left)* of the golden age of the nineteenth-century missionaries differed from the unofficial one. The unofficial symbol became in the popular mind a cadaverous little preacher wearing a phenomenally tall hat and a frock coat too short in the sleeves. Both symbols were inadequate.

In Japan, the missionaries helped through their presence to foment a political and social revolution that culminated in the eclipse of the feudalistic shogunate. In Turkey, they helped back the forces that led to the political rise of the comparatively democratic Mustapha Kemal. In Hawaii, it was the missionaries who were responsible for the first written Hawaiian language and for helping to found the islands' laws on the Ten Commandments. To Siam, they brought a knowledge of democracy and technology that has had its humanitarian—and sometimes its diplomatic—results in a shrinking twentieth-century world *(pages 164-5)*

In the Friendly Islands, the London Missionary Society "saved" Tongo for the Methodists—and for the British Empire. But they also helped along their own idea of progress, and not always hand-in-glove with the imperialists. In China, they lived through national hostility against Western imperialism—and through a series of international conflicts and treaties. Though they were themselves frequently caught on the wrong side, the missionaries nevertheless helped to seat the relatively benevolent Sun Yat-sen in 1911, as an indirect result of the missionary-inspired Taiping Rebellion of 1850–1864 *(pages 170-1)*. In the Gilbert Islands of the Pacific they fought "blackbirding"—*i.e.,* slave trading. In Alaska, it was a Presbyterian missionary who helped bolster a depleted economy by stocking the territory with reindeer *(pages 214-5)*.

In Africa, where they were branded tools of European imperialism as much as they were anywhere in the world, they sometimes behaved ineptly in unfamiliar cultures. They told of the African who claimed they had been

The official emblem of the
"Society for the Propagation
of the Gospel" was a full-blown schooner
set in a seal, with natives streaming down to the
beach to welcome a minister of the gospel
who stood on deck with an open Bible in his hands.

cruel to him. Why? he was asked. Did they beat him? Did they hurt him in any way? No, the African replied to each question. Then what had they done? "You say, 'Hurry, hurry,' " he explained. But it was in the missionary hospitals—which had their beginnings in the first small medicine kits on missionary porches—where downtrodden African nationals learned that somebody cared for their plight as human beings. And on a continent where no other schools existed, it was missionary schools, more than any other force, that for a century nurtured African national education, helping to bring about a knowledge of politics that enabled the African to take part in the great independence movement of the mid-twentieth century.

Their early mistakes haunt the missionary movement to this day. In Japan, they catered chiefly to intellectual and middle classes, mistakenly hoping the less educated classes would follow along. In India, by contrast, they concentrated largely on untouchables—but with results that for a time operated in favor of colonial exploitation and only later helped to overcome the caste system and to influence a new and more democratic constitution.

Today, even in the first of the great Protestant missionary countries—India—only a scant two per cent of the population professes Christianity, and in many another traditional missionary land the percentage is even smaller in spite of a century and a half of missionary work. But the influence of the nineteenth-century mission has undoubtedly been far greater than sheer numbers indicate. In China, as a result of opening the first women's schools, the nineteenth-century missionaries helped unbind the feet of Chinese women. In India, they helped abolish *suttee,* or widow-suicide. In Turkey, their schools helped bring women out of purdah. In country after country the missionaries combated illiteracy (and witch doctors), founded schools, colleges, and hospitals, instituted public health programs, and established institutions for orphans, the blind, and the insane. They introduced anesthesia in medical operations, scientific methods of agriculture—and fought the scourge of hunger and disease, notably leprosy. Millions of the world's peoples would have had little hope of rising above disease, want, and ignorance except through the work of the nineteenth-century missionaries.

The Lives of Five Missionaries

In February, 1812, the cargo ship *Caravan* left Salem, Massachusetts, en route to India, carrying aboard two young missionaries, Adoniram Judson and Samuel Newell, together with their wives. A year later three more young missionaries joined them: Gordon Hall, Samuel Nott, Jr., and Luther Rice.

The first five missionaries of the American Board of Commissioners for Foreign Missions were ordained on February 6, 1812, in Salem, Massachusetts, by the Congregationalists. The American Board was the first organization in the U.S. to be formed to send missionaries to non-Christian countries. "These . . . foolish and inexperienced young people," wrote a scoffer of the times, "will actually sail to the far-distant shores of Hindoostan and, marvellous to tell, . . . teach that numerous and ancient people the right way to heaven!"

The five were members of a group known as "The Brethren," which had had its beginnings during outdoor campus revival meetings at Williams College a few years earlier. At a meeting in 1806, a thunderstorm had forced the students to take shelter under a nearby haystack where, they were later to claim, they felt a call to minister to the people caught in "the moral darkness of Asia."

As the first five American missionaries of the newly formed American Board of Commissioners for Foreign Missions, they had their fill of troubles. Upon arrival in Bombay, Hall and Nott were immediately arrested and imprisoned because the East India Company feared their teachings might interfere with their commercial exploitations. Little more than a decade later both Hall and Newell died, and Nott was forced by ill health to return to America, leaving Rice—and Judson *(next page)*—to carry on.

So did the American Board have its troubles. Convinced on their way to India of the rightness of total immersion, both Judson and Rice forsook the Congregationalists who had sponsored them and applied for admission to the Baptist church. The result was the founding of a separate mission board by the Baptists, thus increasing the missionary movement.

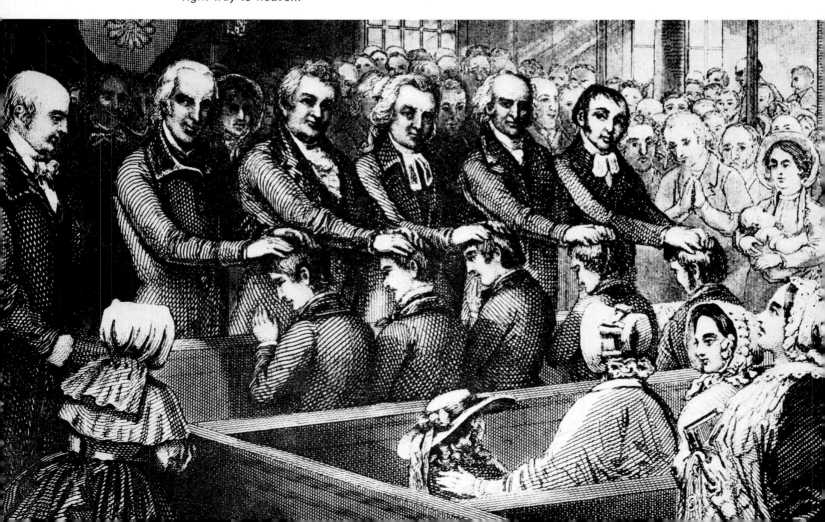

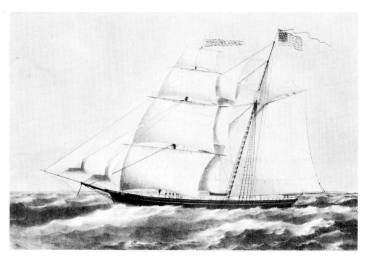

The first two American Board missionaries to Calcutta set sail, with their wives, on the ship Caravan (above) out of Salem, Massachusetts, on February 9, 1812. Well-wishers gave them six thousand dollars—and a considerable quantity of gingerbread for the journey.

The Morning Star was one of many successive schooners of the same name bought with pennies from Sunday-school children, to transport missionaries around the Gilbert and Marshall Islands.

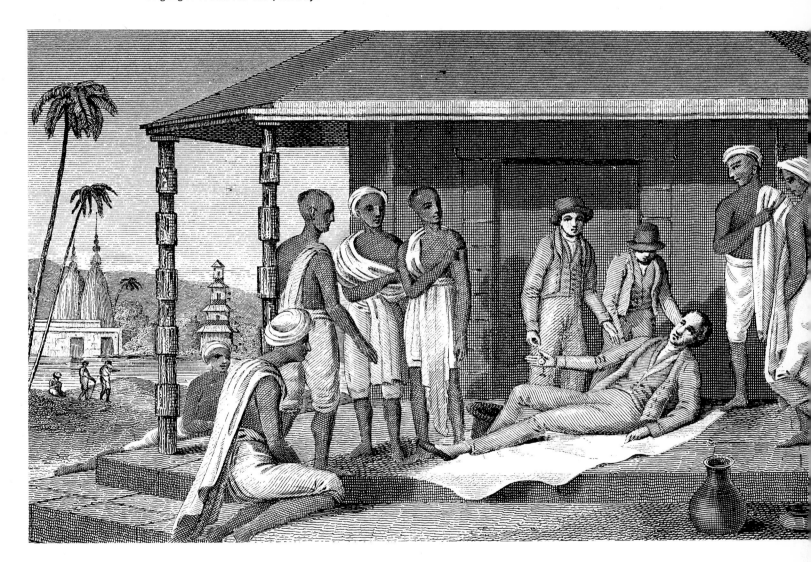

Gordon Hall, one of the first five American Board missionaries, left Bombay to work in a remote hill village, contracted cholera, and died (above) in 1826.

The Arrest of Adoniram Judson

In 1824, when political war broke out between the British and the Burmans, Adoniram Judson, one of the first American missionaries to India, was suspected of being in the pay of the English. As an "enemy alien," he was arrested (opposite page) and spent a total of seventeen months in prison, frequently in irons. Throughout all this time he secreted his Burman translation of the Bible in a pillow. Meanwhile his wife begged the royal family for his release, bribed jailers, and smuggled in food and medicines. The saga of Judson, as told here in a letter from his young wife to her brother-in-law, described some of the troubles experienced by at least one early missionary to India—and also convinced everybody at home that the American Protestant mission was a worthy cause.

Rangoon, May 26, 1826

"My beloved Brother,

"On the eighth of June, just as we were preparing for dinner, in rushed an officer, holding a black book, with a dozen Burmans, accompanied by one, whom from his spotted face, we knew to be an executioner, and a 'son of the prison.' 'Where is the teacher?' was the first inquiry. Mr. Judson presented himself. 'You are called by the king,' said the officer; a form of speech always used when about to arrest a criminal. The spotted man instantly seized Mr. Judson, threw him on the floor, and produced the small cord, the instrument of torture. . . . The hardened executioner, with a hellish joy, drew tight the cords, bound Mr. Judson fast, and dragged him off, I knew not whither. . . .

"The officer and his gang proceeded on to the courthouse, where the governor of the city and the officers were collected, one of whom read the order of the king to commit Mr. Judson to the death prison, into which he was soon hurled, the door closed. . . . Mr. Judson, and all the white foreigners, were confined in the *death prison,* with three pairs of iron fetters each, and fastened to a long pole. . . . I begged and entreated the magistrate to allow me to go to some members of the government to state my case; but he said he did not dare to consent, for fear I should make my escape. I next wrote a note to one of the king's sisters, with whom I had been intimate, requesting her to use her influence for the release of the teachers. The note was returned with this message—She 'did not understand it'—which was a polite refusal to interfere; though I afterwards ascertained that she had an anxious desire to assist us, but dared not on account of the queen. . . .

"After continuing in the inner prison for more than a month, your brother was taken with a fever. I felt assured he would not live long, unless removed from that noisome place. To effect this, and in order to be near the prison, I removed from our house and put up a small bamboo room in the governor's inclosure, which was nearly opposite the prison gate. Here I incessantly begged the governor to give me an order to take Mr. J. out of the large prison, and place him in a more comfortable situation; and the old man, being worn out with my entreaties at length gave me the order in an official form; and also gave orders to the head jailer to allow me to go in and out, all times of the day, to administer medicines. I now felt happy, indeed, and had Mr. J. instantly removed into a little bamboo hovel, so low, that neither of us could stand upright—but a palace in comparison with the place he had left. Notwithstanding the order the governor had given for my admittance into prison, it was with the greatest difficulty that I could persuade the jailer to open the gate. I used to carry Mr. J's food myself, for the sake of getting in, and would then remain an hour or two, unless driven out. We had been in this comfortable situation but two or three days, when one morning, having carried in Mr. Judson's breakfast, which, in consequence of fever, he was unable to take, I remained longer than usual, when the governor in great haste sent for me. I promised him to return as soon as I had ascertained the governor's will, he being much alarmed at this unusual message. I was very agreeably disappointed, when the governor informed me that he only wished to consult me about his watch, and seemed unusually pleasant and conversable. I found afterwards, that his only object was, to detain me until the dreadful scene, about to take place in the prison, was over. For when I left him to go to my room, one of the servants came running, and with a ghastly countenance informed me that all the white prisoners were carried away.

[By boat and cart, Mrs. Judson managed to follow him to the next prison.]

"The prison was an old shattered building, without a roof.... Under a little low protection outside of the prison sat the foreigners, chained together two and two, almost dead with suffering and fatigue.... I asked one of the jailers if I might put up a little bamboo house near the prisoners; he said, 'No, it was not customary.' I then begged he would procure me a shelter for the night, when on the morrow I could find some place to live in. He took me to his house in which there were only two small rooms—one in which he and his family lived—the other, which was then half full of grain, he offered to me; and in that little filthy place, I spent the next six months of wretchedness.

[Mrs. Judson, her children, and Judson himself soon came down with a tropical fever.]

"My constitution seemed destroyed, and in a few days I became so weak as to be hardly able to walk to Mr. Judson's prison. In this debilitated state, I set off in a cart for Ava, to procure medicines, and some suitable food.... I reached the house in safety, and for two or three days the disorder seemed at a stand; after which it attacked me violently, that I had no hopes of recovery left—and my anxiety now was, to return to Oung-pen-la to die near the prison. It was with the greatest difficulty that I obtained the medicine chest from the governor, and then had no one to administer medicine. I however got at the laudanum, and by taking two drops at a time for several hours, it so far checked the disorder as to

The American Bible Society began in 1816, eleven years after the founding of the English Society. At first, the American group made a systematic attempt to put a Bible in every home in the nation—and into the pocket of every immigrant arriving on American shores. With the beginning of foreign missions, the Society began translating the Bible into as many languages of the world as possible. By 1967, its Bibles were appearing in 1,280 languages and dialects.

enable me to get on board a boat, though so weak that I could not stand, and again set off for Oung-pen-la when my strength seemed entirely exhausted. The good native cook came out to help me into the house but so altered and emaciated was my appearance that the poor fellow burst into tears at the first sight. I crawled on the mat in the little room, to which I was confined for more than two months....

[Judson was then moved to a third prison and Mrs. Judson again fell sick.]

"My fever raged violently and without any intermission. I began to think of settling my worldly affairs, ... when I lost my reason, and was insensible to all around me. At this dreadful period Dr. Price was released from prison; and hearing of my illness, obtained permission to come and see me. He has since told me that my situation was the most distressing he had ever witnessed, and that he did not then think I should survive many hours. My hair was shaved, my head and feet covered with blisters, and Dr. Price ordered me to take a little nourishment, which I had obstinately refused for several days. One of the first things I recollect was seeing this faithful servant standing by me, trying to induce me to take a little wine and water. I was in fact so far gone that the Burmese neighbors who had come in to see me expire said, 'She is dead; and if the king of angels should come in, he could not recover her.'

[With the treaty of peace about to be signed, Judson was suddenly released and given into the protection of a British general.]

"When Mr. Judson was sent from Maloun to Ava, it was within five minutes' notice, and without his knowledge of the cause. On his way up the river he accidentally saw the communication made to government respecting him, which was simply this: 'We have no further use [for him], we therefore return him to the golden city.' ... The governor of the north gate presented a petition to the high court of the empire, offered himself as Mr. Judson's security, obtained his release, and took him to his house, where he treated him with every possible kindness, and to which I was removed as soon as returning health would allow.

"It was on a cool, moonlight evening, in the month of March, that with hearts filled with gratitude to God, and overflowing with joy at our prospects, we passed down the Irra-waddy, surrounded by six or eight golden boats, and accompanied by all we had on earth. We now, for the first time for more than a year and a half, felt that we were free, and no longer subject to the oppressive yoke of the Burmese. . . . For several days, this single idea wholly occupied my mind, that we were out of the power of the Burmese government, and once more under the protection of the English. Our feelings continually dictated expressions like these: *What shall we render to the Lord for all His benefits toward us?* The treaty of peace was soon concluded, signed by both parties, and a termination of hostilities publicly declared. We left Yandaboo, after a fortnight's residence, and safely reached the mission house in Rangoon, after an absence of two years and three months."

These two early missionaries, each with an upraised arm, used a favorite early missionary technique on their audiences—but in different countries and with different results. In the old engraving at top, the Rev. John Thomas, who arrived in India with the first group of English missionaries in 1793, came across an assemblage of Brahmans making obeisance to a statue of a Hindu god at a roadside shrine. Facing the crowd, Thomas beckoned for silence, gravely pointed a finger at the image. "It has eyes, . . . but it cannot see!" he preached. "It has ears, but it cannot hear! It has . . . a mouth, . . . but it cannot speak; neither is there any breath in it!" At this moment, an elderly Brahman in the crowd exclaimed, "It has feet, but it cannot run away!" According to the mission historians, the crowd so approved of this sagacity that the Brahman priests were "put to shame" by their shouts. Twenty years later, John Ince (right), another early English missionary, tried the same technique on an assemblage of Chinese in Pulo Pinang off the western coast of Malay—but with different results. At a Buddhist temple where the festival of Shaou and Tseaou was being held, Ince saw a huge paper idol hanging in the air. "It has eyes, but it cannot see!" he said. "It has ears, but it cannot hear! . . ." Then, realizing he was making no impression, he bluntly asked, "What is your idol made of?" "Paper," replied the Chinese, smiling tolerantly and resuming their festivities.

161

Henry Opukahaia's People

"If I receive and patronize you missionaries," King Liholiho, formally known as Kamehameha II, told the first American Board missionaries to Hawaii who arrived on April 14, 1820, "I shall not be allowed but one wife." Then he grinned affectionately at all his five wives who sat fanning him and holding up a gourd spittoon as he chewed black betel juice. Liholiho's wives were more fascinated by missionary women than by missionary men. On a formal visit to the missionary ship *Thaddeus* soon after it sailed into their harbor, they pulled up the skirts of missionary wives, stared at their high-button shoes, giggled.

Liholiho himself was so enchanted with American knives and forks that he tried to walk off with a set when the visit ended. He insisted on taking English lessons from his hosts and was proud as a child when he could say at the top of his lungs, "How do you do! Aloha!" When the missionaries set up a school, he became so jealous the island children might learn English faster than he that the Rev. Asa Thurston, the leader of the group, had to point out the children were being taught Hawaiian, not English. English, he assured Liholiho, was much harder to learn. Later, Liholiho won the day by writing a letter to his rival, the king of the Society Islands, fully aware his correspondent would need an interpreter to read it to him—thus assuring Liholiho he had shown his own superior knowledge. The letter read:

> O Mahina—I now make a communication to you. I have compassion towards you on account of your son's dying. Love to you and the *alii,* chiefs of your island. I now serve the God of you and us. We are now learning the *palapala* [Bible]. When I become skilful in learning I will then go and visit you. May you be saved by Jesus Christ.

True to his word, he made a tour of the islands, taking with him spelling books written by the missionaries as presents for the chiefs instead of the usual gift of ceremonial robes.

By persuading the royal family, as well as the chiefs, to set an example by learning to read —and by doubling as teachers as well as preachers—the missionaries achieved one of their goals. By 1832, there were nine hundred schools with as many native as missionary teachers—and fifty-four thousand pupils, mostly adults. By 1846, eighty per cent of the people could read and write—more than in New England, as Richard Henry Dana observed.

Among the early converts was the Chieftess Kapiolani. To her and the missionaries it seemed tragic that worship of Pele, the first goddess of the great volcano Kilauea, should frighten the people. Kapiolani, helped along by the missionaries, decided to challenge Pele. Climbing to the top of the volcano, she met a priestess of Pele who warned her to stop. Kapiolani quoted missionary tracts to the priestess. Then she clambered down to a black ledge inside the volcano, threw stones into the seething mass, and announced: "Jehovah is my God. He kindled these fires. I fear not Pele. Should I perish by her anger, then you may fear her power. But if Jehovah save me when breaking through her taboos, then you must fear and serve Jehovah."

The first missionaries to Hawaii, then the Sandwich Islands, arrived because of the well-publicized pleadings of a sixteen-year-old boy named Henry Opukahaia *(left)*. The time was propitious. Western commercial inroads had contributed to the destruction of the indigenous religion. King Kamehameha I had just died. His widow, Queen Kaahumanu, and the new king's mother, Keopuolani, had broken taboo, overthrown the old idols, and left the people with no religion at all. The missionaries established the first public

Henry Opukahaia had been trained to be a pagan priest. In 1808, seeing his parents slain in a tribal war, he jumped into the sea from a rocky shore of the island of Hawaii, swam to an American ship lying at anchor in Kealakekua Bay, and begged the captain, who was out of New Haven, Connecticut, to take him to America. In New Haven, Professor Edwin W. Dwight of Yale took him to his home. Soon Henry was the irresistible drawing card at New England church services as he made passionate pleas for missionaries to go to his native islands. When the American Board of Commissioners for Foreign Missions established a Foreign Mission School at Cornwall, Connecticut, Henry became one of its pupils. In 1818, before he could return to Hawaii, he contracted typhus and died.

schools. They reduced the previously unwritten Hawaiian language to written form by devising an alphabet, a grammar, and a dictionary; they introduced Western doctors and modern medicine, encouraged the islanders' latent talent for music—and laid the groundwork of the new political and centralized state. They also initiated the production of sugar cane as the principal basis of the islands' economy.

With the backing of the royal family, it was a great victory for the missionaries. The queen mother had been so affected by the solemnity of the first Christian wedding ceremony held in Hawaii that she wept loudly during the entire service; and later, before she died, she requested Christian baptism. Then she sent for her son and her chiefs. "Protect the teachers who have come to this land of dark hearts . . . ," she told them. "Our former gods were vain. . . ." She charged her son to "take care of these lands. . . . Observe the Sabbath. Serve God. . . . Obey God's word that you may prosper and meet me in heaven. . . ." Taking her charge seriously, the king and the chiefs shortly after her death proclaimed the first written laws of the land: rulings against "murder, theft, and adultery," which were unmistakably reminiscent of the language of the Ten Commandments.

In 1870 the missionaries withdrew from active administration, convinced they had done their job—an opinion that was to be challenged by a host of American writers, led by Herman Melville (*pages 186-7*), up to the present day. The question was whether they had been truly Christian in converting Hawaiian "barbarism" to civilization. The missionaries were said to have found four hundred thousand Hawaiians there when they arrived, and disease unknown. In a few years smallpox and syphilis had reduced the entire population to less than one hundred thousand. They were accused of appropriating Hawaiian-owned land for themselves. (It had been given to the missionaries by the royal family.)

For better or worse the islands became, with missionary prodding, a part of Western civilization, and the missionaries themselves entered into government: one was the first justice of the supreme court, one was government minister of education, one was minister of the interior; they were also land surveyors and map makers—and they became industrialists and businessmen, as well as agriculturalists and teachers and doctors. By 1850, only thirty years after the arrival of the first missionaries, the Hawaiians were themselves sending missionaries to the Carolines and later to the Gilbert and Marshall Islands.

The King and Dan Bradley

"The American missionaries have always been just and upright men," said King Mongkut of Siam in the 1860's. They have never meddled in the affairs of government, nor created any difficulties with the Siamese. They have lived with the Siamese just as if they belonged to the nation."

The sweet reasonableness of this statement had come only after considerable trouble. In 1850, for example, an American Baptist mission had been burned when serious anti-foreign feeling erupted in Siam. The king at the time, who was Mongkut's older half brother, had refused an audience to an American envoy who had arrived to discuss opening trade with the West.

One of the most influential characters in this sweet reasonableness was a missionary, the Rev. Dan Beach Bradley, who had arrived in 1835 with a small working model of the solar system. This device demolished the entire Buddhist cosmos, which had as its center the sacred Mount Mehru (beneath which swam huge fish causing earthquakes), with many hells below and many heavens above. Bradley also had an electric machine (from which the then Prince Mongkut had a shock) and a printing press. In the first newspaper that Bradley proceeded to set up in 1844 in Bangkok, he published the first set of laws for the government—and some of the future king's poetry. He also dispensed information on lightning rods, the United States government, iron warships, and the abolition of slavery in the French colonies. In addition, he brought in chloroform, a cotton gin which Eli Whitney & Son sent to Siam, and a set of false teeth for Mongkut's brother, King Nang Klao. Bradley also introduced the first smallpox vaccine, while a later Baptist missionary brought along a skeleton, which became a prime attraction for the Thais, who had always believed that they were constructed differently from Westerners and thus could not be expected to respond to Western medicine.

The truth was that Mongkut was anxious to stave off Western imperialism and at the same time preserve indigenous Thai culture. Dan Beach Bradley helped him do it. Mongkut was at the time of Bradley's arrival a Buddhist monk with little hope of succeeding his half brother as king. But he was most anxious to understand the West—and, on occasion, to show off his knowledge. (It was a time when a

queen of Thailand had drowned because nobody had dared to lend a helping hand when a royal barge sank. No Thai would have thought of touching the king or queen. When occasionally it was necessary to execute a royal personage, he was put inside a red bag to avoid touching him, and beaten to death with a sandalwood stick wrapped in silk.)

On his arrival Bradley had not even known that Siam was a separate country from China. With the help of another royal brother, Prince Itsaret, Bradley met the royal heir Mongkut, and cured him following a stroke. Thus he became the friend of the future king, who favored the new Siam and the Westernization of ideas.

Bradley had opened his own clinic, handing out with his prescriptions an appropriate Bible text in Siamese. At the clinic all patients were treated alike, noblemen awaiting their turn with commoners, and the poor paying nothing. To the people of Thailand his ideas of human rights were as novel and exciting as his medicines. Within a few months after landing he had also published tracts and works on urgent medical problems, including midwifery in a country where it was at the time the custom of midwives to "roast" the bare back of a woman in labor before a hot charcoal fire. He cultivated a diplomatic friendship with the great nobles. American mission boards, learning of these friendships, hopefully sent reinforcements, until by 1840 there were twenty-three male and female Baptists, Congregationalists, and Presbyterians in Bangkok.

And Bradley did indeed help to introduce science—and some democracy—to Siam without tearing up the living roots of an ancient culture. King Mongkut announced that he liked to see the faces of his people instead of having them bow to touch the ground when he passed. (Human beings, the missionaries had exclaimed, were not made to bow to the ground and walk in his presence on all fours like cats and dogs.) More important, Mongkut cut taxes, built roads and canals, improved the lot of slaves, and, in one magnanimous reform, gave the ladies of the palace permission to leave his household if they so wished.

In return, mission presses produced exactly what Mongkut needed for himself and his people: textbooks, a history of Siam, Siamese-English dictionaries—in addition to the Bible. Hospitals were started, and so was the first

King Mongkut proved to his nobles that Western science, as taught by the missionary Bradley, was correct. But he died from a fever contracted on his trip from the observatory (opposite page), where he and his party observed the solar eclipse. His son Prince Chulalongkorn (right) carried on his enlightened Western policies.

school. In 1857, the missionaries helped the Siamese send the first Thai technical trainee, a student nurse, to the U.S. for advanced schooling.

If Mongkut's reasons were largely that he had an eye on menacing British imperialism, which he could best ward off by allying with the Americans, he nevertheless carried his reforms off well. In addition, as a result of a sound public relations program which was aided and abetted by the Americans, including Bradley, he managed to become famous and well thought of in the United States. As for Dan Bradley, however, the result was different. He considered himself a failure. The Buddhists' tolerant attitude toward other religions had made it easy for them to absorb Christian influence. They simply compromised with it, rather than becoming actual converts to it. Thus Bradley and his fellow missionaries made few converts. Even the descendants of those who did become nominal Christian converts in Bradley's time rarely today call themselves Christians.

To demonstrate the reliability of Western science to his people in 1868, a hopeful King Mongkut gathered his leading nobles at a specially built observatory (below) outside the Thai capital, where they anxiously awaited a solar eclipse which the missionaries had assured him would take place. When it did—and at the scheduled time—Mongkut was so delighted that the moment was commemorated in the painting below in the Temple Rajapradith. The Siamese had previously believed eclipses occurred when a large snake or demon tried to swallow the sun or moon. At such times they did their best to ward off the event by beating gongs, setting off firecrackers, and chanting Eastern scripture.

"Dr. Livingstone, I Presume?"

David Livingstone was a Scotsman who wanted to go to China as a missionary. But the Opium War broke out in 1839, and he had to settle for Africa, after first walking the wards of London hospitals to learn medicine. In Africa, he was responsible for calling the attention of the civilized world to what he called "the running sore of Africa"—the gigantic slave trade that was destroying African civilization. In the scene at right a contemporary magazine romanticized his mission to the Africans and helped make Livingstone into probably the most glamorous missionary of the nineteenth century.

David Livingstone was a kindly, deeply understanding gentleman who was not without humor. In 1841, he arrived in Algoa Bay in South Africa, shortly after the early missionary there, Robert Moffat. As a missionary Livingstone was actually something of a failure, though he became the prototype of the entire nineteenth-century Protestant effort. More than any other single man he focused the attention of the world on one of the great scandals of Western Christendom—the African slave trade, which had reached its peak when Livingstone first arrived. The entire African civilization had been disrupted. Out of fear and terror the natives had been forced into the bush. Trails were named after slaves who had died resisting the slave traders.

Livingstone was an imperialist. But he had worked in a Glasgow cotton mill while a student, and he thought of the Africans as his brothers. For a few years he tried his best to open up mission stations in the "dark interior," where none had been before; then he became so outraged by the slave trade that he turned from traditional missionary work to more practical ways of combating the slavers.

The only way to undercut highly profitable slave trading, he decided, was to open up trade routes from the coast so that the rich continent might develop commercially. To this end he became explorer and geographer. In the bargain, he discovered the Zambesi River and Victoria Falls. For three decades he traveled the continent, making friends with native chiefs, standing up staunchly to the Boers, whom he considered the real threat to Africa. Bitten by a lion, battling malaria and the tsetse fly as well as hostile warring tribes, Livingstone became his century's most famous missionary. When reporter Henry M. Stanley (*right*) came upon him in 1871 after being told by editor James Gordon Bennett of the *Herald* to "Find Livingstone," the entire world watched in fascination. By that time Livingstone was an old man, broken in health and spirit and obsessed with the idea of finding the sources of the Nile and the Zambesi rivers. Paradoxically, through his explorations he had opened up new slave routes and actually prepared the way for greater slave trading than ever before. A tired old man, he tried once more—accompanied by Stanley—to find the sources of the two rivers, but failed.

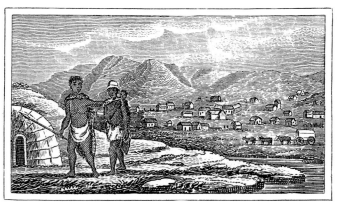 

In the 1790's, the London Missionary Society had sent a Dutchman named John Theodore Vanderkemp as a missionary to South Africa. At Algoa Bay, four hundred miles east of Cape Town, Vanderkemp founded a mission station named Bethelsdorp, which became famous as a refuge for neighboring Hottentots when they were mistreated by European colonialists.

The glamour of David Livingstone was immeasurably boosted when newspaper reporter Henry M. Stanley was sent in 1871 by the New York Herald to find him in the jungle. Stanley's casual greeting, "Dr. Livingstone, I presume?" became a classic of the era.

A Puzzle for Japan

The cartoon shown at right appeared in 1872, a year when Japan, despite its growing interest in becoming Westernized, had outlawed Christianity. It pointed up the misunderstandings, not only in Japan itself but in all Asia, as well as in many other parts of the "missionary" world, regarding the perplexing divisions within Christianity itself.

A few months earlier the Japanese Prince Iwakura had conferred in Washington, D.C., with Secretary of State Hamilton Fish regarding new treaties for the opening of Japan to Western trade, following the original opening of Japan's ports in 1854 by Admiral Perry. Prince Iwakura urged the immediate cancellation of the extraterritorial clauses of the existing treaty, by which Westerners were not subject to Japanese law. But Fish pointed out that the U.S. government could not consent to place its citizens under Japanese jurisdiction as long as laws against Christianity remained unrepealed. The prince denied there was any persecution in Japan. The American ambassador to Japan cited the case of Ichikawa Yeinosuki, a Japanese Christian who then died in prison on November 25, 1872, from neglect due to the fact that he was a Christian—and therefore unwanted. On February 24, 1873, the famous edict was issued which led to the withdrawal of Japanese proclamations against Christianity.

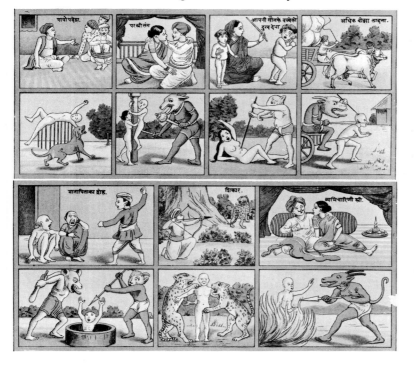

These drawings interpreting Hinduism were brought home by Western missionaries. They show a catalogue of sins with their punishments directly below, including cruelty to animals (bottom center) and adultery.

168

This 1872 cartoon bore the title "A Puzzle for Japan." When Japan, by treaty, reluctantly opened her doors to the West in 1859, she nevertheless adopted Western culture more quickly than did China. Then, during the second half of the century, while China was endeavoring to hold the Westerners at arm's length, Japan feverishly imbibed much of Occidental civilization. Though the treaties did not give permission for missionaries to propagate their faith, Protestant missionaries nevertheless established themselves in the open ports. But the Japanese were confused by the differences between Western Protestantism and Western Catholicism, as this cartoon, showing a gaitered clergyman, makes clear. Speech in hand, the poor man falters— to the delight of the Japanese at left—as the conflict between Protestants and Catholics is satirized in the background. The Western misinterpretation of Oriental religions, especially in the misinterpretation of Hinduism in the drawings at far left, revealed a confusion on the part of the Westerners which was even less understandable than the Japanese confusion regarding Western religions. Such drawings were sometimes sent home by the missionaries.

The Taiping Rebellion

In 1850, as an indirect result of the Protestant mission in China, the great Taiping Rebellion broke out. It was a rebellion that inspired further uprisings in late nineteenth-century China, culminating in Sun Yat-sen's overthrow of the politically corrupt Manchu dynasty in 1911–1912. The rebellion was a national religious-political upheaval that, on one hand, has been praised as a national agrarian and proletarian revolution and, on the other, condemned as the work of "long-haired" bandits. It was also one of the bloodiest rebellions in history, as well as one of the strangest.

The rebellion had its origins in 1843 when a visionary Cantonese village schoolteacher named Hung Hsiu-ch'üan, who had tried to gain political office, failed for the sixth and final time to pass the Manchu government civil service examinations. Dismayed, Hung, who had read some Christian tracts written by Liang A-fa, the first Protestant convert in China, then fell ill, suffered delirium, and thought he saw a vision of two men in heaven, one of whom, he said, ordered him to kill "demons" on earth. He decided the older man in his vision was the Christian God, the middle-aged man was Jesus, and he himself was the second son of God, thus completing a trinity. Hung was soon baptized, then organized a society known as "The God Worshippers."

On September 15, 1851, Hung's rebels, spurred on by the famine and the agrarian troubles of the peasantry, resisted Manchu troops in the mountainous Kwangsi province and captured the city of Yung-an. By March, 1853, they had established their "heavenly capital" in Nanking, where Hung proclaimed himself the king of the "Taiping T'ien-kuo," which meant literally "Heavenly Kingdom of the Great Peace."

During their years in power, the Taipings inaugurated reforms based on their concept of Christianity. They preached the equality of all men. There was to be equality between men and women. Monogamy was the rule. They planned equal distribution of land. Prostitution, foot-binding, and slavery were prohibited. Westernization and industrialization were advocated.

The Taiping government lasted until 1864. It fell when it met opposition from another—and more traditionally Chinese—religious group, a Confucian army trained by the Confucian scholar Tsêng Kuo-fan. Hung's attempts to take Shanghai were stopped with help of the British under General Gordon, and the Taiping forces were finally hemmed in at Nanking. Hung himself committed suicide.

The rebellion failed partly because of its alienation of the Confucian literati—and partly because Western military and commercial interests were willing to ally themselves with the Manchu dynasty in order to protect the profitable opium trade. Some modern scholars argue that, had they succeeded, the Taipings, misguided though they were, might in time have combined Confucianism with Christianity to bring about a truly indigenous Christianity—which, in turn, might have withstood the Marxism that found fertile ground in later Chinese agrarian rebellions. Even in its failure, however, the Taiping Rebellion perhaps helped weaken Confucianism—and thus to pave the way for the anti-imperialist movement of Sun Yat-sen.

In many important ways, wrote historian Max Weber, the Taiping Rebellion involved "a break with Confucian orthodoxy and offer[ed] better prospects of the growth of an indigenous religion relatively closer to Christianity than the hopeless missionary experiences of the occidental Confessions. It may well prove to have been the last chance for such a religion to emerge in China." In the Chinese painting shown here, government Manchu forces reduce Taiping "Christian" strongholds near Tientsin with fire, cavalry, and siege guns.

The Millerites Await Their Glorious Day

On the eve of March 20, 1843, a crowd of almost fifty thousand farmers and townspeople gathered on rooftops in and around churches in Low Hampton, New York. Others headed for nearby graveyards where the resurrection of the dead promised a far more interesting spectacle.

"O glorious, . . ." their leader William Miller, a self-taught, well-meaning farmer had cried joyfully from pulpit to pulpit in New England, "the trump of jubilee will be blown." Miller had been deeply influenced by early nineteenth-century camp-meeting revivalism. In 1816, while reading his Bible, he had made what he believed to be an astounding "discovery"—that the words of Daniel 8:14 predicted the exact day on which the world would come to an end. The passage was a comparatively straightforward one for the apocalyptically minded—and completely symbolic tone of—the Book of Daniel. It read: "And he said unto me, 'Unto two thousand and three hundred days; then shall the sanctuary be cleansed.'"

Miller's "discovery" was that he had decided the word "days" in the text actually meant "years." The second coming of Christ (and the end of the world), he thus decided, would take place exactly two thousand three hundred *years* from the date of the vision described by Daniel, or on March 21, 1843. Millerite followers, who were mainly simple farm folk, left their land untilled and sold off their property. Then they squandered the proceeds so they might be found in the proper abject condition of Christian poverty, come Judgment Day.

But midnight of March 20 came without event. So did dawn. Badly shaken, Miller announced he had apparently made a mistake in his calculations. The trump of jubilee, he now figured, would sound forth a little more than one year later, on November 5, 1844. When his second prediction proved equally wrong, he admitted defeat. Crushed with disappointment, he died in 1849, unaware that from a New Hampshire contingent of his followers would rise a large—and fundamentalist—creed of Protestantism, the Seventh-Day Adventists. Millennially minded like Miller, they cling to this day to his interpretation of the Bible. On or about March 21, 1843, they believe, Jesus actually fulfilled the prophecy of the Book of Daniel by entering into his heavenly, though not earthly, sanctuary, whence he will sooner or later come to judge us all. On this comparatively minor point alone, say the Seventh-Day Adventists, did Miller err. Still awaiting the awful Day of Judgment, they cling to strict observance of Saturday as the Sabbath, to vegetarianism, and to total abstinence from tobacco and alcohol. They ban cardplaying, dancing, attendance at movies. Characteristically they also give more money per member to Christian benevolences than any other large Protestant denomination.

"Judgment Day," envisioned by an artist member of the Millerites, displayed an angel trailing through the sky a scriptural banner whose predictions were interpreted by the artist as falling meteors and toppling buildings.

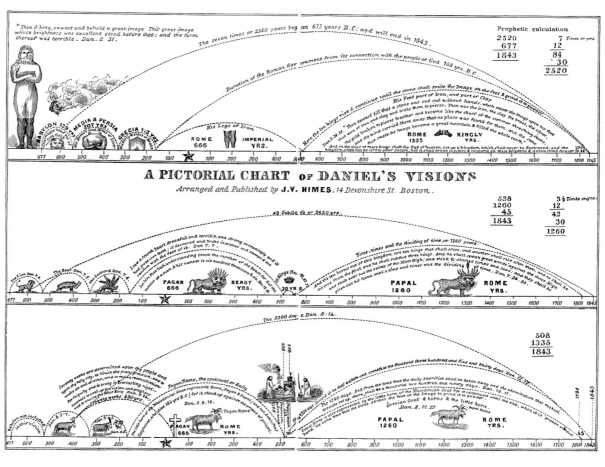

A PICTORIAL CHART OF DANIEL'S VISIONS

Arranged and Published by **J.V. HIMES**, 14 Devonshire St. Boston.

The millennial calculations of William Miller were elaborately based on the Bible. They began with the year 677 B.C., which Miller calculated as the date of the prophet Daniel. By three different routes, here charted by a contemporary Boston printer, he arrived each time at the year 1843 as the date of the end of the world.

This drawing of a Millerite "ascension robe" was the result of a newspaper artist's lively imagination. It was widely published to poke fun at the nineteenth-century Millerites.

A smug occupant of a well-stocked "Judgment Day" larder was equipped by a newspaper cartoonist with a palm-leaf fan and a barrel of ice if he found himself hellbound.

William Miller was the most famous of several nineteenth-century "prophets" who believed in the imminent second coming of Christ; another was Edward Irving of England who, less definite than Miller, predicted that the awful Day of Judgment would occur sometime between the years 1835 and 1901.

The Anti-Catholic Riots

Now, even in an America where freedom of religion had supposedly been guaranteed by the Constitution, the Protestants were persecuting the Catholics. In 1831, Lyman Beecher preached a series of fiery and intolerant sermons against Boston Catholics, thereby becoming at least indirectly responsible for the sacking of an Ursuline convent at Charlestown, Massachusetts, by a Boston mob. In Ellsworth, Maine, in 1854, a Jesuit was tarred and feathered. In St. Louis, Missouri, in the same year, police were helpless to stop a series of pitched battles between Americans and Irish Catholic immigrants, and several were killed. The reason lay in the fact that many of the large number of Irish and German immigrants after 1820 were Roman Catholics. Protestants were alarmed when Catholic priests made use of the Irish vote to demand state support for their own voluntary parochial schools. They were also alarmed by the widespread belief that most of the immigrants would become paupers, since it was true that the journey to the U.S. of thousands of the new immigrants had been paid for by European authorities in order to relieve their own taxpayers of supporting them in Europe.

The intolerance was at its height following the Civil War, though before then the worst single bloc of anti-Catholic feeling had coalesced in a political party known as the "Know-Nothings." As with all bigoted movements the flame spread until, in a country supposedly founded on religious freedom, anti-Catholicism became synonymous in the minds of the Protestant "Know-Nothings" with Americanism. They charged Irish and German immigrants with stealing American elections and running the big-city political machines. In time the party's avowed goal was to bar all naturalized citizens from office and extend to twenty-one years the legal time an immigrant had to live in the U.S. before becoming a citizen. The liberal press fought the prejudice against the Catholics with cartoons like the one below. But the enmity was not resolved. Anti-Catholic political feeling in an America with a Protestant majority was to crop up again in 1928 during the presidential campaign of Al Smith. It was not to be overcome until the 1960 election of John F. Kennedy, a grandson of a Boston Irish Catholic mayor, to the U.S. Presidency.

In this cartoon, published by the liberal press to stem the anti-Catholic feeling, the freedom-of-worship clause of the U.S. Constitution became a reptile choking a young German Catholic immigrant boy.

In Philadelphia, "Know-Nothings" wearing tall beaver hats fought off the state militia, burned two famous old Catholic churches, and killed twenty-four people.

"No Church Need Apply" was the caption of this anti-Catholic cartoon showing the pope carrying a hatbox full of hats, caps, and gowns at the entrance of a U.S. public school. At the door he is stopped by a schoolboy who explains, "Miss Columbia will not try your teaching, as it has proved to be so injurious in Dame Europe's school that our adopted children who left her don't care to learn under that system again."

This scene purported to show "Romish" priests burning Protestant Bibles in Upper New York State.

The Anglo-Catholics

On July 14, 1833, the Rev. John Keble of the Church of England preached a sermon entitled "National Apostasy" at St. Mary's Church, Oxford. One of those who heard the sermon was John Henry Newman, who then launched the Oxford—or "Anglo-Catholic"—Movement. The position of the Anglo-Catholics was frequently so fine a distinction between Anglicanism and Roman Catholicism that it bewildered high-church Anglicans and Roman Catholics alike. The causes behind the movement were deep. The Industrial Revolution had thrown multitudes out of work, and riots flared in all parts of England. In the eyes of a large segment of the population the church now became the scapegoat. They saw in it a symbol of entrenched vested interests, and they resented the church's hostility to social and political reforms which were designed to grant the new industrial cities proper representation in Parliament, to repeal inhumane criminal laws, to reduce the working hours of women and children, and to abolish the slave trade. They were also angered by the state church's refusal to give up any of its special privileges or to reduce the number of high ecclesiastical dignitaries who were drawing large salaries while many people starved.

In its initial phases, the Oxford Movement sought to revitalize the church spiritually. But its members had looked askance at the evangelistic methods of the Wesleyan Methodist movement. As a result the movement gradually developed a definite "high-church" trend, with almost exclusive emphasis on liturgical practices carried over from Roman Catholicism—and strongly insisted on maintaining the privileged position of the church. It vigorously defended the "divine" character of the episcopacy, which it claimed had been preserved by "apostolic succession" from the Roman Catholic Church. This, the new Anglo-Catholics insisted, was the only source and basis for a continuing revelation of truth and of religious authority.

It had actually been the purpose of the movement to take a position halfway between Roman Catholicism and Protestantism. But in doing so, they soon came to stand for the authority of the church as opposed to the right of individual judgment. The whole tendency of the movement was to exalt the clergy as a sacerdotal class and to bring the laity under the rule of the priesthood, though many of its leaders also cherished the idea of a reunion of all Christendom in one church, presumably under the authority of the pope. Of Newman, at his death, the American writer James Russell Lowell said: "[He was] a beautiful old man, as I remember him." But, he added, ". . . surely a futile life if there ever was one, trying to make a past unreality supply the place of a present one that was becoming past. . . ." In America, the cause of the Anglo-Catholics was taken up by Bishop John Henry Hobart, of the Protestant Episcopal Church, thus splitting the low-church Episcopalians from the high-church—or Anglo-Catholic—branch. Hobart's *High Churchman Vindicated,* published in 1827, was a clear call to Anglo-Catholics. It was complete with slogans like "Apostolic Succession," "Only the Episcopal Ministry Valid," and "The Prayer Book is the only divinely approved form of worship."

In this cartoon, British journalists mocked the Christianity of English Prime Minister William Ewart Gladstone's government, which the Anglo-Catholics strongly supported. Its caption read: "Mr. Gladstone has requested the Archbishop of York to order thanksgiving in the churches for the success of British arms in Egypt—Is it Christian to thank God for Islam slaughter?"

John Henry Newman, author of the hymn "Lead, Kindly Light," was a gentle, pale, emaciated, and extremely sincere man who had a deep disdain for conventionalities—and a willful temper. He tried to make the Church of England into the Catholic Church of England. But in 1845, he left the Church of England. He finally became a Roman Catholic cardinal.

Edward Bouverie Pusey, grandson of an earl, tried valiantly to force his Anglo-Catholic beliefs on others, partly because he deeply feared the progress of rationalism in Germany. From his own congregation, two groups of clergy turned Roman Catholic in five years.

John Keble was a brilliant but inflexible conservative who believed literally in the divine origin and authority of the church. In 1827, he published a famous book entitled The Christian Year which comprised devotional poems intended for each Sunday and each festival observed in the liturgy of the Church of England.

The Rev. Samuel Wilberforce was disgruntled by hearing of an instance in which American Episcopalians had admitted non-Anglicans to occasional communion. To him, such fraternizing with "dissenters" was deplorable. But as Bishop of Winchester he was forced to steer a course between low- and high-church factions.

Much to Charles Kingsley's annoyance, his Anglo-Catholicism was sometimes called "muscular Christianity." He had hoped to rouse the English upper classes to their duties toward the working classes without depriving them of their own social and economic privileges. But in the end he simply bowed to the status quo.

The European Theologians

Out of eighteenth-century Deism there had arisen in Germany during the early nineteenth century a group of philosophers and theologians who were to leave their imprint on changing Protestant theology throughout the world. But it was a new theology that obviously, too, bore the stamp of idealism. God, they said, was to be found in nature, in history, and in the mind and heart of man. Man, said these liberals, should be regarded as potentially a son of God. The kingdom of God would, they believed, be achieved not so much by a divine cataclysmic event as by the dedicated service of human beings through social relationships with each other. In Jesus, they said, it was possible for man to capture the truest insight into the meaning of God, and find an example worth emulating. The principal difference between ordinary man and Jesus was, they said, that Jesus had more fully realized his divine potentialities.

Of the new philosophers, both Georg Wilhelm Friedrich Hegel and Immanuel Kant (*right*) stood at the top. "The Good," said Hegel, "and absolutely good, is eternally accomplishing itself in the world; and the result is that it need not wait upon us, but is already by implication, as well as in full, actually accomplished." He taught that the universe was, as Deism had said, inherently rational and that the irrational would be overcome by reason. In a way, as modern theologians are discovering, he was the precursor of existentialism, whose first exponent was to be a Danish theologian named Sören Kierkegaard (*pages 182-3*). But there was nevertheless a heartlessness in Hegel which, in a later generation, was to make him the idol of Nazism and Italian Fascism, though he himself was not a racist or totalitarian but a complex conservative. Even Karl Marx (*pages 208-9*) was to recognize that Hegel's system was a speculative expression of Germanic Christianity which glorified the patterns of history as the path of God. Marx was not, however, to recognize how much of Hegel's immoralism had seeped into his own conception of the historical process.

Hegel did much to substitute a sense of their fundamental unity for the older sharp distinction between the divine and the human. It was a concept prevalent, too, in other nineteenth-century Protestant theology. As a child, Immanuel Kant (*right*) had been influenced by

German Pietism. Later, as a young professor, he was influenced by the Deistic rationalism of Leibnitz and Wolff. But he was even more influenced by Rousseau's "discovery of the deep hidden nature of man." Then, in 1781, in his *Critique of Pure Reason*, he struck a hard blow at pure rationalism. Knowledge, he said, is the product of two elements: reality and mind. From these two elements comes human experience. But, said Kant, men do not have knowledge of what things actually are, but only what their minds make of objective reality. It is thus, he said, impossible to demonstrate God by "pure reason"—or by natural religion, or by the constitution of the universe. Evil and the inner moral law in man, he said, combat for the obedience of man. Yet, he said, man is conscious of a *feeling* of moral obligation because he asks himself what he ought to do. This inner moral law—or "categorical imperative"—is, he said, the noblest of man's possessions. Man can, therefore, live virtuously if he has the freedom to do so, and, he said, such virtue should result in happiness. But since experience does not actually provide happiness, the accomplishment of the happiness demands a power that can unite happiness with virtue. Therefore, said Kant, there must be a God—a God whose existence is only a hypothesis in "pure reason" but whose existence nevertheless becomes a logical conviction. One ruled by the principle of moral good is pleasing to God—and is, in fact, a son of God.

In effect, Kant was a Deist who had reduced religion to ethics. But he had nevertheless given a new status to human feeling in religion. Out of his philosophical trend came the most influential German theologian of the early nineteenth century, Friedrich Ernst Daniel Schleiermacher (*right*). Schleiermacher's chief significance lay in the fact that, for him, religion belonged to the realm of "feeling." The basis of belief was thus shifted from the Bible to the experience of the believer himself. Man in himself, he said, is a microcosm, a reflection of the universe. But, as contrasted with that which is universal, man feels himself finite—and dependent. It is this feeling of dependence which, said Schleiermacher, is the basis of all religion. In itself, he said, religion is neither a body of doctrines, revealed or rationally certified, nor a system of conduct. In human experience, he said, man perceives the antitheses of the manifold and the changing over against a principle of unity and permanency. These antitheses give us the absolute and eternal—*i.e.*, God—without whom all would be empty. It is, he said, the aim of all religions to bridge the gap between the universal and the finite, to bring man into harmony with God. And, he said, the worth of each religion is to be measured by the degree in which this goal is accomplished. Thus, all religions are not to be divided into true and false but into relative degrees of adequacy. Doctrines, he said, are these fundamental religious experiences defining and interpreting themselves intellectually. But, he said, these explanations have only a relative and secondary value because they have changed and may still change. They are, he said, simply the forms in which abiding truth from time to time expresses itself. Yet, he insisted, since the problems fundamental to all religion are sin and pardon—*i.e.*, separation from God and reconciliation with him—Christianity is the best of all religions thus far known to man, since it most fully accomplishes its goal. Morality, he said, as demonstrated by the life of Jesus, is the result of the proper understanding of that of which man is a part: the family, the community, the state, the world. Such an enlarging view of man's real place in these relations will drive out selfishness and self-centeredness—*and* achieve an immortality. But, said Schleiermacher, immortality may be a quality of life rather than a question of duration.

Reacting against these philosophers, Arthur Schopenhauer held that the true nature of the world consists in an unspiritual will to live, that the function of religion is to deliver man from the bondage of universal power, and that the supreme moral principle is compassion, because it overcomes separation of individual men and leads them back to the original unity from which they originate. Said another reactivist, Friedrich Wilhelm Nietzsche: "God is dead." He had, said Nietzsche, been killed by striving, self-centered man. That, he said, was that.

Samuel Taylor Coleridge introduced the nineteenth-century German philosophies to England. He was, said Charles Lamb, "an archangel, a little damaged." At one time Coleridge had thought of becoming a Unitarian clergyman.

A timid, colorless personality, Georg Wilhelm Friedrich Hegel was nevertheless a colossus of German nineteenth-century thought who became the semiofficial philosopher of the Prussian state because he came to see Prussian nationalism as the model of free society. For him, the universe was a constant logical development of the Absolute Mind—i.e., God—through human struggle and effort. Man, he said, is the union of mind and matter. Since men are thus portions of the Absolute, a prime duty of the finite spirit is to realize its relationship to the Absolute. Such realization is, he believed, religion. For the older sharp distinction between the divine and human, Hegel did much to substitute the sense of their fundamental unity that became prevalent in nineteenth-century Protestant theology.

Immanuel Kant was a little man with a strict morality who developed a new respect for human feeling as well as human reason in nineteenth-century philosophy. On the one hand, he was the climax and fulfillment of the rationalistic religion of the eighteenth-century Deists (pages 120-1) and a critic of Protestant orthodoxy. But he was also a critic of the Deists, giving a new value to feeling, which had not previously been recognized.

Friedrich Ernst Daniel Schleiermacher was condemned by the rationalists of his day as too visionary—by the orthodox as too radical. Educated by Moravians, Schleiermacher fell under the influence of rationalists, was then greatly impressed by the philosophies of Spinoza, Kant, and the Romanticists.

The Changing Devil

More people, it has been said, have their ideas about heaven and hell from John Milton than from the Bible—though they fail to realize the fact. The Angel Gabriel, for example, first blew his horn at Milton's behest, not at the Bible's. But the most important aspect of Milton's interpretation was his streamlining of the devil. Before Milton's time, Satan had appeared in medieval plays as a shaggy, masked, menacing character forking doomed souls to destruction. To this interpretation, Christopher Marlowe, as in some earlier morality plays, had added in the sixteenth century (right) a sense of humor for his Mephistopheles. But Milton added to that. He modernized him and made Satan a gentleman, and since that time more than one Protestant continues to believe in his heart that the Satan of Milton is the "true" Satan, and feels a sense of loss in turning back to the Bible's prosaic Lucifer.

After Milton, it was the German poet Johann Wolfgang von Goethe (left) who changed the world's concept of the devil in literature. In Goethe's *Faust*, the devil became a soul searching for salvation for himself. He was evil personified seeking salvation through knowledge. The philosophies of Spinoza and of Leibnitz had furnished Goethe with a religion that made individual creeds and dogmas seem unnecessary. They had also provided him with a faith in the divine purpose of human life. His protagonist Faust became the image of Western civilization's modern man searching for the good. In that search, he pointed out, man constantly errs. From that time on, among liberal Protestants, the devil and hell became far different concepts from those entertained by the traditionalists—and, in opposition to Roman Catholic theology, damnation was no longer considered to be eternal. In the end Goethe's Faust, tempted by Mephistopheles, triumphs over the powers of evil—a triumph for which even Mephistopheles himself is searching.

Until the end of the seventeenth century almost everybody, Christian and non-Christian, had believed that a human being could make a pact with the devil, thus becoming a "witch" who was able to cause good or evil for friends or enemies. In Germany, a woman was executed as a witch even as late as 1793. In 1685, Cotton Mather of New England had, like others, written a book on the subject, setting forth exactly how witches were expected to behave, including their ability to ride broomsticks. Mather's book had unfortunately gotten into the hands of some adolescent girls in Salem, Massachusetts. Soon these girls were accusing dozens of innocent people in or near Salem of witchcraft. Fourteen women and five men were hanged as a result, and one man, Giles Corey, was pressed to death for refusing to plead either guilty or not guilty. For liberal Protestants, the Salem witch trials of 1692 had marked the beginning of the end of a literal belief in the devil. In 1697, Samuel Sewall, one of the judges at the trials that had convicted the "witches," publicly acknowledged his guilt in the affair by standing up in church and admitting his error. From that time on, the devil and his hell tended to become more and more the symbol and the spirit of evil inherent in every human being, not a literal person and place.

The Rise of Existentialism

"To be a Christian is the most terrible
of all torments, it is—and it must be—
to have one's hell here on earth. . . ."

During the nineteenth century, probably no man made a more devastating attack on Christianity than frail, persecuted, suffering—and conceited—Sören Aabye Kierkegaard (*right*), whose name in Danish meant "churchyard." ". . . What torture!" he wrote. "If a man is really to be the instrument of God, for the infinite will that God is, then God must first take all his will from him. What a fearful operation! And it is natural that no one knows how to examine so painfully as one who is omniscient and omnipotent. Certainly with other forms of torture there are doctors present to estimate how long the tortured man can hold out without losing his life. Yet mistakes can happen, and the tortured man can die before their eyes. This never happens with one who is omniscient." Again he wrote, "If I were a pagan and had to speak Greek, I should say that God has arranged everything for his own entertainment; he amuses himself like a man who puts a piece of bacon in a mousetrap and watches all the tricks of the mice to get the bacon out without being trapped—so God amuses himself at the leaps and springs and contortions of these millions of men [who hope] to get hold of the truth without suffering."

Suffering, Kierkegaard believed, is the basis of life. But suffering is a paradox. It is irreparably connected with the majesty of God: "It is the paradox of the majesty which is bound to make the beloved unhappy. . . . Suffering depends on the fact that God and man are qualitatively different, and that the clash of time and eternity in time is bound to cause suffering."

Modern analysts, anxious to find the root of Kierkegaard's troubles, have hypothesized that he felt "original sin" because he was embarrassed by the fact that his parents were elderly when he was born. Others have guessed that he was shocked by learning that his father, whom he both loved and hated, had once cursed God. Regardless of the reason, he was the first of the great modern existentialists, finding a God and the meaning of life from his own inner experience. For him, life was characterized by the "dread," the "absurd"—and religion was the "leap" from objective thinking to subjective faith, with the consciousness of sin as the driving force in the leap. Doubt, he said, cannot be defeated by reason. It can be overcome only by the "leap of faith."

"Through a crime," he wrote, lending credence to the analysts' hypotheses, "I came into

In sharp contrast to Sören Kierkegaard, Nikolai Grundtvig argued that human life was joyful. He became a bishop in the Danish church at the time Kierkegaard was criticizing it.

existence. I came into existence against God's will. . . . The punishment fits the fault; it is to be deprived of all joy of life, to be brought to the supreme degree of disgust with life. My task," he also wrote, "is to put a halt to a lying diffusion of Christianity, and to help it to shake off a mass of nominal Christianity." This was his constant argument against the Established Church. That church, he said, is "an impudent indecency." He had long hesitated before directly attacking the Established Church. Then he determined to break through "a conspiracy of silence." He could, he said, no longer repress his rage against the everyday blasphemy that Christianity had become. "Whoever you may be, and whatever the life you live, my friend," he wrote, "by omitting to attend the public divine service—if indeed it be your habit to attend it—by omitting to attend public divine service as now constituted (claiming as it does to represent the Christianity of the New Testament) you will escape at least one, and a great, sin in not attempting to fool God by calling that the Christianity of the New Testament which is not the Christianity of the New Testament."

At times Kierkegaard was willing to admit that God was, as John Calvin had said, "Love." But generally he found only "Hatred." It was an attitude almost as magnificent as Luther's bombastic shout of "Love God! I hated him!" But with Kierkegaard's existential emphasis, the concept of Christian suffering was once more emphasized. It was a concept that was ardently opposed by Nikolai F. S. Grundtvig *(left)*. But in an age of disillusionment following World War II, the existentialism of Sören Kierkegaard was rediscovered by the world. As some modern critics have said, the discovery was to make Christianity intellectually possible for the twentieth century.

As the chief critic of the church, Sören Aabye Kierkegaard was roundly criticized—and caricatured—by his contemporaries. Children taunted him on the streets, and parents took to admonishing stubborn boys, "Don't be a Sören." As a figure of controversy, he was nicknamed "Either-Or," after the title of one of his critiques. In typical fashion, Kierkegaard himself lamented in his journal: "To let oneself be trampled by geese is a slow way of dying. . . . When I have sought recreation by driving ten or twelve miles, and my body has gradually become somewhat weak . . . when I alight from the carriage, there is sure to be someone at hand who is jolly enough to call me names."

The New Freedom

The nineteenth century was the age of the proliferation of theological seminaries, the first being Andover—now Andover Newton—in 1807, which was founded because of Harvard College's steady drift toward Unitarianism. Up to the beginning of the nineteenth century most colleges, including Harvard, Yale, Williams, and Amherst, had been founded for the purpose of educating students for the ministry. The trouble was the colleges were being swept by a new freedom and were breaking away from denominationalism. In 1800, Lyman Beecher wrote of Yale: ". . . Most of the class before me were infidels, and called each other Voltaire, Rousseau . . ." He meant "Deists."

In the fight against the rising tide of liberalism there arose three men, Horace Bushnell, Charles G. Finney, and Beecher himself. But each in his own way was more liberal than past generations. Bushnell rejected the extremes of Calvinist total depravity and taught that a child is susceptible to good even though he is plagued by "sinful tendencies" from his birth. He also taught, contrary to old orthodoxy, that men are not saved by Christ's sacrifice but by coming to know God's love through an understanding of Christ's suffering. In 1834, even Beecher was charged with heresy for his belief against old-line Calvinism, but his trial ended in acquittal. At the same time, Presbyterian Albert Barnes was brought to trial for holding that a "sinner is not personally answerable for the transgressions of Adam." Like Beecher, he was acquitted.

In the early nineteenth century there were Germans who came to America because they refused to abide by the Prussian-government-enforced union in 1817, under Friedrich Wilhelm III, of the Lutheran and Reformed Churches, known as the Prussian United Church. But the new German theologians had strongly influenced the churches of both Calvinist and Lutheran origin. When, as a result of the German political situation, a group of liberal refugees from Germany came to the United States to settle, some of them brought with them a more liberal brand of Protestantism. In America, these put the stamp of the nineteenth-century German theologians on their theological seminaries, one of which is shown in the old print below.

In New York City in the 1830's, a huge new church called the Broadway Tabernacle was built for a Presbyterian-Congregationalist preacher named Charles G. Finney. But before the church was completely finished, Finney chose instead to go to the new Oberlin College in Ohio, where he was to become its most famous president. Finney fought the rise of Deism, but he also championed the doctrine of man's free will against the old Calvinist doctrine of determinism. His break with the past was indicative of the new freedom coming about in the nineteenth century.

A White Whale Becomes Black Evil

In 1851, Herman Melville published his greatest novel, *Moby Dick.* Melville had already published two adventure stories of the South Sea Islands, *Typee* and *Omoo,* both of which had earned him the disfavor of the Protestant missionaries. In them, he had written of his God as a deity far bigger than many nineteenth-century Calvinists were willing to admit —and of the South Seas as the home of "strong, wicked, beautiful men" doomed to ruin by the encroachment of the narrow-mindedness and "stupidity" of Protestant missionaries.

Moby Dick told the story of a crazed whaling captain who bore the biblical name of Ahab, and who obsessively tried to hunt down a giant whale which had bitten off one of his legs. At the beginning of the novel a crusty old whaling preacher named Father Mapple climbs a rope rigging to reach his high, old-fashioned pulpit in the whalers' chapel in New Bedford, Massachusetts, and strikes the key-note of Melville's message. "Beloved shipmates," Mapple shouts to Ahab and the assembled crew, "clinch the last verse of the first chapter of Jonah: 'And God had prepared a great fish to swallow up Jonah . . . ,' " thus giving a biblical setting to the entire novel. Then Mapple, à la Melville, makes his point: "All things that God would have us do," he preaches, "are hard for us to do—remember that—and hence he oftener commands us than endeavors to persuade. And if we obey God, we must disobey ourselves; and it is in thus disobeying ourselves wherein the hardness of obeying God consists."

The words might have come straight from original Calvinism. But to each reader the whale became a different symbol. By many he was regarded as the symbol of evil. But was he also the symbol of the soul, or of the subconscious? Or was he the devil—or God? Whatever the whale symbolized, Ahab was ruined by his tragic battle against it. In the midst of the nineteenth century, Melville had given new breadth to Protestantism. His words have, in fact, frequently been read as a *secular* Calvinism. He had written of the paradox of life itself—and from a viewpoint outside the orthodox church.

In his novel Moby Dick, *Herman Melville challenged the narrow-mindedness of nineteenth-century Protestantism—and incidentally stirred up a hornet's nest with the Protestant missionaries—by conceiving of a Christian God far too enormous to feel the need for foisting one civilization—or religion—on another.*

In The Scarlet Letter, *his contemporary Nathaniel Hawthorne branded "sin" as far different from the concept of it held by his Puritan forefathers, illustrating the long road some liberal New England Protestants had traveled from the strictness of John Cotton and Jonathan Edwards.*

In his book Melville played upon the seaman's terror of the whale, as illustrated by this old drawing of a leviathan attacking a ship.

The whale Moby Dick, as conceived by a contemporary artist, breaches the waves. Of such a moment, Captain Ahab said, "I now know thee, thou clear spirit, and I know that thy right worship is defiance. To neither love nor reverence wilt thou be kind; and e'en for hate thou canst but kill; and all are killed."

The Collapse of Calvinism

The old Calvinist ideas of man's predestined fate had lost out. A new liberality was sweeping New England. It was codified in Unitarianism, whose origins could be traced to Michael Servetus in the sixteenth century (*pages 46-47*) as well as, more immediately, to the Deists (*pages 120-1*), to the new German theologians (*pages 178-9*), and to the French philosophies of Rousseau. All these had now worked their way into prosperous New England drawing rooms—and given them a new intellectualism, although sometimes against some New Englanders' determinedly commercial interests.

In America, Unitarianism's godfather was William Ellery Channing *(right)*. In 1819, Channing officially launched the new movement by preaching an ordination sermon in Baltimore, Maryland, for his friend Jared Sparks. It was a sermon that became the platform of the new creed. ". . . How mournfully the human mind may misrepresent the Deity," he said in that sermon.

To the dogmas of rigid Calvinism, Unitarianism—like Universalism with which in the present century it allied itself—said "Nonsense!" Every human being, it argued, is potentially divine and capable of working out his own salvation. Jesus was, in fact, according to Unitarianism, only a man—albeit a man with the divine spark in him. And, as in Jesus, every man has the opportunity to grow by his own choices, his own ideals, his own loyalties—with the help of God.

To liberal Christians the new doctrine seemed sound. To others, it seemed as heretical as Luther's doctrines had seemed to medieval Catholicism. Clearly denying the unique divinity of Jesus, the Unitarians thereby denied the Trinity. They also denied other traditional Christian doctrines, including the doctrine of the Atonement. How, they asked, can a man bargain with God?

The positive emphasis of the Unitarians was on the brotherhood of man and on salvation by character. In their beliefs, reason was exalted. Religion, they said, is not a body of doctrines. It is based on man's own conscience. The Unitarians argued that what is truly important in Christianity is the *ethics* of Jesus. As a corollary to their lack of dogma, they were exceptionally broad-minded toward other religions, including those of the Far East *(following page)*. They were also, as a result, less mission-minded than other churches, feeling comparatively little need for evangelizing others to their own religion. Christianity, they argued, will develop differently in every culture—and it is right, they said, that it should do so.

The rising Unitarians formed a small, intellectual, unorthodox group. But they were to become one of the most forceful groups of the new liberalism.

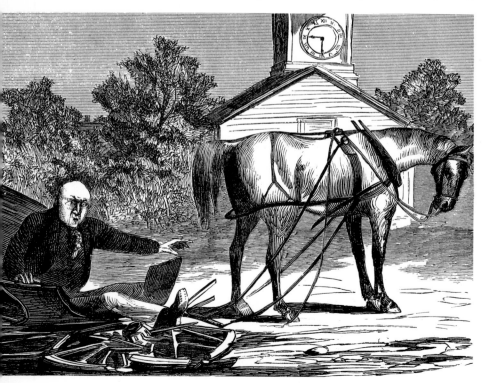

The collapse of Calvinism was humorously announced in 1858 by Oliver Wendell Holmes in a poem entitled The Deacon's Masterpiece, *or* The Wonderful One-Hoss Shay:

> *First a shiver, and then a thrill*
> *Then something decidedly like a spill,—*
> *And the parson was sitting upon a rock,*
> *At half-past nine by the meet'n-house clock, . . .*

> *You see, of course, if you're not a dunce,*
> *How it went to pieces all at once,—*
> *All at once, and nothing first,—*
> *Just as bubbles do when they burst.*

Ostensibly the poem told of a staunch Calvinist deacon's "one-hoss shay" which was so perfectly built (just as Calvinism was seemingly so perfectly logical) that instead of wearing out piece by piece it collapsed all at once after exactly a hundred years to the day. But The Deacon's Masterpiece *was actually a broad parody of Jonathan Edwards (pages 110-3) and his rigidly logical brand of Calvinism.*

William Ellery Channing, the founder of the Unitarian Church in America, was snubbed on New England streets for his espousal of the new creed. But twenty of the twenty-one oldest churches in Massachusetts went over to the Unitarian side. In Dedham, Massachusetts (above), as in other New England towns, the split between old Calvinism and the new Unitarianism was apparent by two churches which stood almost side by side, behind the courthouse, the one the "orthodox" Congregational church, the other the Unitarian church, shattering the tranquillity of the traditional New England scene (below).

The Oriental Influence

By the 1830's a left-wing movement was developing within Unitarianism. It was formed by a group of New England savants who called themselves the Transcendental Club but who were ridiculed by some onlookers as little more than "a mutual admiration society." So radical was the transcendentalist point of view that it was antagonistic even to the Unitarianism of Channing.

They were a back-to-nature group who owed much of their doctrine to Plato and the Neoplatonists, to the pantheistic German philosophers (pages 178-9) including Goethe (pages 180-1), and, in the case of Emerson, to Emanuel Swedenborg (pages 142-3). They were also influenced by the new affinity between the West and the Orient, and sometimes their statements showed the direct influence of Hinduism and Buddhism. Said a member of the group, the ardent feminist Margaret Fuller: "I accept the universe!" To this, shock-headed Scottish Thomas Carlyle, who had affinities with members of the group, replied tartly from across the Atlantic: "By God! she'd better."

In America, the shining star of transcendentalism was Emerson. As a young preacher he had made a reputation second only to the Unitarian leader William Ellery Channing. But he was fighting even more than Channing to free himself from old orthodoxy. Emerson had been influenced by the Newtonian mechanistic conception of the universe and by the psychology of "sensation" as promulgated by John Locke (pages 120-1). God, said Emerson, incarnates himself in every man just as he did in Jesus and reveals himself progressively from within man. In his sermons he argued for each individual's own intuition of the moral law. The test of that law, he said, is a life of virtue and character. He was, he argued, searching for a more certain conviction of God than that granted by any historical evidence of Christian "miracles." In 1836, in his essay entitled Nature, he idealistically set forth his philosophy. "Who," he asked, "can set bounds to the possibilities of man?" When man is filled with the influx of spirit, "we learn that man has access to the entire mind of God, is himself the creator in the finite." "Nothing," he said, "can bring you peace but yourself." "Reason," he added, "is the highest faculty of the soul, what we often mean by the soul itself: it never reasons, never proves; it simply perceives, it is vision. The Understanding toils all the time, compares, contrives, adds, argues; near-sighted but strong-sighted, dwelling in the present, the expedient, the customary."

Emerson had faced up to the real terror of freedom—and survived. His nineteenth-century optimism stood in interesting juxtaposition to the later existentialists' concept that "every man is condemned to be free." He had made an attempt to destroy the ironclad, deterministic universe of New England Calvinism. Essentially, it was a belief in the goodness of change itself and in man's greater role in that change as a part of the divine "Mind" or "Over-Soul"—a concept that was intensely more individualistic and far less deterministic, but nevertheless had a great deal in common with the pantheism of Hinduism and Buddhism .

"Evil will bless, and ice will burn," announced transcendentalist
Ralph Waldo Emerson, influenced by European and Oriental
pantheism, including the Hindu vision of the universe (above).
He refused to believe in disorder—or "evil."
Order, he said, is the absolute law; good is absolute; evil is but
good in the making. "In all nations," wrote Emerson, "there are
minds which incline to dwell in the conception of the fundamental
Unity. . . . This tendency finds its highest expression in the
religious writings of the East, and chiefly in the [Hindu]
Scriptures. . . ." He also wrote: "Were not a Socratic paganism
better than an effete, superannuated Christianity?" From the midst
of nineteenth-century Russian Orthodoxy, the novelist Leo Tolstoy
inquired half a century later why the American people paid so little
attention to the voice of Emerson. But from Scotland, Thomas
Carlyle, to whom God was "God the Terrible," reportedly inquired,
after showing the visiting Emerson the worst of London slums,
"And do ye believe in the deil [devil] noo?" Emerson, according
to the story, gently shook his head, "No."

Mind, Matter —and Muscle

One winter day in 1866, Mary Baker Glover Patterson, later to become Mary Baker Eddy, slipped on an icy path in the town of Lynn, Massachusetts. She was so badly injured that she was carried into a nearby house and ex-amined by a medical doctor who, it was later reported, said she would never walk again.

But she recovered fully.

"On the third day," she later wrote, "I called for my Bible and opened it at Matthew 9:2." There she read the story of the healing of the man sick of palsy. "As I read," she said, "the healing Truth dawned upon my sense."

In a book originally entitled *Science and Health,* Mrs. Eddy set down her central be-liefs—beliefs which became known as Chris-tian Science and which derived much from the emphasis of mind over matter as espoused by the New England Transcendentalists, with whose tenets she was familiar. On these ten-ets she also imposed her own highly personal —and feminist—interpretation of Christianity.

Nothing, she argued, possesses reality or ex-istence except the divine "Mind" and "His ideas." "There is," she wrote, "no life, truth, intelligence, nor substance in matter. All is infinite Mind. . . ." From this transcendental viewpoint she worked out the reasoning of Christian Science: Spirit is real and eternal and, as she put it, "All-in-All"; matter is unreal and temporal. Since Spirit is God (or Good) and since man is made in the image and like-ness of God, man is therefore spiritual, not material. If God, being Good, is All-in-All, then evil is an error of mortal mind and does not exist. Man, therefore, creates his own experi-ence. "As a man thinketh," she wrote, "so is he. Mind is all that feels, acts, or impedes action."

Like Mother Anne Lee of the Shakers, Mrs. Eddy envisioned God as feminine as well as masculine. For her, God was a mother as well as a father God. The Trinity, she argued, is composed not in the traditional form of Fa-ther, Son, and Holy Spirit but of "Life, Truth, and Love." "These," she said, "constitute the triune Person called God." The third person of this Trinity—Love—she equated with divine, or Christian, Science.

As the founder of Christian Science, Mrs. Eddy lived to old age. When she died, it was said she had a telephone buried with her in her tomb. The telephone was supposedly put there in case she should come to life—so firmly did she believe in the final triumph of mind over matter. But the truth was she did not remotely consider the body important. "Those who look for me in person, or elsewhere than in my writings," she once said, "lose me in-stead of find me."

Mary Baker Eddy was a spare-built woman with deep-set gray eyes. She wrote the first edition of Science and Health *in her home in Lynn, Massachusetts, in the attic room shown above.*

In England, a concept of "mind over matter" was espoused by poet-critic Matthew Arnold. "The pursuit of perfection, . . ." wrote Arnold, "is the pursuit of sweetness and light. . . . He who works for sweetness and light indeed works to make reason and the will of God prevail." For his efforts he was satirically caricatured swinging athletically from a trapeze. Of a published collection of his religious essays entitled Mixed Essays, another critic said, "An unhappy title —suggesting biscuits."

On June 6, 1844, a young drygoods clerk named George Williams founded the Y.M.C.A., in the belief that a sound mind in a sound body helped young clerks and factory workers to become better Christians. In 1894, the Y.W.C.A. was formed to help working girls too.

The Mormons

Joseph Smith often accompanied his mother to early nineteenth-century revival meetings in Upper New York State. In 1823, Smith, still a youth, began, he claimed, to have a series of visions. In them, he said, the Angel Moroni, whom he identified as the last survivor of one of the ten lost tribes of Israel mentioned in the Bible, told him of the existence of six golden plates that had been deposited in a nearby New York hillside in 385 B.C. With the plates, Smith claimed, were buried two stones called Urim and Thummin that enabled him to translate their message.

The plates, said Smith, revealed that Jesus had appeared to Moroni's people in the Western Hemisphere shortly after the crucifixion. Founding a church in 1830, the youthful Smith headed West, and, after years of persecution in which he himself was killed *(right)*, his followers, known popularly as Mormons from the title of the book Smith translated from the plates, arrived in Utah under the leadership of his successor, Brigham Young.

Though Mormons are frequently regarded as Protestants, they themselves stoutly deny it. They consider themselves a Christian church whose origins date back to the beginnings of Christianity. Like Mormon "history," its theology is uniquely its own. All existence, said Smith, is material. Spirit is merely a finer or truer kind of matter. God, Smith said, was once a physical man who became divine by gaining all knowledge. Therefore, other men can achieve godliness, and earthly life is intended to develop in man those qualities which will exalt him in the next phase of eternal life. In practice, the Mormons therefore tended to emphasize physical as well as spiritual needs, including economic justice, physical education—and sex. Furthermore, said Smith, man himself, like God, has lived eternally. Before being born into this world, he had a pre-existence in a previous world. It is, Smith therefore believed, man's duty to bring unborn spirits into the world. It was this belief which gave impetus to the nineteenth-century Mormon practice of polygamy. The belief was actually practiced in early Mormonism by a scant three per cent of the group—and it was the cause of a split within the ranks of the Mormon church itself. But, for Mormon purposes, this same polygamy, added to religious zeal, proved to be a practical expedient. It enabled them, a persecuted people in an isolated environment, not only to survive but to multiply—and thus to be able to turn the desert haven in which they were forced to settle into one of the most prosperous regions of the world.

Cane in hand, Joseph Smith stands in front of the Mormon temple at Nauvoo, Illinois, with his elder brother Hyrum. Later the temple was destroyed, and Joseph and Hyrum were killed (opposite page). Brigham Young, their successor (below), was a Vermont house painter who proved to be one of the greatest leaders ever produced by the American frontier. The only way to avoid persecution, he decided, was to go to a region so bleak that nobody else would want it. In 1847, he led the first Mormons to Utah.

Smith and his brother Hyrum were killed by a mob in Carthage, Illinois, in front of state militiamen, after the brothers had been imprisoned by the governor of Illinois. In addition to their practice of polygamy, Mormon opposition to slavery turned neighboring Protestants against them.

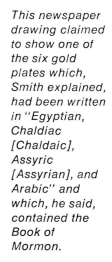

This newspaper drawing claimed to show one of the six gold plates which, Smith explained, had been written in "Egyptian, Chaldiac [Chaldaic], Assyric [Assyrian], and Arabic" and which, he said, contained the Book of Mormon.

IT LOOKS AS IF HE *WAS* IN EARNEST AT LAST.

Polygamy was declared illegal by Congress in 1862, and the Mormons accepted the ruling in 1896 in order to be admitted as a state of the union. The anti-polygamy cartoon at left, published at Christmas time and featuring "One Wife Only" in a stocking hung by a Mormon hearth, bore the caption "St. Nick's Compliments to the Mormons." The one at right, showing Uncle Sam hewing down the "tree of polygamy," was entitled "It Looks As If He Was in Earnest at Last." Below, a brigade of Brigham Young's twenty-seven wives backs him in a fictitious attack on U.S. troops.

BRIGHAM YOUNG FROM BEHIND HIS BREASTWORKS CHARGING THE UNITED STATES TROOPS

The Good Lives of the Quakers

Even the sedate ranks of the Quakers were split apart by the ground swells of Unitarianism. In 1828, Quaker Elias Hicks decided that founder George Fox's "inner light" was actually the eternal spirit of Christ which dwells potentially in all human beings. He drew a sharp distinction between the man Jesus and this eternal spirit of love, and he argued that the entire process of salvation thus lies chiefly within man.

It was the Quaker custom to allow disagreements to go unsettled at meeting rather than to force a small but sincere group to act against its convictions. Now the new Hicksites claimed the custom was being observed in the breach. Their minority opinions, they said, were going unheard, so they split off to form their own group. One result was the founding of Swarthmore College in 1864 in addition to the orthodox Quaker Haverford College.

In the nineteenth century the Quakers achieved remarkable political power—through their women. The American Quaker Lucretia Mott (above) was a cheerful, sprightly, impulsive woman. She was also a spirited feminist, and she asserted her feminism in the antislavery movement as well as in the nineteenth-century woman's rights movement. Denied a seat as a delegate to a world antislavery convention in London, she nevertheless attended it—and left it with the reputation of having been the "lioness" of the gathering. The indirect result was her calling of the first woman's rights convention ever to be held in the U.S.—in Wesley Methodist Church, Seneca Falls, New York. Her counterpart in England, Elizabeth Fry, was equally feminist and independent-minded. Wellborn, fond in her youth of un-Quakerlike clothes, she outgrew an initial shyness to teach women prisoners in London's notorious Newgate Prison to read (below), and became the prime force in English prison reform. She influenced Parliament to pass laws by which women prisoners received the training necessary to fit them for profitable employment once they were released, brought pressure to bear on Parliament to institute reforms of the English custom of shipping women prisoners to Australia, where they were unable to support themselves, and helped found the first nurses' training school, out of which came Florence Nightingale.

In both England and the U.S., the habits of the Quakers were natural targets for ridicule throughout the nineteenth century. Their patience, thrift, customs—and their old-fashioned clothes, which they continued to wear into the nineteenth century (below)—were lampooned in the press as well as elsewhere. In the U.S., when Henry Clay fought against admission of Texas to the union, cartoonists seized upon the incident to lampoon Quaker attitudes again (left).

The Amistad Mutiny

Cinqué, the leader of the mutineers, testified through an interpreter found for him by a Yale Divinity School professor. He eventually became a chief among his people—and ironically, according to one historian, a slave trader himself—when he returned to Africa.

In 1839, a Portuguese merchant ship, having outwitted the British slave patrol, arrived in Cuba carrying a cargo of forty-nine African slaves. In Havana, the slaves were sold to dealers, put aboard a schooner named *La Amistad,* and shipped along the Cuban coast to be resold to plantation owners. On the way a young slave named Cinqué, believing a tale told by the ship's cook that all slaves were to be murdered on arrival, led a mutiny, killed the captain, took control of the ship, and tried to steer it back to Africa.

By day, Cinqué was able to chart his course by the sun. By night, however, he was forced to depend on the regular crew, who tricked him, turning the ship's course northward. On August 25, 1839, *La Amistad* grounded on Montauk Point, Long Island, where she was boarded by U.S. Coast Guard officers. The slaves were arrested and taken to New Haven, Connecticut, for trial. U.S. President Martin Van Buren tried to have the slaves deported to the owners in Cuba. But after a series of dramatic appeals, including an impassioned defense before the U.S. Supreme Court by the aged—and half-blind—John Quincy Adams, the Africans were declared free. "The law of Nature and of Nature's God," Adams had pleaded, "[will] I trust . . . be the law on which this case will be decided by this Court."

In 1841, the mutineers were returned to Africa in the care of three missionaries. Public indignation against slavery had been aroused by the case. In 1846 the committee that had been organized by New England abolitionists for the defense of the slaves on *La Amistad* merged with three other antislavery societies and thus formed the interdenominational American Missionary Association, one of the great U.S. Protestant home mission societies. The society achieved its greatest success after the Civil War. In 1865, in cooperation with the government Freedmen's Bureau, it set up some five hundred colleges to advance Negro —and poor white—education throughout the South, among them Hampton Institute, Dillard and Fisk universities, Huston-Tillotson, Le Moyne, Talladega, and Tougaloo colleges.

In May, 1860, a newspaper reporter described the crowded conditions of four hundred and fifty Africans on the slave ship Wildfire *, which had just landed in Key West, Florida. Ninety slaves had died on the voyage, a loss considered comparatively small for the time. Ten more died after arrival, and forty were sent to the hospital in serious condition.*

Joshua Commands the Sun to Stand Still

In a way, it was the last time the Bible was to be taken absolutely literally in the political arena. The Southerners, many of them fundamentalists in belief, claimed that the institution of slavery was based on biblical text. They cited the Old Testament story of Noah's sons, of whom the punished Ham was the legendary father of the Negro race. Somewhat shakily, they also cited the New Testament text that Christ had come to fulfill rather than destroy the law of the Old Testament.

Slavery, therefore, said the Southerners, was an "ordinance of God." Later, some of them were to cite similar biblical texts for the founding of the Ku Klux Klan.

There were Northerners who took the Bible as literally as the Southerners. On October 16, 1859, a demented and obsessed man who had trained for the ministry, though without any formal schooling, instigated a raid on Harpers Ferry, Virginia, to seize guns and ammunition in the cause of abolition. In the end, even the stern New Englanders announced they would not have done it that way—though

Transcendentalist Ralph Waldo Emerson approved—and John Brown himself, looking like a wounded eagle, went to the gallows. After his death, the soldiers of the North sang the marching song, "John Brown's Body."

From Boston, Julia Ward Howe, visiting the battlefield, sat down in her tent after viewing, as she said, "the watchfires of a hundred circling camps." She gave the soldiers' songs religious import in "The Battle Hymn of the Republic," whose words smacked of the millenarianism that had also influenced such nineteenth-century Protestants as William Miller and the Seventh-Day Adventists. If the hymn was saccharine, it expressed the feelings of the time.

The Civil War furthered once again the increasing splits in Protestantism. In the midst of the slavery controversy, a Southern Methodist bishop named James C. Andrew was brought before the Methodist General Conference because of the fact his second wife was a slaveowner. The resulting controversy divided the Northern antislavery Methodists in the nation from the Southern proslavery members. In time, the issue of slavery divided several other major Protestant denominations, notably the Presbyterians and the Baptists, both appropriately Calvinist in strain. Of the others, the Congregationalists had so little membership in the South that it hardly seemed worth the effort; and Quakers, equally in both North and South, were opposed to slavery. The Episcopalians, on the other hand, took no definite action on the issue of slavery; the Lutherans continued to make a sharp distinction between the sacred and the political, and so avoided the issue of slavery, as did the Disciples of Christ who, during the nineteenth century, were more interested in personal evangelism than in mass social reform.

John Brown welcomed his execution as good publicity for the antislavery cause. Of him, New England abolitionist Ralph Waldo Emerson wrote: "That new saint, than whom nothing purer or more brave was ever led by love of men into conflict and death . . . will make the gallows glorious like the cross."

The Confederate army was said to be the most pious army since Oliver Cromwell's time, and the brigade of Stonewall Jackson was the "prayin'est" in the Confederacy. Officers who visited Jackson's tent any time of day or night were likely to find the general on his knees, or, as Jackson himself put it, "wrestling with the Lord."

In 1848, John Calhoun, champion of states' rights, pleaded on the floor of the U.S. Senate, as he had many times in the past, for the right of Southern planters to own slaves. A cartoonist, parodying his words as well as his meaning, pictured him in biblical setting like the prophet Joshua, commanding the sun in the heavens—symbolized by a printing press above the capitol dome—to stand still.

"Sun of Intellectual light & liberty,
stand ye still, in Masterly inactivity,
that the Nation of Carolina may continue
to hold Negroes & plant Cotton till the
day of Judgment!"

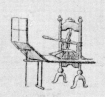

The Temperance Movement

In 1900, Carry Nation, a local "jail evangelist" of the Medicine Lodge, Kansas, chapter of the W.C.T.U., stopped before an illegal but prospering saloon in the town, swung her umbrella and shouted, "Men and Women of Medicine Lodge, this is a Joint!" So saying, she sailed through the swinging doors and led what was to be the first of her many raids on "dens of iniquity." But the W.C.T.U. relied more strongly on Bible instruction than on types like Carry. In a series of engravings entitled "The Bible and Temperance" a visiting parson reads the Bible to the wife of an alcoholic named Brown who, in the picture at top, lies in bed drunk. As a result, the reformed Brown, taking a stroll with his happy wife in the picture below, is congratulated by the same parson for becoming a "steady, sober, and industrious" citizen.

Following the Civil War, when the amount of capital invested in the liquor business soared from $29,000,000 in 1860 to $190,000,000 in 1880, the temperance movement really came into its own. The churches joined up with a vengeance, and, in the following decades, determined women marched into "dens of iniquity" (and into the halls of Congress), fell on their knees and prayed, and, in enough cases to merit the telling, persuaded the saloon keeper to pour his product into the gutter and quit the business. In the 1840's and 1850's the "Cold Water Pledge" of total abstinence had been coined, and even children (largely in Sunday schools) were recruited into a "Cold Water Army"—a phenomenon that particularly pleased members of those Protestant creeds which, as a condition of membership, had long banned the use of liquor, though the Lutheran idea, like that of non-Protestants, was that of the Continental: wine was the gift of God, and even its misuse did not change their opinion.

In 1842 a former bookbinder and bit actor named John B. Gough began appearing in church pulpits throughout the country. In pulpit after pulpit Gough acted out a skit he had picked up on the Bowery of New York—in which he raucously took the role of a drunken parson circulating a ribald pledge to a group of drunken friends. He finished his show by delivering evening-long lectures hard and strong for temperance.

Gough's story was a heartbreaker *(right)*. It was also a huge success with his audiences, which numbered approximately nine million people in a total of 9,600 lectures. Traveling not only in America but also in Great Britain, he personally collected an estimated 140,000 temperance pledges. A further record of 215,-000 pledges were calculated to have resulted from his efforts.

Most of his life Gough resisted the passage of prohibition laws. Only personal and individual reformation, he argued out of experience, could do the trick—with, as he was to say time and again in his lectures, "the help of God." But late in life he finally joined forces with Frances E. Willard who, in 1874, having been influenced, so she said, by hearing the singing of "How Firm a Foundation," had helped organize the Woman's Christian Temperance Union. Miss Willard disagreed with Gough regarding temperance by law. "I am," she firmly said, "profoundly interested in politics as the mightiest force on earth except Christianity"; and she and the W.C.T.U. openly advocated political action and supported the Prohibition party.

John B. Gough was a nervous little man who always dressed in black. He had a musical voice that could make audiences laugh or cry. His early theatrical training (right), combined with a sincere desire to help others who had fallen into his state, catapulted him to the top of the nineteenth-century temperance movement. By his own account, he had worked as a bookbinder, then had become a drunken sot and lost his job. During one of his binges, his wife and baby died of neglect. Later he also let his mother and sister starve. According to his own story, he reformed only when, lying dead drunk in the gutter of a Worcester, Massachusetts, street, a Quaker found him, spoke kindly to him, and thereby gave him the courage to sign the pledge.

Gough called intemperance "suicide," and compared it to lying down on a railroad track when the train was coming. In this drawing, a contempory artist, inspired by Gough's metaphor, labeled the railroad's ties from "A" for "All-Aboard" through "L" for "Loafing, Lying, and Lust," "S" for "Sorrow, Stealing, Suicide," "T" for "Tremens, Trouble, and Torment" and finally, "Z" for "Zero of Hell."

The Great Revivalists

Dwight Moody was a businesslike, energetic, traveling shoe salesman with a man-to-man approach—and an executive attitude—toward Christianity. As an evangelist, Moody began his career just before the Civil War by renting four pews in Plymouth Church in Chicago, then making sure they were filled every Sunday with other itinerant salesmen whom he sought out in boardinghouses and on street corners. Soon he was also collecting a Sunday-school class of youngsters (*left*) from neighboring slums and meeting with them in a hall above one of the city markets.

In 1870, Moody joined forces with Ira Sankey, a former choirmaster and superintendent of a Sunday school in Newcastle, Pennsylvania. Sankey was equally businesslike. He was also a wizard at singing. Everywhere he went he captivated audiences with his unexceptional—but full-throated—rendition of sure-fire hymns which he accompanied on a small reed organ. It was, he said, more difficult to find suitable words than tunes. His favorites were "Let the Lower Lights Be Burning," "I Need Thee Every Hour," and "What a Friend We Have in Jesus." He liked "Tell Me the Old, Old Story" almost as much. When he and Moody made a long tour of England and Scotland, their trip was hailed as a success equal to that of the Wesleys a century before them.

Unlike other evangelists, Moody emphasized the fatherly love of God instead of the terrors of hell—to the immense relief of some listeners. Businessmen, especially, were pleased when he reasoned very practically with them: "There is no use in asking God to do things you can do for yourself." The worst most scoffers could really find to say about him was that P. T. Barnum was probably backing the entire Moody movement.

"Moody's Bodyguard," sometimes called "Moody's Waifs," were pictured in these before-and-after photographs. The top one showing "the crude material from which [Moody] evolved his first Sunday-school class in Chicago" bore the caption "Will It Pay?" The bottom one, showing twelve of the same boys, with books and without brooms, was entitled, "It Does Pay."

John Wanamaker was a Philadelphia merchant who became known as a "Christian businessman." He taught Sunday-school classes. The fact that he printed homely Sunday-school truths in his department store advertisements did not hurt his business. He was cartooned here (in foreground) for trying to keep the public library and museums closed on Sunday.

Some of the methods of Moody were exaggerated in a later era by the evangelist Billy Sunday (left) who preached a fundamentalist brand of Christianity. "Soaking it into Satan," as he said, he smashed pulpit furniture to attract attention, advertised with calliopes, and once when he claimed to have seen so much sin in one community, he prayed at a meeting, "O Lord, the next time you come here, bring along plenty of antiseptic and rubber gloves." Sunday persuaded thousands to "hit the sawdust trail," but he also helped bring discredit on the revivalist movement.

Moody impressed business-men because he ran his prayer meetings in a businesslike way. He also achieved—with the backing of businessmen—a program of home social work, recreation, and welfare.

A Bridge to Darwinism

In 1859, Charles Darwin published his *The Origin of Species*, and to many Protestants his thesis that man had evolved from the ape seemed to shake the very foundations not only of the biblical story of creation but also the historical accuracy of the entire Bible—and of Christianity itself. As interpreted by Thomas Huxley, Darwin's thesis of "agnosticism"—a word coined by Huxley—was equated by many with outright "atheism" and with a purely naturalistic philosophy.

There were champions on both sides. In America, the liberals included Henry Ward Beecher inside the church and Robert G. Ingersoll outside it. Ingersoll, a big, boisterous man, seized the opportunity to augment his lecture tour around the country by making speeches with titles like "Some Mistakes of Moses"—and to launch into long diatribes against the bigotry of the church and strict interpretation of the Bible. "This manna," he liked to jibe, "was a very popular thing. It would melt in the sun, and yet they could cook it by seething and baking. One would as soon think of frying snow or of boiling icicles." He berated the "Calvinist" conception of a "cruel God." The Episcopalians, he said, were all right and the Methodists relatively harmless, but he took special delight in hitting at Presbyterians—and at Catholics.

If Ingersoll was colorful, he was almost outdone by the equally colorful Henry Ward Beecher (*right*). A gaudy figure, son of Lyman Beecher and brother of Harriet Beecher Stowe, Henry was, if not the foremost champion, certainly the most engaging. For the cartoonists of the day he became almost as favorite a churchly subject as had Martin Luther and Anglican Archbishop William Laud in their days. In real life, he was almost as flamboyant as he was in the cartoons. He romped

Bewhiskered Charles Darwin, author of The Origin of Species, *was surrounded by jungle plants in this English drawing of 1872. Below, grinning and looking to many a fundamentalist like Satan himself, he was caricatured in the magazine* Vanity Fair.

with the young at Sunday-school picnics, frequently pushed a wheelbarrow through the streets for the sheer joy of it, went to fires and held the hose like a pre-LaGuardia, and shucked peanuts as he walked along the streets of Brooklyn, leaving a trail of shells behind him. He was, also, usually a liberal, and people flocked to hear him at Brooklyn's Congregational Plymouth Church. He made his platform (he would have no pulpit in *his* church) the place for discussion of public questions, including antislavery, temperance, free trade with England, and other questions of the day—most of them on the side of freedom. He also got himself into trouble, especially when he—seemingly—bumbled into a scandal with the wife of one of his parishioners. The subsequent trial resulted in a hung jury (nine to three in his favor), which his friends interpreted as a victory for him.

Theologically, Beecher was a free agent, and he made the most of it. He accepted the Trinity. "I accept without analysis the tri-personality of God," he said. "I accept the Trinity; perhaps because I was educated in it. No matter why, I accept it." But he refused to believe in Calvinist predestination. God, he was fond of saying, loves "a man in his sins for the sake of helping him out of them, not out of compliment to Christ or to a law, or to a plan of salvation, but from the fullness of his great heart."

Naturally, Beecher accepted evolution wholeheartedly. In time, following his example, liberal Protestants came to accept the evolutionary theories of Darwin. At the same time, new revisions of the Bible were being made (*pages 224-5*) in an attempt to understand it less literally and more meaningfully. "It may be," said a Methodist minister of the era, "that we have claimed too much for the Bible. . . ." But the controversy was perhaps summed up best by a nineteenth-century prenuclear view of science: "Atoms," it read, "may or may not be divisible; creation may or may not be through natural selection; religious belief may be justified in either case. Yet because the beliefs of religion cannot be intelligibly expressed except in current concepts, there is always chance for confusion between the truth which is essential and the passing forms in which it is clothed. At times the protagonists of religion, falling into this confusion, have resisted the progress of scientific discovery because it seemed to them at some point to contradict and subvert religious faith."

In 1885, a harried Henry Ward Beecher, who is shown with a plank labeled "Evolution Sermons," valiantly tried to bridge the gap between the church and the new discoveries of science, here represented by an imposing mountainside of philosophers, with Spinoza and Copernicus at the peak and Darwin at the bottom. As the most famous—and chunkiest—American Protestant clergyman of his day, Beecher was so well known to the public that he was frequently cartooned from the rear, unnamed (left), and still recognized by almost everybody.

The Marxist "Heresy"

In 1848, Karl Marx, together with Friedrich Engels, published *The Communist Manifesto,* the basic doctrine of Communism. In doing so, Marx unmasked much of religion as a projection of man. With him, religion shifted from an emphasis on "heaven" to an emphasis on natural right, from theology to politics. He turned German idealism *(pages 178-9)* inside out. He took Hegel's historical idealism and transformed it into historical materialism.

But the fact was that Hegel's speculative metaphysics was really a secularized Christian theology. And, according to some scholars, Marx's approach can, in part, be understood as a typically Christian phenomenon. It had in it a secularized biblical view of ultimate ends —a pattern in which the proletariat assumes the aspect of the "Servant of the Lord," whose vicarious suffering for the whole creation inaugurates the new age. In this connection it is important to remember that Russian messianism—in which Marxism was to find a fertile field and of which the Russian Orthodox Church was a part—had been formed under Christian influences and was closely akin to the Jewish messianism that had been notable in Russia since at least the thirteenth century. Marxism, denying the extrahistorical category of this messianism, tried to force the fulfillment of history within the historical process itself.

Marx's Communism has been regarded by many as a phenomenon which was brought into being as a reaction to—and a derivative of—Christian thought regarding God, man, the world, and history. The dialectical fashion in which the Russian Revolution sets itself over against Christian history has been called by theologians a pseudotheological reiteration of the contract which Christianity sees between the "Old Covenant" of the Old Testament and the "New Covenant" of the New Testament. The result has thus been regarded by some theologians as a Christian "heresy" —a heresy that fastened with fanatical single-mindedness and in necessary and fully justified protest—against a prevalently bourgeois version of Christianity. It fastened upon a partial truth which it then exalted into the one complete, exclusive, and infallible dogma at the expense of all other aspects and points of view.

In his study *Christianity in World History,* historian Arend Th. van Leeuwen has pointed out that it is exactly in this heresy that Christianity is genuinely challenged. It is a heresy that, says van Leeuwen, "calls upon Christianity to mend its ways and to turn from its own heretical one-sidedness and emasculation of the truth in its fullness . . ." When, he adds, "Christianity stoops to sterile anti-Communism, at once defensive and aggressive, it does indeed show itself to be that very caricature of the prophetic, biblical message—as rigid a heresy as any—which Communism has rejected with justifiable indignation."

Sören Kierkegaard was a staunch monarchist who believed in suffering as the basis of the Christian faith. Karl Marx (above), by no means a monarchist, was the son of Jewish parents who became Christians when he was a child.

"Soap, Soup and Salvation"

White-haired William Booth once dramatically knelt in Winston Churchill's office during the time Churchill was British Home Secretary, prayed loudly for Churchill's conversion. Anxious to spur his world-wide organization to further efforts of service but aghast at the cost of cablegrams, he compressed his Christmas message into the one succinct word: "Others."

General William Booth was a strong-minded man who had been expelled from the Methodist Church. But he was determined to carry John Wesley's Methodism to its ultimate conclusion: to help the poverty-stricken by living with them, not just by preaching at them. In 1865, Booth founded the Salvation Army.

Like Methodist-founder John Wesley, Booth worked outside traditional church buildings, preferring the secular atmosphere of the world —and bringing religion to people where they were. In New York, he chose a notoriously disreputable variety theater as his church headquarters. On one occasion a tough escape artist brought down the house with an action sermon on "Trapdoors to Hell." "Come drunk or sober," said an early handbill advertising the Army. A genius at publicity, he equipped his Army women with iron kettles, coal-scuttle bonnets, and announced for public ears: "Taken as a whole, I say that woman is equal to man in the value of her gifts and the extent of her influence, and I maintain that if she is given a fair chance she will prove it to be so." Soon women outnumbered men two to one in his Army.

Of the followers of the new organization, George Bernard Shaw was later to write, "[They] actually fight the devil instead of merely praying at him." But to many, Booth's method of organizing his Army with uniforms, banners, brass bands, and marchers seemed overly militant—even in terminology. A church building was a "citadel." A congregation was "a corps." Sunday-school class was a "company meeting," and prayer a "knee-drill." Even death had its military connotations; a member who died was "promoted to glory."

The organization, however, was as efficient as it was military. The prime purpose of the Army was to feed the poor, physically as well as spiritually, with soup kitchens as well as with prayer meetings. Its motto, it said, was "Soap, soup, and salvation." In fact, it was a mopping-up organization for outcasts. It offered no new theology, only practicality. As a result, it founded innumerable social-service centers, including boys' camps and youth centers, homes for unwed mothers and for alcoholics. Need, not creed, the Army pointed out, was the criterion it asked of those it helped, and it helped countless thousands with social reform, religion—and doughnuts. In its "secular" Christianity, it actually took more seriously than almost any other religious group the teaching of Jesus: "I was a stranger, and ye took me in: naked, and ye clothed me: . . . in prison, and ye came unto me."

In America, the early Salvation Army found its most fertile fields in slum sections of the cities and among immigrants. Later, Booth's daughter Evangeline (left), who wore a velvet uniform, proved a notable fund-raiser during World War I days.

The Social Gospel

In 1902, George F. Baer, an Episcopalian who happened also to be president of the Reading Railroad, said in court, "The right and interest of the laboring men will be protected and cared for not by labor agitators but by the Christian men to whom God in his infinite wisdom has given control of the property interests of this country." The statement was to become one of the most famous of its kind, and Baer was laughed out of court.

In the late nineteenth and early twentieth centuries, Walter Rauschenbusch, a German-American Baptist, and Washington Gladden, a Congregational minister, founded the "Social Gospel" movement. Rauschenbusch had worked in Hell's Kitchen (*below*) in New York City. Sin, he said, was ingrained not just in the individual but in social institutions: "No man can be redeemed and saved alone; no community can be reformed and elevated save as the individuals of which it is composed are regenerated." He called upon the church to "realize in ourselves a new type of Christian manhood which seems to overcome the evil in the present world, not by withdrawing from the world, but by revolutionizing it."

Originally, the Protestant Reformation had evolved as much from the political ills of the sixteenth century as from the strictly religious ills of medieval Catholicism. To many a well-heeled Protestant, such a concept now seemed to forecast concerted Protestant stands in later days on such political issues as disarmament, labor-management relations, technical aid to underdeveloped nations, and racial justice—and stands regarding the Christian attitude to welfare aid by the government.

Christianity, these said, was for the individual's own soul, not for government action. "Many men in business and in the professions, . . ." said industrialist J. Howard Pew, "could afford to give far more [to the church] than they do. Most of them give liberally to charity, moderately to their local churches, and not at all to the corporate church. . . . They cannot understand how our corporate church could tolerate such statements and pronouncements on social issues as they have seen in the press."

In a time of notable labor-union troubles, the Social Gospel movement pointed out that arbitration meant little if the worker had no position of power from which to arbitrate. For now backing unions—and the rights of immigrants—both Gladden and Rauschenbusch got into trouble. They tried to make Protestantism an organized body that could actively engage in Christian concern for the social problems of the day. In the competitive basis of laissez-faire capitalism, Gladden understandably found a lack of true Christianity. In 1879, he wrote what seemed a perfectly good Christian hymn to arouse Protestants to his cause. It read:

> O Master, let me walk with Thee
> Before the taunting Pharisee;
> Help me to bear the sting of spite,
> The hate of men who hide Thy light,
>
> The sore distrust of souls sincere
> Who cannot read Thy judgments clear
> The dullness of the multitude,
> Who dimly guess that Thou are good.

Many a congregation refused to sing it.

This satirical magazine drawing contrasted
Washington Gladden's preaching in New York's
Hell's Kitchen to the comparative comfort—and
comparatively good behavior—of a conventional
minister and his congregation. Its pro-Gladden
caption read: "A Hint for a Certain Class of
Reformer: Shirt-Sleeves Talk in the Slums May
Do More Toward Redeeming the Human Race
Than Swallow-Tail Eloquence in the Sanctuaries
of Good Society." Below, a photographer pictured a
more sedate Hell's Kitchen meeting in the early
1900's, and an artist drew a scene in a home for
orphan children at Christmas time.

In 1897, Charles M. Sheldon published what
proved to be far and away the world's best-selling
book except only for the Bible itself. In His Steps,
which has sold an estimated thirty million copies,
told of an average American town in which the
appearance of a seedy and homeless tramp
forced the townspeople to figure out how Jesus
would have acted toward him. The implications of
the book gave added impetus to the "Social
Gospel" movement.

The Anti-Missionary Cry

The cartoon at right appeared in the 1890's in the magazine *Puck.* It bore the long title: "According to the Ideas of Our Missionary Maniacs, the Chinaman Must Be Converted Even If It Takes the Whole Military and Naval Forces of the Two Greatest Nations of the World to Do It." The guns on the British ships at left were labeled "Good Samaritan" and "Revivalist"; on the U.S. ships at right, "Psalm-singer," "Sermonizer," and "Deacon." The British missionary in the foreground relies on scriptural passages to prove his point, the American couple on hymns and missionary tracts. At their feet were the inevitable moneybags.

The cartoon was by no means the only one of its time to cry that the missionary movement was imperialistic. Why, Americans were asking, foist a Christian God on peoples who had their own religions? Why should the missionary frequently assume the guise of a great white father to people of non-Christian countries? Mission, the antimission movement also argued, should begin at home.

But during the latter part of the nineteenth century, signs of a new reexamination of overseas mission were appearing. The practical Presbyterian Sheldon Jackson *(below)* was a part of the movement. After serving as missionary to Choctaw Indians at Spencer, Wyoming, Jackson headed for Alaska. In 1884, in cooperation with the United States government—but by no means as an imperialist—he served simultaneously as first government superintendent of public instruction in the territory and as superintendent of the Presbyterian mission.

Jackson's greatest achievement was his bringing of the reindeer to Alaska. The territory's caribou had vanished, and salmon, whale, and walrus were being depleted. When Jackson arrived, Alaskan Eskimos were literally starving for want of proper food. Frustrated by delays of politicians in Washington, Jackson acted on his own in stocking the territory with reindeer from Siberia, to replace the caribou. The first shipment of sixteen reindeer was lost in a storm en route through the Aleutians. But before Jackson died he was able to build up a nucleus of 1,280 reindeer, which has since increased to many thousands. In the spirit of new mission, Jackson had helped the Eskimos to help themselves. It was a spirit aimed not only at charity but at mutual reconciliation between peoples.

Sheldon Jackson was described by a newspaper reporter as "short, bewhiskered, and bespectacled." Then he added, "By inside measurement, a giant."

In the antimissionary cartoon above, complete with warships and moneybags, Protestant missionaries from England and the U. S. at work in the Far East were charged with working hand-in-glove with Western imperialism, in stark contrast to the photograph from the album of an American Board missionary (left), in which starving Indian children bore eloquent testimony to the need for missionary homes, hospitals, and agricultural skills in India.

The Boxer Uprising

In more peaceful days, these two American Board missionaries sent home a photograph of themselves in Chinese garb.

The greatest setback in missionary history was to come in the 1940's with the rise of Communist China. But there had been plenty of forewarning. In the Opium War of 1839–1842, the British had proved that nothing, least of all the Imperial government of China, could stop them from peddling narcotics or any other profitable trade goods, wherever a good market existed. The main result of the Opium War had been the opening of five treaty ports where foreign merchants could live and do business. After a series of violent incidents, China was compelled to open more ports. They also gave the missionaries access to the entire interior, thus sowing seeds that would sprout into the bitterly anti-Christian Boxer Uprising of 1899–1900.

By 1893, the Western powers were exploiting China to the fullest. In order to meet the situation, the reactionary Empress Tz'u Hsi made herself regent and opposed all Western ideas. "The foreigners," she was to say, "are like fish in the stewpan." Her attitude encouraged antiforeign activity, especially among the "Boxers," a secret military group known as "Righteous, Harmonious Fists." They had sprung up against the traditional background of peasant unrest: floods, drought, famine and banditry. Now it was the presence in their countryside of the Western missionaries, whom they identified with Western imperialism, that gave focus to their hatred and frustration. Aided by the empress and her forces, they slaughtered scores of missionaries, along with Chinese Christian converts. Then, in the summer of 1900, they besieged Westerners, including the British and American missionaries, in the legation compounds of Peking. After fifty-five days, during which all had been given up for dead, an international army of British, French, German, Austrian, Russian, American, and Japanese troops raised the siege and rescued the survivors *(right)*. For the moment the rebellion proved to the Chinese the necessity of reform, so that the period beginning with 1900 was one in which the missionaries were at the peak of their activity in China. But in the 1940's, with the rise of Communism, their successors were soon forced to leave the country.

For fifty-five days during the Boxer Uprising,
the British and American missionaries, as well
as Western diplomatic personnel, were besieged
in Peking's legation compounds until all were
given up as dead. In August, an allied column
reached Peking, raised the siege, and rescued
the survivors, among them the missionaries
shown here.

"Nearer, My God, to Thee"

It was the era of "O Little Town of Bethlehem," of "Stand Up, Stand Up for Jesus"—and of "Abide With Me," which was to displace the eighteenth century's "Rock of Ages" in popularity among the hymn singers. It was also the era of a host of hymns whose first lines revealed their spirit: "Onward Christian Soldiers," which was written for a parade of Sunday-school children (and whose music was written by Sir Arthur Sullivan of light-opera fame), "I Need Thee Every Hour," "He Leadeth Me," "What a Friend We Have in Jesus," "I Think When I Read That Sweet Story of Old," and "In the Cross of Christ I Glory," which was written by a missionary in China when he saw a cross still standing on a cathedral after a ruinous typhoon. By the turn of the twentieth century, no hymn had become better known—or better loved—than Sarah Adams' "Nearer, My God, to Thee" (right). Interestingly enough, it was also considered controversial; written by a Unitarian, it was criticized for being unchristian because it never specifically mentioned Christ—an omission that several clergymen tried their hand at remedying, but with little popular success. The original lines consistently won out:

> Nearer, my God, to Thee,
> Nearer to Thee!
> E'en though it be a cross
> That raiseth me; . . .

Before President William McKinley, having been shot by an assassin, died in 1901, his doctor heard him say, " 'Nearer, my God, to Thee, E'en though it be a cross' has been my constant prayer." The hymn was played at his funeral. Later, when it was sung as passengers went down with the sinking *Titanic,* it became so closely identified with the era that, as in many things Protestant, the original controversy surrounding it was dimmed by a foggy, if heartfelt, glaze of sentimentality.

The hymns they sang throughout the nineteenth century reflected the theology, the emotion—and the historical trends—of many Protestants.

> There is a fountain filled with blood
>   Drawn from Emmanuel's veins;
> And sinners, plunged beneath that flood,
>   Lose all their guilty stains.

The lines, written by poet William Cowper, who had died in 1800, were only one example.

Cowper had also written:

> God moves in a mysterious way
>   His wonders to perform;
> . . . God is His own Interpreter,
>   And He will make it plain.

It was an age of missionary hymns, one of the first examples of which was:

> From Greenland's icy mountains,
>   From India's coral strand,
> Where Africa's sunny fountains
>   Roll down their golden sand,
> From many an ancient river,
>   From many a palmy plain,
> They call us to deliver
>   Their land from error's chain.

It was also the era of the great revival hymns:

> Just as I am, without one plea
> But that Thy blood was shed for me,
> And that Thou bidd'st me come to Thee,
> O Lamb of God, I come, I come!

The lines comprised one of the first hymns written by a woman in a century that was to bring forth women hymn writers by the dozens as a result of the revival meetings. In some cases, the story behind the writing of the hymn was better than the hymn itself. In 1868, Fanny Jane Crosby, making a charitable visit to a prison, heard one of the inmates plead with her, "Good Lord! don't pass by me." She went home and wrote "Pass Me Not, O Gentle Saviour." But if some of their hymns were sentimentalized, there were others that were not. In 1872, John Greenleaf Whittier, a Quaker, wrote:

> Dear Lord and Father of mankind,
>   Forgive our foolish ways;
> Reclothe us in our rightful mind,
> In purer lives Thy service find,
>   In deeper reverence, praise.
>
> In simple trust like theirs who heard,
>   Beside the Syrian sea,
> The gracious calling of the Lord,
> Let us, like them, without a word
>   Rise up and follow Thee.

The lines became one of the century's greatest and most lasting hymns, in spite of the fact that Quakers did not sing hymns at their meetings.

PRESIDENT
WM McKINLEY'S FAVORITE HYMNS
WORDS AND MUSIC
William McKinley
BORN AT NILES, OHIO, JAN. 29, 1843.
DIED AT BUFFALO, N.Y. SEPT. 14. 1901.
BURIED AT WESTLAWN CEMETERY, CANTON, O. SEPT. 19. 1901.
HIS LAST WORDS!
"GOD'S WILL, NOT OURS, BE DONE"
"NEARER, MY GOD, TO THEE"
AND
"LEAD KINDLY LIGHT."
COPYRIGHT SEPT. 25, 1901. EDWARDS DEUTSCH & HEITMANN CHICAGO.

Freud Enters!

"The completest religions," wrote philosopher William James in his *The Varieties of Religious Experience,* "would seem to be those in which the pessimistic elements are best developed." Then he cited the case of Martin Luther, among others:

> One day when Luther was dining with [the Electress Dowager of Saxony], she said to him: "Doctor, I wish you may live forty years to come." "Madam," replied he, "rather than live forty years more, I would give up my chance of Paradise."

If James was to examine Luther, he was also to examine George Fox, Johann Wolfgang von Goethe, and Leo Tolstoy—and come to the same conclusion.

"On the whole," he concluded, "one is struck by a psychological similarity between the mind-cure movement and the Lutheran and Wesleyan movements. To the believer in moralism and works, with his anxious query, 'What shall I do to be saved?' Luther and Wesley replied, 'You are saved now, if you would but believe it.'" Under these circumstances the way to religious experience, James concluded, is by "an anti-moralistic method, by . . . 'surrender.'" "The mind-curers," he wrote, "have given the widest scope to this sort of experience. They have demonstrated that a form of regeneration by relaxing, by letting go, psychologically indistinguishable from the Lutheran justification by faith and the Wesleyan acceptance of free grace, is within the reach of persons who have no conviction of sin and care nothing for the Lutheran theology."

But the fact was that James believed in what he called "the Reality of the Unseen." "God," he wrote, "is the natural appellation, for us Christians at least, for the supreme reality, so I will call this higher part of the universe by the name of God. We and God have business with each other; and in opening ourselves to his influence our deepest destiny is fulfilled. God is real since he produces real effects. . . . Notwithstanding my own inability to accept popular Christianity or scholastic theism, I suppose that my belief that in communion with the Ideal new force comes into the world, and new departures are made here below, subjects me to being classed among the supernaturalists of the piecemeal or crasser type. Universalistic supernaturalism surrenders, it seems to me, too easily to naturalism. In this universalistic way of taking the ideal world, the essence of practical religion seems to me to evaporate."

"Both thought and feeling are determinants of conduct, and the same conduct may be determined either by feeling or by thought. When we survey the whole field of religion, we find a great variety in the thoughts that have prevailed there; but the feelings on the one hand and the conduct on the other are almost always the same, for Stoic, Christian, and Buddhist saints are practically indistinguishable in their lives. The theories which religion generates, being thus variable, are secondary; and if you wish to grasp her essence, you must look to the feelings and the conduct as being the more constant elements. It is between these two elements that the short circuit exists on which she carries on her principal business, while the ideas and symbols and other institutions form loop-lines which may be perfections and improvements, and may even some day all be united into one harmonious system. . . ."

With the rise of psychiatry, all manner of new interpretations were coming to the fore. James provided organized religion with apologetic analysis which did not stand in conflict with science. If, however, he was pragmatically prepared to advocate any religious doctrine that tended to make people virtuous and happy, there were many other points of view to be heard from, and they grew with the twentieth century *(see especially pages 254-7).* One of these, however, came from Sigmund Freud. In 1927, Freud wrote *The Future of an Illusion,* in which he set forth a powerful general criticism of the validity of religious beliefs, based on psychiatric repression and its results. The result, said Freud, is a religion of "fantasy," in which, for Christians, the story of Adam and Eve became the greatest of all birth myths, and the church a mother symbol. The devil, hypothesized the Freudians, is actually the projection of the bad-father image. With Freud, the Protestants took a special beating. Those who manifest a strong emotional antipapal bias or who think of the Church of Rome as the "scarlet woman," Freud suggested, betray an unconscious mother identification, and are clearly reacting against their fathers, as symbolized by the pope—and against the father's power over the mother (the church). Thus Protestantism, in particular, became a "reaction formation," attractive to human beings suffering from a strong mother fixation. Worse yet, by this line of reasoning the entire Christian church seemingly attracts those very people who are most unlike its supposed ideal: the strong, fearless, independent, and creative Christ.

220

Sigmund Freud (right) wrote of a religion of "fantasy" in which Protestantism, as a "reaction formation," attracts those very people who are most unlike the Christian church's supposed ideal, the strong, independent Christ. But William James (above) argued in his The Varieties of Religious Experience for what he called "The Reality of the Unseen," thus attempting to provide organized religion with an apologetic analysis that did not stand in conflict with science or psychiatry.

The Defeated Presbyterian

"It is a fearful thing to lead this great peaceful people into war . . . ," said President Woodrow Wilson on the eve of World War I. "But the right is more precious than peace. . . ." Son of a Presbyterian minister, he believed that God and the people were with him. Ironically, it was Holy Week. To justify a national policy of preparedness, which he had long hoped to avoid, he quoted Ezekiel 33:6: "But if the watchman see the sword come, and blow not the trumpet, and the people be not warned; . . . his blood will I require at the watchman's hand."

Wilson perhaps served as the best symbol of the strengths and weaknesses of the whole tradition of social ethics that had developed in American Protestantism. He was, historian John Maynard Keynes was later to write (though there were those who disagreed with the Keynesian interpretation as an oversimplification), "like a nonconformist minister, perhaps a Presbyterian. His thought and his temperament were essentially theological, not intellectual, with all the strength and weakness of that manner of thought, feeling, and expression." Some of his "Fourteen Points," including the League of Nations, were conceived not only in Calvinist terms but in Calvinist language. They were: 1. "Open *covenants* openly arrived at"; 2. Freedom of the seas; 3. No economic barriers; 4. Disarmament; 5. The adjustment of colonial claims; 6,7,8. Evacuation of Russia, Belgium, and France, including Alsace-Lorraine; 9. Readjustment of the Italian frontiers; 10. Autonomy of parts of the Austrian Empire; 11. Evacuation of the Balkans; 12. Emancipation of Turkey's subject peoples; 13. An independent Poland, with access to the sea; 14. A League of Nations. The League of Nations itself was conceived of as a "Covenant."

It was, however, a Calvinism that, as in John Calvin's own sixteenth-century Geneva, was doomed to failure in practicality, if not in ideal. "President Wilson and his Fourteen Points bore me," announced Georges Clemenceau, Premier of France, one of the "Big Four" at the Peace Conference. "Even God Almighty has only ten!" Years later, Ambassador William Bullitt was to accuse Wilson of having been warped by his Presbyterian father so that he was, by sheer personality, unable to win a lasting peace—and of having consented "to deliver the suffering peoples of the world to new oppressions, subjections, and dismemberment—a new century of war."

"The President's programme for the world, . . ." Keynes was also to write, "had displayed a spirit and a purpose so admirable that the last desire of his sympathizers was to criticize details—the details, they felt, were quite rightly not filled in at present, but would be in due course. . . . But in fact the President had thought out nothing; when it came to practice, his ideas were nebulous and incomplete. . . . He could have preached a sermon on any of them, or addressed a stately prayer to the Almighty for their fulfillment, but he could not frame their concrete application to the actual state of Europe." To Keynes, Wilson seemed "a Presbyterian elder, bamboozled" by "Tiger" Clemenceau and by Lloyd George of England. In addition, Wilson refused to compromise with the forces in the Senate, and so lost his League. With his failure, many said his strain of liberal Calvinism had failed, too. But there were others who were to hold Wilson high in their ideals as the personification of American Calvinism.

"The world," said Woodrow Wilson, "is run by its ideals; only a fool thinks otherwise." In 1919, during the negotiations at the Versailles Peace Conference, even the Europeans had hopes for the man who almost personified the essential difference between American and European civilizations—and American and European Protestantism: the American emphasis on morality and the nineteenth-century American emphasis on perfectionism, by which political issues, too, were constantly thought of as hopes toward perfection.

As the world fell apart, John R. Mott represented the U.S. at the World Missionary Conference in Edinburgh in 1910. The conference became the turning point for modern ecumenism. Despite deep doctrinal differences, the churches of the different Christian faiths began to serve together in common ethical action. From the beginnings at Edinburgh, combined with strong ties with the Y.M.C.A. movement and the Student Christian Movement, grew the later World Council of Churches, the first great world-wide ecumenical organization of Protestants and Eastern Orthodox.

The New Bibles

When early twentieth-century Bible readers opened Scottish scholar James Moffatt's new translation of the Old Testament in 1924, they found themselves in for a shock. In it, the familiar "Garden" of Eden became a "park," Esau's "mess of pottage" became a "red omelet," and Noah's ark was no longer an "ark" but a "barge." The changes were symptomatic of a host of other changes which were to startle many a fundamentalist—and many a liberal too. In the last line of Edgar J. Goodspeed's translation of the Twenty-third Psalm a few years later, they found Goodspeed holding out comfort only for earthly—not immortal —life. It read simply: "And I shall dwell in the house of the Lord *down to old age.*" Other familiar biblical passages were also seemingly going by the board. In J. B. Phillips' translation in 1952 of the Gospel According to John, the opening phrase, "In the beginning was the Word," now read: "At the beginning God expressed Himself. That Personal Expression was with God and was God, and He existed with God from the beginning."

Moffatt, Goodspeed, and Phillips—and Roman Catholic translator Ronald Knox—were representative of a host of new translators who were attempting to make the Bible more understandable and more acceptable for the reader. For liberals, the narratives of Jesus' birth were, as one result for example, coming to be considered legends. During the latter part of the nineteenth century it had become clear to scholars that the King James Version, which in its time had been charged with "bad theology, bad scholarship, and bad English" *(pages 70-71),* was by no means an accurate and understandable translation of the original Greek and Hebrew texts. In the 1880's, the German biblical scholar Julius Wellhausen had ascribed dates to the various books of the Old Testament. Wellhausen had thus proved that the Jewish concept of God, as set forth in the Bible, actually progressed from polytheism to monotheism. He also discovered that the first five books of the Bible were not, as had always been believed, written by Moses. (In fact, some scholars argued, it was unknown whether Moses could even read and write.) In addition, it became clear that the early Hebrews, like many another people, had exaggerated their national greatness—and that, as only one example, it was doubtful that Goliath had been killed by David, since there

was evidence he had been killed by another man.

The result was a new spate of biblical scholarship. Misunderstandings promulgated by older versions, including the King James Version, had, they discovered, been legion. The first two chapters of Genesis, for example, offered contradictory accounts of the story of creation. In the Elizabethan English of the King James Version, hypothetical remarks had been rendered as positive statements. The "one died for all" of II Corinthians 5:14, for example, was far less positive in original texts. The original text read: "If one died for all, then were all dead." The scholars who produced the English Revised Version of 1881 and the American Standard Revised Version of 1901 had found corrections to be necessary at more than five thousand points. Among other changes, they eliminated the word "Saint" from the titles of the four gospels, and substituted the words "Holy Spirit" for "Holy Ghost." Gradually, in varying versions, obsolete words, some of them important, others unimportant, were changed: "amazed" became "distressed," "outlandish" became "foreign," "wealthy" became "at ease." The "challenger" on which Salome placed John the Baptist's head became more understandably a "platter," and, in one instance, the Old Testament Joseph was no longer the familiar "fruitful bough" but an unfamiliar "wild colt." Early English texts had indiscriminately used the word "hell" both for "Hades" (the abode of the dead) and for "Gehenna" (a place of punishment). "Take no thought for your life" should have correctly been translated less sweepingly. Its correct version: "Be not anxious." In one of the more unfortunate results of modern biblical scholarship, the phrase "strain at a gnat" became a prosaic "strain out a gnat." Sometimes the meaning conveyed in Elizabethan English had resulted in a meaning exactly the opposite of what had been intended: The familiar "letteth" was now translated correctly "restraineth." By the 1960's biblical scholars were questioning the biblical record that the Israelites had crossed the Red Sea in their flight from Egypt: their route had actually been farther north in the region of what is now the Suez Canal. They were also eliminating the word "spirit" from Genesis 1:2, since the word was, they said, of Christian, not Jewish, origin. And they were, among other things, questioning the real meaning of the Third Commandment: "Thou shalt not take the name of the Lord thy God in vain." Actually, they now believed, the commandment did not refer, as popularly understood, to profanity but to perjuring one's self in court. And in the Protestant Revised Standard Version of the New Testament, the much-disputed eleven final verses of the Gospel According to Mark describing the Resurrection were relegated to a footnote.

The new translations brought about a fuller and deeper understanding of the Bible as the history of the struggle of a people to find meaning for human life. They also heaped coals on the growing controversy *(right)* between the modernists and the fundamentalists. In 1967, the United Presbyterian Church in the U.S.A. went perhaps the furthest of all as an official denomination in making scriptural thought understandable to modern man. Within its new statement of faith, representing the first change in the official doctrinal platform of Presbyterianism since the Westminster Confession of 1647, many found denial of the virgin birth. But there were greater numbers who backed its liberality and its content. Its most eloquent passage read: "In Jesus of Nazareth true humanity was realized once for all. Jesus, a Palestinian Jew, lived among his own people and shared their needs, temptations, joy, and sorrow. He expressed the love of God in word and deed and became a brother to all kinds of sinful men. But his complete obedience led him into conflict with his people. His life and teaching judged their goodness, religious aspirations, and national hopes. Many rejected him and demanded his death. In giving himself freely for them he took upon himself the judgment under which all men stand convicted. God raised him from the dead, vindicating him as Messiah and Lord. The victim of sin became victor, and won the victory over sin and death . . . the Risen Christ is the savior of all men. Those joined to him by faith are set right with God and commissioned to serve as his reconciling community."

The argument between modernists and fundamentalists centered between modernist Harry Emerson Fosdick (left) and fundamentalist J. Gresham Machen. Fosdick questioned the literalness of the virgin birth—and he was joined by others who questioned the literalness of the Resurrection, of the Trinity, and of Original Sin. Machen stated the five test points of fundamentalism. They were: belief in the virgin birth and the complete deity of Jesus; belief in physical resurrection; belief in the inerrancy of the Scripture; the belief that Jesus died for the sins of the world; and belief in the imminent physical second coming of Christ. Like all fundamentalists, Machen also believed in a literal heaven and a literal hell. In 1924, the Presbytery of Philadelphia charged Fosdick, a Presbyterian, with heresy. Said Fosdick in a sermon published as "Shall the Fundamentalists Win?": "Creedal subscription to ancient confessions of faith is a practice dangerous to the welfare of the church and to the integrity of the individual conscience. . . . What is permanent in Christianity is not mental frameworks but abiding experiences that phrase and rephrase themselves in successive generations' ways of thinking. . . ." Vacating his Presbyterian pulpit, he accepted a call from the Baptists and became nationally famous as the minister of Riverside Church in New York City. In Baltimore, the critic H. L. Mencken parodied the entire argument by writing: "C. S. Fothergill, instructor in history at Baylor University, Texas, resigned today because he did not believe that Noah's ark with the dimensions mentioned in the Bible was capable of accommodating a pair of all animals extant in the world in Noah's time, and because he had been criticized for expressing that feeling."

The real meaning of the biblical story of Jonah, said the liberals, has been missed by fundamentalists. The literal truth of whether Jonah was actually swallowed by a whale* was, they said, unimportant. It was, they argued, a symbolic tale by which biblical prophets tried to convey to early Jews the universality of the Jewish God—and that, being universal, he cared for foreigners as much as he did for the people of Israel. The story, said the liberals, was basic to the entire Jewish theological concept that they were a people chosen by God to suffer for others. It was a concept, they further pointed out, that crystallized in Jesus' concept of himself as a redeemer who, by suffering, took upon himself the sins of others in order to save all mankind from separation from God.

* Not until the Bible was translated into English did the Greek word "KHTOS," meaning "sea monster," become a "whale."

"The Monkey Trial"

In the Bible-belt town of Dayton, Tennessee, in 1925, a young red-haired substitute high-school biology teacher named John Scopes admitted that, contrary to Tennessee law, he had taught Darwin's theories of evolution to his public-school pupils, and he was brought to trial. Actually, the trial had been dreamed up by enterprising local merchants, who hoped thereby to pull the town's business out of midsummer doldrums. It did. It also brought forth enterprising hucksters, one of whom set up a booth, complete with monkey, outside the courthouse and offered passers-by the opportunity to take a good look at their "ancestor."

At the trial, fundamentalists made a public stand, based on a completely literal—and unsymbolical—interpretation of the Bible. It was a stand personified by the great orator William Jennings Bryan, a three-time loser as a candidate for the U.S. Presidency, who headed the prosecution as a one-man team. It was also a

Palm-leaf fan in hand, fundamentalist William Jennings Bryan posed in the steaming courtroom with agnostic Clarence Darrow, the defense attorney. At the beginning of the trial, Darrow objected to an opening prayer offered by the presiding judge, on the grounds that any prayer at the moment was likely to prejudice the jury against the defendant. In the course of the trial he summoned Bryan as a witness and subjected him to a relentless cross-examination that revealed Bryan's lack of familiarity with modern science.

stand which brought scorn on—and saddened—liberal Protestants throughout the country.

"Why," pleaded a tearful Tennessee lawyer inside the courtroom, "have we not the right to bar science if it comes from the four corners of the earth to tear the vitals of our religion? . . . If we bar that upon which man's eternal hope is founded, then our civilization is about to crumble. Tell me that I was once a common worm that writhed in the dust? No! Tell me that I came from the cell of the ass and the monkey? No! I want to go beyond this world where there is eternal happiness for me and others. . . . Who says we can't bar science that deprives us of all hope of the future life to come?"

On some of the hottest days of the summer, Bryan, who had delivered the commencement address at Scopes's own high-school graduation six years previously, fanned himself with a palm-leaf fan and argued before twelve unschooled jurymen. Believing that he was choosing between "God and the gorilla" and between Darwinism and the biblical story of the Garden of Eden, he argued majestically for a literal interpretation of the Bible. "The modernists," he cried, "have taken away my Lord, and I know not where they have laid Him." Evolution, he argued, made God unnecessary. He insisted that the biblical account of creation should be believed as a revelation inspired by God and that he would consider no proposition whatsoever to be preposterous, provided it were found in the Bible. At one point he insisted he believed literally that Joshua had made the sun stand still in the heavens.

The opposing lawyer was the liberal, and self-styled agnostic, Clarence Darrow. The Tennessee law, said Darrow, was "the most brazen and bold attempt to destroy liberty since the Middle Ages."

Scopes, who had received two washtubs of mail every day during the trial, was found guilty and fined one hundred dollars. Later he became a geologist, married a Catholic. "I believe," he said, "but I reserve the right to doubt." The country as a whole—and the world—favored his stand. Only Bryan himself seemed to suffer in the ordeal. A few days later he died of a stroke induced by his exertions.

This newspaper cartoon (right) showed Bryan "gathering data for the Tennessee trial."

John Scopes, the defendant, was convicted for teaching Darwin's theory of evolution in the Tennessee public schools, though the conviction was later reversed on technical grounds. Forty years later he admitted he wasn't quite sure whether or not he had actually taught evolution at all.

In 1896, Bryan had gained the Democratic nomination for the U.S. Presidency by his championing of free silver rather than the U.S. gold standard. It was his biblically oriented "cross-of-gold" speech that won him the nomination. "You shall," he had said, "not crucify mankind upon a cross of gold."

"Peace, It's Wonderful!"

In 1931, a bright-eyed, chipper little man who had named himself Father Divine was arrested and put into jail. While he repined in his cell, the judge who had sentenced him died of a heart attack. Said Father Divine from his cell: "I hated to do it!" Father Divine almost—but never quite—admitted he was "God" to his self-estimated twenty-one million "angels" who had joined his self-styled "heaven." And in Washington, D.C., his counterpart, Daddy Grace, who sometimes baptized two hundred converts at a time with a fire hose, was fond of saying, "Grace has given God a vacation."

Father Divine's and Daddy Grace's cults, together with Aimee Semple McPherson's "Angelus Temple" in Los Angeles (where Aimee once roared down the aisle on a motorcycle to advertise her "Four-Square Gospel"), were only three of some four hundred so-called sects which, in keeping with Protestant individualism, were flourishing in twentieth-century America. There were sects whose members talked in "unknown tongues." There were sects formed, seemingly, chiefly for opposing a whole list of human sins, including, as in one case, "education, smoking, hilarity at weddings, and the social features of funerals," and, in another case, "filthiness of speech, foolish talking or jesting, or the use of slang . . . ," "attending fairs, swimming pools, or shows of any kind . . . ," "jewelry, gold, feathers, flowers, costly apparel, neckties, hobble skirts, split skirts, low necks, short sleeves, and indecent dress." Most sects also put great store by the apocalyptic biblical Book of Revelation.

By 1949, the foremost authority on sects in America, religious historian Elmer T. Clark, had categorized the Protestant sects of America into seven groups. There were the "pessimistic or adventist" sects, whose members, said Clark, believed the world "is rushing speedily to hell" according to the will and plan of God. These despaired of obtaining any earthly benefits through normal social processes. Their followers, reminiscent of nineteenth-century William Miller *(pages 172-3),* liked to predict the imminent—and catastrophic

—end of the world. There were the "perfectionist or subjectivist" sects, whose emphasis is on personal perfection or "holiness," with, usually, a strong stand against "desires of the flesh." Many of these sects are, understandably, offshoots of early Methodism. There is, however, a left-wing division in this group that Methodist Clark has characterized as the "charismatic or pentecostal" sects. More hopeful than the perfectionists, these seek the "gift" of glossolalia (based on the biblical account of the apostles' ability to "speak in unknown tongues" at the time of the birth of the Christian church), "divine blessings"; and they sometimes pride themselves on the ability to prophesy. In the manner of early nineteenth-century American revivalism, their members frequently fall into trances and visions—and experience convulsions.

Though the fourth category, the "communistic" sects whose chief characteristic is a tendency to withdraw from "the world" into colonies like the early Shakers, have largely disappeared, there still remain such communistic groups as the Dukhobors of western Canada, who have become notable for trying to secure the social approval and the economic justice they believe is denied them elsewhere, by occasionally demonstrating, unclothed, in public, especially when they believe their religious and economic freedom is threatened by government interference. But most such sects, descendants of Reformation-day Anabaptists, have died out.

Like the communistic sects, the "legalistic or objectivist" sects tend to stress certain rules based on specific verses of the Bible, and tend to regard themselves as the restorers of first-century Christianity. In addition to insisting on such biblical rites as foot washing, for example (and that women should wear caps to cover their heads), the legalistic sects often set great store on the "apostolic succession" of their clergy. The remaining two categories include the "egocentric" sects, who emphasize freedom from pain, disease—*and* ennui— (in the manner of the Christian Scientists and the Unity school of Christianity), and the "mystic" or "theosophist" sects, which, influenced by non-Christian as well as Christian doctrines, are in reality more the offshoots of Hinduism than of Christian Protestantism.

By the mid-twentieth century the largest—and fastest-growing—of all the so-called sects (which, as old-line denominations are well aware, may in the future develop into "respectable" denominations) were the Jehovah's Witnesses. Founded in 1872 by Charles Taze Russell, a Congregationalist haber-

dasher of Allegheny, Pennsylvania, who had become convinced that the second coming of Christ would take place—in invisible form—in the summer of 1874, the Jehovah's Witnesses believe in a literal devil but not in hell—and that, in reality, there is no need for a hell, since, in the end, the wicked will be totally destroyed when Christ sets up his theocracy right here on earth following the biblical battle of Armageddon as described in the biblical Book of Revelation.

"De Lawd" of The Green Pastures

In 1930, the Broadway hit *The Green Pastures* told of an anthropomorphic God, "De Lawd," who looked with mercy—and with humor—upon the world he had created. It also told of the hope of a three-dimensional heaven in the clouds *(below)* which, in keeping with its setting in the Deep South, smacked of fish fries and ten-cent cigars.

"De Lawd" himself *(left)*, dressed in a long Prince Albert coat and black trousers was "de big boss." Almost unintentionally, as a "kind of experiment," as he explains to his angels, he has created Adam and Eve, just because he can "pass miracles." But in one of his most frequently quoted lines, he ruefully admits, "You know, *dis* thing's turned into quite a proposition. . . . I only hope it's goin' to work out all right."

For many a man of the 1930's, *Green Pastures,* despite its obvious appeal to the "Amos 'n'Andy" interpretation of the Southern Negro, was as good as any interpretation of the Christian religion, including "De Lawd's" answer when the Angel Gabriel asks, "How about cleanin' up de whole mess of 'em and sta'tin' all over ag'in wid some new kind of animal?" Replies "De Lawd": "An' admit I'm licked? . . . No, suh. No, suh. Man is a kind of pet of mine and it ain't right fo' me to give up tryin' to do somethin' wid him. Doggone, mankin' *mus'* be all right at de core or else why did I ever bother wid him in de first place?"

The Green Pastures *told of a three-dimensional heaven and of a God who looked with some humor upon the world he had created. In the play, even "De Lawd" learned to his surprise that mercy, too, is an attribute ascribed to him.*

"Even bein' Gawd ain't a bed of roses," said "De Lawd" of The Green Pastures *in 1930. To Noah, he explained as he started the flood, "It's enough to discourage you. I'm startin' all over, Noah."*

The Gospel of Success

In 1925, a New York advertising man named Bruce Barton published a book which was to be hotly debated, entitled *The Man Nobody Knows.* In it Barton presented Jesus to his readers as a backslapping, go-getting Rotarian businessman. The relationship of business to Christianity—and the efforts of business to make Christianity conform to business ethics instead of vice versa—had long been evident in Protestantism.

In the U.S., Barton was the prototype of a whole school of so-called "gospel of success" interpretations of Christianity. By mid-century, Norman Vincent Peale, of New York's Marble Collegiate Church, was, in a somewhat similar vein, preaching "The Power of Positive Thinking"—a theme which attracted so many followers that Peale became a nationwide, jet-flying clergyman who, according to his writings, seemed to be continually chatting with successful businessmen seated beside him on planes—and, to the consternation of many Protestants, equating Christianity with a materialistic success that denied the biblical message of victory through defeat as symbolized by the crucifixion itself. Satirizing Peale's message, *The New Yorker* magazine once referred to his book as "The View from Vincent's Head," and more than one critic was to characterize him as a Protestant clergyman who had perverted the basic meaning of Christianity.

The phenomenon was not peculiar to America. In France, back in the late 1800's, Frenchman Ernst Renan had made Jesus into a debonair French gentleman. On a visit to England shortly after World War I, dapper, well-manicured Frank Buchman, who was dubbed a "soul-surgeon" by the English upper classes, formed a new "Oxford Group" movement known popularly as "Moral Rearmament" (but which had nothing to do with the Anglo-Catholic Oxford Movement of the nineteenth century, *pages 176-7*). Insisting that "ninety per cent of ultimate sin" is based on sexual irregularities, Buchman coined the "soul-winning" slogan: "Confidence, Confession, Conviction, Conversion, Conservation" —a slogan which he considered "life-changing" and which seemed to be geared to meet the needs of, for example, one businessman who said he was thus helped "not only to find God but to meet the Queen of Rumania and make a better impression on customers"; and, equally, to "help" a woman who testified at one of the group's meetings that she was successfully "led" to buy a one-thousand-dollar coat for a mere three hundred dollars. And in Germany—albeit on a far higher level—historian Max Weber contributed a historicity to the materialistic concept of Protestantism—a historicity that had truth in it. In his historical study entitled *The Protestant Ethic and the Spirit of Capitalism,* Weber wrote, somewhat as a result of a visit to the United States, that Calvinism, beyond the intention of its founder, could be partly explained by the thesis that throughout the centuries it had provided large numbers of believers with a religious rationale for economic gain through methodical hard work, and that the creed's moral asceticism, by discouraging the use of that gain for worldly pleasures, had made capital available for further economic investment. The thesis —which was repeated in hundreds of books and pamphlets—precipitated one of the great and continuing scholarly controversies of the century, and the words "The Protestant Ethic" became synonomous in some minds with Puritanical, mid-Victorian thrift.

Actually, Weber did not assert that Calvinism created capitalism but that there was an "elective affinity" between the virtues esteemed by Calvinism and by Puritanism—self-restraint, frugality, sobriety—and the requirements of an economy undertaking industrialization. It was, in fact, an assertion that was to set contemporary scholars searching for equivalents of Puritanism in the so-called underdeveloped societies.

In an America of the late 1950's the problem of the "businessman's version" of Christianity and the Bible was to crop up again, though in slightly different form, in a widely acclaimed Broadway play by poet Archibald MacLeish. In MacLeish's *"J.B.,"* the biblical story of Job was presented as that of an average American businessman who found in a kind of watered-down concept of Christian love the answer to life—thereby entirely missing the very grandeur of the story of Job through which anguished Old Testament Jewish prophets had tried to explain the problem of "Why must the good man suffer?" by the magnificent answer that it is not man's prerogative to question the ways in which God helps man to know him— and that no man can truly be "good."

Billy Graham became the most famous evangelist of the post-World War II era. Graham, who liked to say "May the good Lord bless you—real good!" was a firm-jawed, handshaking, conservative North Carolina Southern Baptist. He began his career with a huge youth rally in Chicago, soon moved on to cities throughout the world. During a New York crusade in 1957 at the zenith of his career, 56,707 people made "decisions for Christ" after a two-year preparatory campaign that was said to cost $2,500,000, including 650 billboards heralding his arrival, 40,000 phone-dial cards bearing the words "Pray for Billy Graham," and twice-a-day personal appearances by his manager on television to promote the crusade. "Here, in this year of 1957," he announced at the end of the New York crusade, "God has done a great work." His message was a simplified one, accompanied by heart-rending music and a corps of counselors, that gave little if any evidence of discernment of complex contemporary problems, and the real value and permanence of his followers' highly publicized "decisions for Christ" was frequently questioned. By the mid-1960's he had become a frequent guest of U.S. President Lyndon B. Johnson at the White House and was being advertised as "the man who put Christ into Christianity for thirty million people."

The Atomic God

Aboard the battleship Missouri *on September 2, 1945, General Douglas MacArthur addressed the people of the United States. "Today," said MacArthur, "the guns are silent. Men since the beginning of time have sought peace. . . . We have had our last chance. If we do not devise some greater and more equitable system, Armageddon will be at our door." Then he added, "The problem basically is theological and involves a spiritual recrudescence. . . ."*

In July, 1943, Dietrich Bonhoeffer, a young German theological student, joined with others in an unsuccessful plot to assassinate Hitler. Bonhoeffer was imprisoned and, in April, 1945, hanged. In the Nazi concentration camp he began writing letters which were later published as *Letters and Papers from Prison* and which, as much as any single body of writing, were to influence the course of postwar Protestant theology. Among other things, the letters stood in notable contrast to the traditional state church of Germany— and to the actions of German pastor Martin Niemöller, who had at first bowed to Hitler.

Like Niemöller, the young Bonhoeffer had accepted the traditional Lutheran view that there is a sharp distinction between politics and religion. He had himself first hoped that the nonviolence of Gandhi, which he had studied, could defeat Hitlerism. But he soon became one of the first German teachers of theology of his time to teach his students the history and creeds of non-Lutheran churches as well as of Lutheranism itself. Christianity, he came to believe, was not a concern of the believing pious soul who shuts himself away from the world. The church, he said, had become more concerned with its own existence than in preaching against war. The Bible, he said, needs to be adapted to requirements of a secular world. "I am," he wrote, "going through another spell of finding it difficult to read the Bible. I never know quite what to make of it. I don't feel guilty at all about it. . . ."

His theology crystallized into a new—and highly contentious—secular or "religionless Christianity," through which he preached of Jesus as "the man for others." For him, Hitler became the "Antichrist." It was, he came to believe, a Christian's duty to oppose tyranny —a form of government he characterized as one no longer based on natural law, or, as he believed, God's law. He proposed a practical person-centered morality based on love rather than law, which has in some cases evolved into a new school of "situation ethics." It was, he believed, morally right in his particular situation to assassinate Hitler. This belief was to make him not only one of the most frequently quoted theologians of his generation but also one of the most controversial.

"The Christian," wrote Dietrich Bonhoeffer (below), "is not a homo religiosus *but simply a man as Jesus . . . was a man. . . . Not the flat and banal 'This-sidedness' of the Enlightened, of the Active, of the Comfortable and the Sluggard, but the deep 'This-sidedness' which is full of discipline and in which the knowledge of Death and Resurrection is always present. . . . When a man really gives up trying to make something out of himself—a saint, or a converted sinner, or a churchman (a so-called clerical somebody), a righteous or unrighteous man . . . when in fulness of tasks, questions, success or ill-hap, experiences and perplexities, a man throws himself into the arms of God . . . then he wakes with Christ in Gethsemane. That is faith, . . . it is thus that he becomes a man and a Christian. How can a man wax arrogant if in a this-sided life he shares the suffering of God?"* In 1946, German pastor Martin Niemöller (left), who opposed Hitler only after the German state had subjugated the church, joined a group of Protestant delegates at a World Council of Churches meeting in Geneva and posed beneath heroic statutes of Luther, Calvin, and other Reformation leaders (above) . In 1948, speaking from the pulpit (left) about his experiences in a Nazi concentration camp, he said, "We [German Christians] have discovered sin and guilt are not merely words. . . ."
In the U.S., however, there were those who said he did not even understand the real depth of his own guilt.

The Last Anabaptists

In 1950, a sad but philosophical old Shaker lady explained how she felt about the fact that the sect founded by Mother Ann Lee back in 1776 had finally dwindled down to little more than a handful of members, almost all of them old. "The good," she explained, "just won't be concentrated in one place any more." Victims of their own policies of abstinence from sex, the Shakers had been unable to bring into their groups enough converts—or adopted children—to keep their colonies alive. They had also been the victims of an expanding industrialization which had made their simple agricultural economy archaic.

But if the Shakers had lost out, another—and older—sect of Anabaptist descendants, the conservative Amish branch of the Mennonites, steadfastly kept to their separate communities, even in the face of a changing culture. Through war after war they had abided by their pacifist Christian beliefs, refusing to enter military service. Of all the Protestants, they had perhaps also remained most faithful to their sixteenth-century beliefs and customs, refusing even to use telephones and automobiles, on the grounds that such inventions had not been specifically sanctioned by the Bible. But after World War II it was within their ranks that one of the best-known forerunners of the great interdenominational relief and rehabilitation agency, Church World Service, originated with the founding of the Mennonite Central Committee. Through this agency even the conservative Amish faction, having prospered in fertile Pennsylvania farmland, was particularly interested in sending food and farm implements to less fortunate peoples throughout the world.

The Dead Sea Scrolls

On a spring day in 1947, an Arab boy, out for a stroll, stepped into a cave on the western shore of the Dead Sea. There, by luck, he happened upon a cache of ancient leather rolls wrapped in linen cloths. When examined by scholars, the scrolls, which numbered hundreds of thousands of fragments, revealed among other things the history of a little-known sect of ancient Jews called Essenes, whose beliefs were astonishingly Christianlike —and yet predated the time of Jesus. The leader of the Essenes was, like Jesus, called a "Teacher of Righteousness" and was, it was reported, regarded as a divine incarnation. Like Jesus, it was also reported, he had been martyred—though the scrolls themselves contained no evidence to this effect. But, like Jesus, he had inspired belief among his followers that he would return from the dead. In addition, the Essenes had practiced ceremonies and rituals similar to Christian baptism and communion.

To many, these facts seemed to deny not only the uniqueness—and the divinity—of Jesus but also the entire basis of Christianity. In short time the scrolls became the center of one of the hottest controversies of twentieth-century religion—and soon a whole hymrackful of books appeared, arguing the Dead Sea Scrolls pro and con. A few angry Protestant clergymen mistakenly advised their congregations there was nothing to worry about in the scrolls because they could not be translated. Red-faced, they soon learned that seven of the least likely looking scrolls had already been successfully pieced together.

In the controversy the "devil's advocate"—an honorable title in Roman Catholic tradition— was a rotund little ex-Catholic priest named André DuPont-Sommer, who had become a professor at the Sorbonne in Paris. As devil's advocate, M. Dupont-Sommer bore his title with aplomb. He was, he said, *"un pur savant."* Others called him a "sensationalist" and, in mockery, "a great secular seeker of the truth." But throughout it all the little Frenchman remained bland-faced and smiling, urbane and yet priestly-looking. On his findings he published two books, the earlier of which became the basis of a small book written by the dean of American literary critics, Edmund Wilson, and published in the United States. If Wilson's book was not the most scholarly on the subject, it was by far the most widely read,

and it introduced the entire Dead Sea Scrolls controversy to a delighted American public. "Will or will not this process of elucidation inevitably have the effect of making Jesus seem less superhuman?" asked Mr. Wilson. ". . . It would seem an immense advantage for cultural and social intercourse—that is, for civilization—that the rise of Christianity should, at least, be generally understood as simply an episode of human history rather than propagated as dogma and divine revelation. The study of the Dead Sea Scrolls—with the direction it is now taking—cannot fail, one would think, to conduce this."

To which a host of voices shouted, "Amen."

Wrote Unitarian minister Franklin P. Smith, of Albuquerque, New Mexico, in a letter to *The New York Times:* "It ought to be quite obvious to all that the Dead Sea Scrolls, as Mr. Wilson rightly infers, [are] going to cause a new evaluation of Christianity. The Pre-Existent Christ, the establishment of unique sacraments, the development of original rituals, all that the official church has cherished for the last two thousand years will have to be re-evaluated." Proving that the controversy had its repercussions among other creeds, too, some liberal Jews were quoted as being "delighted that the scrolls may close the gulf between Christians and Jews."

The conservatives retorted angrily. "Any stick now seems big enough to use against Christianity," a Roman Catholic cried. Said a conservative Jew: "Seldom have so many readers been led astray by one man." Said the Very Rev. John J. Dougherty, a Catholic professor of Sacred Scriptures in Darlington, New Jersey (thereby bringing the controversy down squarely on the head of M. Dupont-Sommer): "Mr. Wilson has taken one hypothetical interpretation, that of the French scholar André Dupont-Sommer . . . and presented it, dressed up in exciting diction, to the circle of those who can read but not evaluate. . . . That is mischief."

In the midst of the confusion the American literary magazine *Saturday Review* addressed a number of questions to the devil's advocate himself. "Since it is generally believed," asked the magazine, "that your second book is more cautious than is your first book, the *Saturday Review* would like to know whether you . . . continue to believe that there is evidence in the scrolls which may deny the uniqueness and divinity of Jesus? Do you find any new evidence for believing that orthodox Christian thinking may have to be revised in the light of the Dead Sea Scrolls?" To the surprise of many, Dupont-Sommer replied: "I never claimed that the Dead Sea Scrolls could strike a blow against the 'Uniqueness' of Jesus. I simply pointed out, in my *Aperçus préliminaires,* a certain number of characteristics held in common by the Teacher of Righteousness and Jesus. . . . I believe that the Dead Sea Scrolls do not deny the divinity of Jesus [even] in the sense of 'Son of God Incarnate.' In a general sense, viewed as a whole, the originality of the Christian Church seems to me to remain unchallenged."

To the fighting liberals, the devil's advocate thus seemed to have lost his horns. The con-troversy was summed up in theological language by Protestant Frank M. Cross, of McCormick Theological Seminary, who was one of the three American scholars who had thus far worked on the translations of the scrolls: "God chooses to give meaning to history, not suspend it," he wrote to the *Times.* "This means he uses its continuities, its language, its events, its institutions in speaking to men and in building his church." The implication was clearer than the explanation itself. The argument was: An understanding of Jesus in his historical perspective does not deny Christianity; none but the fundamentalists need be concerned that a study of the scrolls would destroy Christian faith.

"I Am Ready to Kneel Down..."

The founding fathers of the World Council of Churches presided over its formation. From top to bottom they were: Greek Orthodox Archbishop Germanos, John R. Mott of the U.S. Methodists, the Archbishop of Canterbury, Dr. Marc Boegner as chief of the Reformed Church of France, Archbishop Erling Eidem of the Church of Sweden, and Dr. Samuel McCrea Cavert of the U.S. At center opposite, representatives of the formerly divided Methodist Protestant Church, the Methodist Episcopal Church, and the Methodist Episcopal Church, South, shake hands in 1939 when the three churches united into one.

"I am ready to kneel down for the purpose," announced Protestant Episcopal Bishop James A. Pike in the 1960's of the proposed union between his church and the Presbyterians that would have resulted, if carried out, in Episcopal clergymen becoming ordained presbyters in the Presbyterian church and, conversely, Presbyterian clergy becoming ordained priests in the Episcopal church. He was echoing the phrase used by Methodist Bishop G. Bromley Oxnam, who, in an earlier decade, had said of similar hopes between Methodists and Episcopalians, "I would be proud to kneel at any altar. . . ." By mid-twentieth century, even the Russian Orthodox had become members of the interdenominational World Council of Churches (left), in which by 1967 a total of 223 communions throughout the world, chiefly old-line denominations which had become separate churches within their own countries, shared common missionary concerns.

"Is it any wonder," leading Protestant Henry P. Van Dusen had asked in 1937, following the failure of a proposed union between Episcopalians and Presbyterians, "that throughout American Protestantism, the Episcopal Church is increasingly likened to an adolescent schoolgirl who proposed a marriage in leap year, and then, when her offer is accepted, searches frantically for some escape from her pledged commitment?" But if the Episcopalians, largely because of their historic stand on apostolic succession, were proving standoffish, the ecumenical movement was nevertheless gaining strength. As far back as 1918, the Lutherans had begun the movement with the union of three branches of their creed in America into the United Lutheran Church in America. Later, in 1930, three other Lutheran bodies formed the American Lutheran Church. In 1931, the Congregational Churches had united with the Christian Church of early nineteenth-century revivalist origin. Three years later the Evangelical Synod of North America had united with the old-line Reformed Church in the United States. In 1939, three denominations of Methodism (right) had also united, healing, among other rifts, the split that had occurred in the denomination during the Civil War. And in 1957, the Congregational Christian Churches and the Evangelical and Reformed Church, already the results of unions, took the greatest single step in U.S. ecumenism by uniting to form the United Church of Christ, the first time that two major Protestant groups in the nation, with different backgrounds, practices, and forms of church government, had found a common meeting ground. Perhaps the most significant of all, however, was the union in 1947 in India of five completely different Protestant faiths—Anglicans, Methodists, Congregationalists, Presbyterians, and Dutch Reformed—into the new Church of South India. It was, said one clergyman at the time, an unbelievable event "little short of a miracle." The union, which brought together a million members, had taken twenty-eight years of discussion and compromise to effect. But it stood as proof that—at least in the Orient—the old splits among Protestants could be overcome. The fact was that, in America, much of the trouble—but by no means all—stemmed from the problem of merging vast denominational property holdings.

In 1947, when the Church of South India formally united, Oriental music was played, the service was printed in three different languages, and even the austere delegate representing the traditionally unliturgical Presbyterians, in respect for Indian Christians, wore a stole whose crimson lining was a color regarded as holy by Hindus. In further respect to Indian tradition, some, though not all, new bishops removed their shoes upon entering the cathedral, and members of the congregation chose between removing their hats in conformity with European custom or removing their sandals in conformity with Indian custom.

"Are You Running With Me, Jesus?"

Benevolent and easy-going Father: we have occasionally been guilty of errors of judgment. We have lived under the deprivations of heredity and the disadvantages of environment. We have sometimes failed to act in accordance with common sense. We have done the best we could in the circumstances; And have been careful not to ignore the common standards of decency; And we are glad to think that we are fairly normal. Do thou, O Lord, deal lightly with our infrequent lapses. Be thy own sweet Self with those who admit they are not perfect; According to the unlimited tolerance which we have a right to expect from thee. And grant as an indulgent Parent that we may hereafter continue to live a harmless and happy life and keep our self-respect.

In 1959, a Methodist clergyman named David Head, seriously intent on exposing the frequently watered-down religion of twentieth-century man, published this "altered" version of the English *Book of Common Prayer* in a small collection of "prayers" entitled *He Sent Leanness.* The collection was loaded down with apt vignettes of present-day man's thinning attitude toward religion. Its mock liturgy included:

O God, we have considerable doubts in our minds about the way You are running the universe.
  Is there any chance that You will show Your mercy to us, O Lord?
. . .

The psychologists tell us that our nagging doubts about Your goodness burrow into the subconscious mind and spit poison.
  Isn't this a bit unfair, O Lord?

From a universe where things can be extremely unpleasant,
  Deliver us, Good Lord.

From everything that calls from us courage and endurance,
  Deliver us, Good Lord.

In England, C. S. Lewis, a wry Christian apologist, said, "A doctrine never seems dimmer to me than when I have just successfully defended it." It was an era in which the past of the Protestant had frequently caught up with him—when, though he frequently misunderstood the real venom in the sobriquet of "WASP" ("White Anglo-Saxon Protestant"), which was hurled at him by others, one or another Protestant did sometimes admit that he was one of *God's Frozen People* sitting in *The Comfortable Pew* on Sundays and commuting back and forth to *The Secular City* on weekdays. The titles of these self-critical Protestant books and the prayers of David Head were only symbolic of the problem. In 1965, a young Episcopal priest named Malcolm Boyd joined the group with another book of prayers entitled *Are You Running With Me, Jesus?* One sample prayer:

They're having a party in a hotel suite which is elegant and located in the best hotel in the heart of the city. There's music, jewelry, glamour, gin, V.I.P. status, and Power, Lord.

But nobody's having any fun. . . . I mean, they're not relating, Jesus. . . . The masks are on parade tonight, Jesus. The masks are smiling and laughing to cover up status anxieties and bleeding ulcers.

Tell us about freedom, Jesus.

To a newspaper reporter, Boyd announced in early 1967 that an "underground church" was developing in Protestantism. "It rejects phoniness," he explained. Furthermore, he announced, its members look upon official church hierarchies as "the old Wizard-of-Oz type of church leadership, fearfully hiding behind high walls."

Following World War II, also, Dietrich Bonhoeffer's concept of "Christ in the community" had brought forth a host of new Protestant movements, including notably the industrial mission of Horst Symanowski in Mainz-Kastel, Germany, the evangelical academy at Bad Böll in Germany, and the Taizé community in France. Sometimes, as in the case of the Taizé community—an ecumenical group that included Roman Catholics and Eastern Orthodox—the Protestants were even dressing like monks. (In the Netherlands, the monastic Remonstrant Brotherhood, direct spiritual

descendants of Jacobus Arminius, who had opposed Calvin back in the sixteenth century but had been forgotten by most Protestants, was suddenly rediscovered.) In an extension of medieval Christian doctrine, the Taizé brethren were looking upon the entire world as a monastery in which to serve as laborers, as farmers, as office workers—and as political organizers in underprivileged rural and urban communities. They had derived part of their belief that every believer should share in ministry to *the world,* not just to the church, from the sixteenth-century Protestant Reformation itself. The "priesthood of all believers," they said, "does not mean 'every man his own priest.' " It means more deeply that every man shares in the Christian ministry and in the responsibility of that ministry.

There could be no denying that vast numbers of Protestants were unaware of these experiments in Christian living. Instead, they remained *God's Frozen People,* who continued sitting in *The Comfortable Pew*—and, according to more than one sociological study, vying for a social status that was supposed to progress up the ladder from Baptists near the bottom, to the now-middle-class Methodists, to Presbyterians, to Episcopalians—frequently completely forgetful of their less social Protestant past. (Sociology popularizer Vance Packard called it "The Long Road from Pentecostal to Episcopal.") In their churches they far preferred to sing such rosy—and originally Sunday-school-inspired—hymns as "All Things Bright and Beautiful," though the Anglicans had finally dropped two outdated lines from the hymn because they at long last agreed that the lines smacked of feudalism. They were:

> The rich man in his castle;
> the poor man at his gate,
> God made them, high or lowly,
> and ordered their estate.

Their liturgy, as parodied by David Head, was, in their hearts, apt to be:
> We miserable owners of increasingly luxurious cars, and ever-expanding television screens, do most humbly pray for that two-thirds of the world's population which is under-nourished;
> *You can do all things, O God.*

Not infrequently, too, their personal prayer, as parodied by Head, was too likely to be:
> I thank Thee that I had more gall-stones than Mrs. Peters.

The Question of "Syncretism"

". . . We have seen" wrote historian Arnold Toynbee in 1956, "how Christian heritage [became] part of the background of a great Hindu saint, the Mahatma Gandhi. We have seen how Gandhiji held the allegiance of the whole Hindu world, though his Hinduism was obviously tinged and blended with elements of Christianity which he himself did not disown. And we have seen the immense effect on the World of this two-fold religious inspiration harmonized in one great soul. On a less exalted plane than Gandhi's we already see Christians of ordinary spiritual stature making individual choices in grown-up life between the Protestant and the Catholic versions of Western Christianity and between the Western and non-Western versions of Christianity. . . . Both the Protestant Western Churches and the Catholic Western Church also have converts from Hinduism and Buddhism and Confucianism, as well as from the primitive religions. . . . I think we can already see a tendency for people to pass, by deliberate choice, from one religion to another, in contrast to the traditional state of religious affairs in which, almost automatically, one remained for life in the religious communion into which one had been introduced by the accident of being born in a particular place at a particular time. I think this tendency towards making a free choice of religion in grown-up life is likely to increase as the World grows closer together."

Toynbee was attempting to answer the ever rising question of syncretism of the world's religions. It was a question that had been dramatically brought to the fore during the first half of the twentieth century by the example of Mahatma Gandhi. For a time syncretism

had seemed to win the day. In a way it reached back to the days of Emerson in America. It was a trend brought to the fore again within Protestantism by William Ernest Hocking in a book published in 1912 entitled *The Meaning of God in Human Experience*. Hocking had argued that all the religions of the world are ultimately the same. He had also predicted that ". . . we shall see in the Orient the rise of a Christianity far outpassing that which we of the West have conceived." By the late 1960's, however, Hocking's hopes had generally given way within Protestantism to the less syncretistic approach of an Arnold Toynbee. God, said the Protestant theologians, was indeed working in history through other faiths as well as through Christianity. But, said most theologians, he was by this very method testing and shaping the crucible of Christianity.

"In the light of history," Toynbee wrote, "I should not expect to see mankind converted to a 'syncretistic' religion, constructed artificially out of elements taken from all the existing religions. Such artificial religions have been, and are being, manufactured; but I should not expect to see any of them capture the imagination and the feelings and the allegiance of Mankind. I should not expect this because such attempts are generally made only partly for religious reasons, and partly for utilitarian reasons which are other than religious. I am thinking of attempts in the past like the Mughal emperor Akbar's attempt in India, in the early years of the seventeenth century, to create a new composite religion blending elements of Islam and Hinduism and Zoroastrianism and Christianity; or the at-

Mahatma Gandhi's political course of action was partially based on a realism that transformed the ascetic ideals of mystical self-deliverance, as espoused by ancient Hinduism (right), into a force capable of rousing the masses of Indian people. His conception of an independent Indian national state—and his tireless struggle for it—became possible only because it formed part of a counterphase to British colonialism. But there is little doubt that his fight against the caste system in India resulted as much from the impact of Christianity on him as it did from the impact of Western civilization.

244

tempt of the Roman Emperor Julian to reverse the triumph of Christianity in the Roman Empire by building up artificially a pagan counter-church in which he tried to weld together all the non-Christian religions in the Roman Empire. It is notorious that such attempts have failed in the past, and I think they are also likely to fail in the future, as far as the past is any guide to the future. . . . I should say that, in learning more and more to respect, reverence, admire, and love other faiths, we should be making progress in the true practice of Christianity. And the practice of the Christian virtue of charity need not prevent us from holding fast to what we believe to be the essential truths and ideals in our own Christian faith. . . . If we can express what we believe to be the essential truths and precepts of our own religion in action as well as in words, and if at the same time we can be receptive to the truths and ideals of the other faiths, we shall be more likely to win the attention and good will of the followers of these other faiths. If we can learn to present Christianity in this spirit, we can perhaps manage to present it with conviction without at the same time relapsing into Christianity's traditional sin of arrogance and intolerance."

"You will," Toynbee continued, "have taken my point that Christianity has never been a monopoly of the Western Christians; and I think we may also confidently predict that Christianity will continue to be a living spiritual force in the World for thousands of years after our Western civilization has passed away. Though our vista of history is rather short up to date—extending back, as it does, over no more than a few thousand years—it is already long enough for us to see that all secular institutions, whether they are states or nations or governments or languages or civilizations, have comparatively short lives compared with religions. We can be sure that Western civilization's role in history is going to be a minor one compared with the role of Christianity."

Wrote Toynbee, however, in warning: ". . . To purge Christianity of its exclusive-mindedness is a much harder task than to purge it of its Western accretions. The vein of exclusiveness and intolerance in Christianity is not, I should say, an especially Western deformation of Christianity; it is a congenital feature. . . . Yet, however hard it may be to purge Christianity of its exclusive-mindedness, it seems imperative for Christians to achieve this spiritual feat, and this for a number of

reasons. The paramount reason is that exclusive-mindedness is a sinful state of mind. It is the sin of pride, and we know that the sin of pride is an arch sin, because it is a gateway for the entry of all the other sins, and a roadblock across the path of repentance."

"The Greatest Man in the World"

The twentieth-century missionary was still mistrusted because of his association with the West, but he had frequently learned to adjust himself to new political and social problems. The old attitude toward missions seemed to many to be reflected in the life of Albert Schweitzer. The new attitude was explained in 1964 by a group of six American missionaries to countries around the world—Europe, Africa, Japan, South America, and Turkey. Asked by an American magazine reporter what practical results they had achieved in the countries where they worked, the six pointed out that the question was a conspicuous example of American Protestantism's narrow point of view. American Prot-

estants, they pointed out, want to see visible results—in accordance with their own standards of "good." The missionaries pointed out that they had not become missionaries "simply to *give* something, as if we are playing Santa Claus to others." "We are," they said, "there to *give* and to *receive* as Christian brothers—to be *reconciled* to each other. . . . We are in other lands—and we must be—to *work together* with indigenous Christian churches in all countries. We're there to join the indigenous Christian community and thus to work for international, inter-racial, inter-tribal, inter-caste, inter-what-ever-you-have *reconciliation*." It was an attitude demonstrable in the rise of indigenous Christian missions *(lower right)* staffed by nationals in many a country throughout the world. It was also an attitude that, in Africa alone, stood in sharp contrast to the words of another "Christian," Rhodesian Prime Minister Ian Smith, who, following his seizure of the Rhodesian government in the fall of 1966, declared: "We Rhodesians have . . . struck a blow for the preservation of justice, civilization, and Christianity, and in the spirit of this belief we have this day assured our sovereign independence."

246

In the 1950's a Rhodesian artist envisioned the universal symbolism of the Bible as an African Christ tempted by a jungle devil.

An Indian serving as a Christian missionary in her own country here teaches a deaf-and-dumb child to "feel" sound. At right, one of the last remaining American Presbyterian missionaries in China just prior to the expulsion in 1951 of Western missionaries from Communist China gives medicine to Chinese orphans.

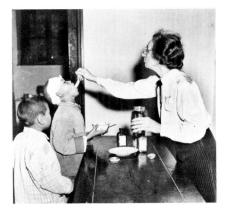

"Letter from a Birmingham Jail"

On April 16, 1963, the Rev. Martin Luther King, Jr., a Southern Baptist clergyman, addressed a letter to eight fellow clergymen, including one Jewish rabbi, from behind the bars of a jail in Birmingham, Alabama. Those who received the letter had called the civil rights activities of King's Southern Christian Leadership Conference "unwise and untimely." The letter, written on scraps of paper supplied to King by a friendly Negro trusty in the jail, pointed bluntly to the state of Protestantism—and Christianity—in mid-twentieth-century America. The Christian church, King said, had become "so often the archsupporter of the status quo." In the letter, too, he set forth his understanding of the meaning of Christianity, with direct reference not only to early Christendom and Reformation days but also to emerging twentieth-century theologies. These included the new theologies of Paul Tillich and Karl Barth (*pages 256-7*), as well as the great—and ecumenical—contribution to Christian theology made by the twentieth-century Jewish theologian Martin Buber (*pages 254-5*).

"My dear Fellow Clergymen:

"... You express a great deal of anxiety over our willingness to break laws. ... One may well ask, 'How can you advocate breaking some laws and obeying others?' The answer is found in the fact that there are two types of laws: There are just laws and there are unjust laws. I would agree with Saint Augustine that 'An unjust law is no law at all.'

"... A just law is a man-made code that squares with the moral law or the law of God. An unjust law is a code that is out of harmony with the moral law. To put it in the terms of Saint Thomas Aquinas, an unjust law is a human law that is not rooted in eternal and natural law. Any law that uplifts human personality is just. Any law that degrades human personality is unjust. ... To use the words of Martin Buber, the great Jewish philosopher, segregation substitutes an 'I-It' relationship for the 'I-Thou' relationship, and ends up relegating persons to the status of things. ... Paul Tillich has said that sin is separation. Isn't segregation an existential expression of man's tragic separation, an expression of his awful estrangement, his terrible sinfulness? So I can urge men to obey the 1954 decision of the Supreme Court because it is morally right, and I can urge them to disobey segregation ordinances because they are morally wrong.

"... If I lived in a Communist country today where certain principles dear to the Christian faith are suppressed, I believe I would openly advocate disobeying these antireligious laws.

"... You spoke of our activity in Birmingham as extreme. ...

"... Was not Martin Luther an extremist: 'I will stay in jail to the end of my days before I make a butchery of my conscience.'*

"... I must honestly reiterate that I have been disappointed with the church. I do not say [this] as one of those negative critics who can always find something wrong with the church. ... I say it as a minister of the gospel, who loves the church; who was nurtured in its bosom ...

".... In the midst of a mighty struggle to rid our nation of racial and economic injustice, I have heard so many ministers say, 'Those are social issues which the gospel has nothing to do with,' and I have watched so many churches commit themselves to a completely otherworldly religion which made a strange distinction between bodies and souls, the sacred and the secular.

"... The contemporary church is so often a weak, ineffectual voice with an uncertain sound. It is so often the archsupporter of the status quo. Far from being disturbed by the presence of the church, the power structure of the average community is consoled by the church's silent and often vocal sanction of things as they are.

"But the judgment of God is upon the church as never before. If the church of today does not recapture the sacrificial spirit of the early church, it will lose its authentic ring, forfeit the loyalty of millions, and be dismissed as an irrelevant social club with no meaning for the twentieth century. ...

"Yours for the cause of Peace and Brotherhood,

"Martin Luther King, Jr."

*In a later version of the letter, King correctly attributed this quote to Calvinist John Bunyan, author of *The Pilgrim's Progress*, instead of to Martin Luther, thereby inadvertently underscoring a historic distinction between the government-conscious early Lutherans and some early Calvinists.

Three Negroes were killed when this Negro Methodist church near Philadelphia, Mississippi, was burned down by fanatical whites in the southern U.S. in the mid-1960's.

"You deplore the demonstrations that are presently taking place in Birmingham," wrote Southern Baptist Martin Luther King in April, 1963. "But I am sorry that [you] did not express a similar concern for the conditions that brought the demonstrations into being." In a public meeting in Savannah, Georgia, that summer, youthful Ku Klux Klan members wore the Christian cross on their robes, while Protestant and Catholic churches joined together in the great "March on Washington" for civil rights and equal opportunities for jobs.

The Vatican Council

In 1959, John XXIII announced the first real attempt at reconciliation between Rome and the Protestant churches in five centuries. In Vatican Council II, which met in medieval splendor from 1962 to 1965, there were signs that the Catholic Church was examining itself in a new way. For the first time, the Roman church admitted past historical errors. In its criticism the Council specified the church's historic condemnation of Galileo, its backing of the Inquisition, and historic scandals of the papacy itself. Moreover, Rome for the first time in history recognized the Protestants as churches—*and* admitted its own "equal" responsibility for the long-standing divisions of Christianity. (It also avowed its "respect" for the positive values of non-Christian religions of the world, including Hinduism, Buddhism, and Islam, and it refused to condemn Communism.)

The Council brought about other reforms that were equally interesting. In an astonishing reform of the church's liturgy, it permitted the mass to be said in the vernacular of each country instead of in Latin. For the first time in history, Protestant hymns were permitted in Catholic worship, notable among them Martin Luther's "A Mighty Fortress Is Our God." Reminiscent of sixteenth-century Lutheran reforms, both these reforms shifted the traditional Catholic emphasis from the church as the basic hierarchy to a new emphasis on the "priesthood of all the faithful"—a phrase remarkably reminiscent of Martin Luther. In addition, plans were proposed for an interfaith translation of the Bible.

As if to prove the Roman church's good intentions, there were also other minor—but dramatic—reforms. In a reform reminiscent of Henry VIII's England as well as of Reformation Europe, the eleven-hundred-year-old abstinence from meat on Fridays was left to the discretion of bishops in individual countries. But there were also problems, and, with the death of John XXIII, there were those who

John XXIII was already an old man when he became pope in 1958, and his election was regarded as a compromise. But more than any other pope he became the hero of Protestants—and Jews—as well as Catholics. He once greeted a group of visiting Jews with the words, "I am Joseph your brother." On his deathbed he won the admiration of the entire world by praying for forgiveness of any sins he might have committed unknowingly during his life. The presence of his peasant relatives at his state funeral emphasized not only his complete lack of pretense but also his total sincerity.

feared that the reforms had come to a standstill. In one of the most disappointing of its compromises—a compromise calculated for Islamic ears—the Council, which continued to meet until 1965, issued a statement regarding the age-old Catholic dogma that the Jews were responsible for Jesus' crucifixion. In it, the Council missed the opportunity to state that, like all Christianity, the Catholic Church had fostered anti-Semitism over the centuries.

Moreover, the Council also failed to take a forthright stand limiting papal autocracy. And it failed to take a stand on the issue of interfaith marriages—and, in the midst of a world faced with overpopulation—to take an unequivocal stand on birth control though it dramatized a difference of opinion within the Council and a more positive attitude toward sexuality and family planning. In March, 1966, nevertheless, the pope's decree *Matrimonii sacramentum* relaxed some of the regulations governing mixed marriages. As a result, Catholics marrying non-Catholics before a non-Catholic minister were no longer to be excommunicated. In 1966, too, the pontifical commission on birth control submitted to Pope Paul a report in which the vast majority recommended leaving the question of the means of family planning to the consciences of married couples themselves.

On March 23, 1966, Arthur Michael Ramsey, Archbishop of Canterbury, and Pope Paul VI sat side by side in gold and red damask armchairs in front of Michelangelo's fresco "The Last Judgment" in the Sistine Chapel of the Vatican. The archbishop spoke in English. Then the pope spoke in Latin. The visit was primarily a friendly gesture. But it resulted in talks regarding unity by Anglicans and Roman Catholics in communities throughout the world. It was the first official visit to a pope by a head of the English church since, under Henry VIII, the church had broken away from Rome. Shortly thereafter, both the Roman and Eastern Orthodox churches officially "deplored" the age-old schism between them that had originated (pages 8-9) in 1054.

"God Is Dead!"

"I can tell you," announced the Rev. Billy Graham in 1966, "that God is [not dead] because I talked to him this morning." Graham was reacting to the new "God Is Dead" movement in the "post-Christian" era. But the "God Is Dead" school of theology had caught the popular fancy. In mid-twentieth century it echoed the same phrase uttered by Friedrich Nietzsche back in the nineteenth century—but with different overtones.

The new movement had originated with three young theological professors whose opinions are summarized at right, each of whom disagreed somewhat with the other two as to its meaning. Theologian Karl Barth *(pages 256-7)* had warned that God is wholly "other-being" and that any search for him that starts with human experience is a vain one. And from Dietrich Bonhoeffer *(pages 234-5),* the new school had taken the concept that modern man needs to develop a nonreligious interpretation of the Bible. The real point of the school was actually a paradox. It was an attempt to escape from a too-strict anthropomorphic past, in which God was envisioned in terms of man. What united the members of the "God Is Dead" movement was their agreement that the biblical God was "unreal" or "dead" for contemporary man, and that man must reconsider the meaning of the concept of a God, that no serious modern theologian would attempt to describe the qualities of God with the assurance of previous generations, and that any attempt to prove God by reason alone was doomed to failure. It was, they therefore explained, now necessary to declare God dead in order to discover him. Perhaps, they said, only when faced with the awful dread that God is dead could modern man really find the deepest meaning of life. In a way they were restating the Christian concept that man must face the brink of death in order to live.

There were critics who challenged them for merely substituting "Jesus-language" for "God-language." One theologian satirized the movement by quipping: "There is no God, and his only-begotten son is Jesus Christ, Our Lord." But there were others who stood just as solidly on the side of the "Death of God" school. One of these was the great theologian Paul Tillich. "I say yes to this movement," said Tillich firmly, "insofar as it points to something above the symbolic language concerning God."

TIME

THE WEEKLY NEWSMAGAZINE

Is God Dead?

The death of God, said Episcopalian Thomas J. J. Altizer, of Emory University, paradoxically, was essentially a redemptive act on the part of God. Instead of trying to put God back into human life, he said the Christian should welcome the total secularization of the modern world, on the grounds that it is only in the midst of the secular that man will be able to recapture an understanding of divinity. As a mystic, he rejected not only much of Christian tradition but also much of Western culture, in order to explore Eastern and primitive religious phenomena.

God's "death," said Baptist theologian William H. Hamilton, of Colgate-Rochester Divinity School, means that man has neither faith nor hope. Only love is left. Therefore man must look to the ethics of Jesus as a model for love and service to his fellow man.

Religion is man's imagination, said Episcopalian Paul Van Buren of Temple University. But, he implied paradoxically, it is in imagination that God actually lives.

253

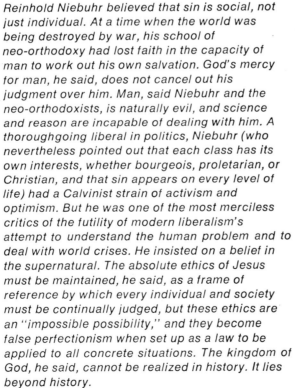

Reinhold Niebuhr believed that sin is social, not just individual. At a time when the world was being destroyed by war, his school of neo-orthodoxy had lost faith in the capacity of man to work out his own salvation. God's mercy for man, he said, does not cancel out his judgment over him. Man, said Niebuhr and the neo-orthodoxists, is naturally evil, and science and reason are incapable of dealing with him. A thoroughgoing liberal in politics, Niebuhr (who nevertheless pointed out that each class has its own interests, whether bourgeois, proletarian, or Christian, and that sin appears on every level of life) had a Calvinist strain of activism and optimism. But he was one of the most merciless critics of the futility of modern liberalism's attempt to understand the human problem and to deal with world crises. He insisted on a belief in the supernatural. The absolute ethics of Jesus must be maintained, he said, as a frame of reference by which every individual and society must be continually judged, but these ethics are an "impossible possibility," and they become false perfectionism when set up as a law to be applied to all concrete situations. The kingdom of God, he said, cannot be realized in history. It lies beyond history.

The myths of the New Testament tempt men to base their faith on the history of the past instead of on the future, said Lutheran Rudolf Bultmann. The Bible, he said, must be stripped— or "demythologized"—of its fictional heaven-above, hell-below framework. Its message must be restated in ideas that make sense today. The mythological concepts of heaven and hell, he believed, are no longer acceptable to modern man, since to speak of a heaven "above" and a hell "below" in a scientific age obscures the meaning. But Bultmann argued for the concept of a transcendent God. God, he said, is an objective occurrence in the world. As a Lutheran he argued that justification is by faith alone. A Christian, he said, has to base his faith upon a trust in the future. His detractors criticized him for going too far in separating God from biblical miracles and for reading the story of Jesus' birth without supposing that its validity depends on a literal interpretation of a supernatural occurrence. It is said that the German Evangelical Church would like to try him for heresy if it could find a prosecutor who would be his match in theology.

"The old distinctions between religion and non-religion are dead," said the great twentieth-century Jewish philosopher Martin Buber. "Religion has nothing to do with church attendance as such nor with doctrinal beliefs as such. These old distinctions are utterly meaningless in the present situation. Those who call themselves religious and those who call themselves non-religious must join hands to find the first steps out of our human situation. In his readiness to do this, the agnostic or even the atheist may be more religious than his believing neighbor." Buber doubted that man was made to conform to canon law or to elaborately worked out plans for existence. On the contrary, he stressed individual responsibility. God, said Buber, is personal, and man can achieve an intimate relationship with God through intimate interrelationship with his fellow man—and each man's relationship with God and his fellow man is distinct. The Bible, he said, is neither an infallible guide to conduct nor a mere collection of legends. It is a "dialogue" between ancient Israel and its God. Thus Buber strove for a "dialogue" between modern man and God. He called this dialogue an "I-Thou" relationship. The "I," he said, can exist only as it comes into relationship with another being. The "I-Thou" relationship treats the "Thou" as possessing an end, purpose, or meaning of its own. This relationship is exactly the opposite of an "I-It" relationship that man experiences in his relationship with objects, things, or "its." Such a relationship, which simply uses objects—or persons as objects—keeps the "I" from being fulfilled.

"The way we treat people is the way we treat God," said Roman Catholic Pierre Teilhard de Chardin, who has been regarded as a twentieth-century Thomas Aquinas. He tried to combine the secular with the spiritual. But he was also surprisingly nontraditional as a Roman Catholic. In the midst of anxiety and confusion, every Christian must, he said, strive for his own synthesis of all the facts of human existence, the universe, and God.

The Twentieth-Century Theologians

If there were those who believed the twentieth century is a post-Christian era in which God has died, there were others who were also treading the path of theology, sometimes more traditionally, sometimes in brand-new ways. In the second half of the twentieth century these theologians, some of them non-Protestant, were contributing their concepts of God to a changing—and more ecumenical —Christian theology. The new theologians included the Catholic Pierre Teilhard de Chardin and the great Jewish philosopher Martin Buber.

"God Is Bigger Than We Think"

What do the two greatest Protestant theologians of the mid-twentieth century say of the nature of God? And, equally important to the present-day Protestant, how do they arrive at their conclusions? In keeping with Protestant history, their views are frequently as different as day and night.

In 1918, a thirty-two-year-old Swiss theologian, Karl Barth, published a revolutionary book which, it was said by one theologian, "fell like a bomb on the playground of the theologians." His book was entitled *Commentary on Romans.* In it Barth announced his school of thought known as neo-orthodoxy, a school whose chief exponent in the U.S. has been the widely known Reinhold Niebuhr. As a neo-orthodoxist he uncompromisingly attacked the modernist Protestant tendency to accommodate Christianity to the pragmatic values of the world. Equally uncompromisingly, he returned to the Reformation doctrine of salvation by grace—through Christ alone. The Bible,

By the mid-1960's the two men shown here had long stood in the forefront of Protestant thought concerning the nature of God. Karl Barth (left) was a Calvinist. The other, Paul Tillich (right), who died in 1965, had been reared a Lutheran but had Calvinist leanings. Barth was neo-orthodox; reacting strongly against Nazism, he insisted on a return to biblical religion in opposition to modernist tendencies. His theology was a "theology of crisis." Tillich was basically an existentialist, finding God through human experience. As a result he had become the favorite theologian of laymen. By contrast, Barth was perhaps a clergyman's theologian. But both agreed on one basic point in their concept of God in the midst of an atomic, fragmented, psychiatric age: the real God, they agreed, is bigger than man can envision.

said Barth, is a human book written in human language—as opposed to divine symbolism. But it is, he argued, the absolutely valid word of God. As a Calvinist, he insisted on God's infinite and transcendent sovereignty. There was, however, an important distinction between Karl Barth and John Calvin. For Barth, the key to God's nature lies in the freedom he has given to man. In almost paradoxical language, Barth announced, "God exists, speaks, and acts as the partner of man." But, said he, the freedom in which God thus exists, speaks, and acts "is" his deity. It is, he said, impossible to speculate about the divine nature, so far separated is man from God. Scornfully, he struck out at the liberal Christian who cannot understand why, as he put it, "one cannot speak of God simply by speaking of man in a loud voice." "Men," he said, "are not competent, even if they are gifted with tongues of fire, to speak of God otherwise than in a parable." God, he said, is objective, not the subjective creation of men's minds.

If, for Barth, God was bigger than man can conceive, so, too, was the God of Barth's greatest contemporary, Paul Tillich. But there was still a vast abyss between the two men. Tillich was an existentialist (and he was frequently embarrassed about such questions as the literal Resurrection and the Virgin Birth, both of which he regarded as symbols of non-literal ideals). His theology—which he frequently considered to be as much a philosophy as a theology—was always in response to man's life in man's actual environment. For him, a religion shut up in itself rather than in two-way communication with the prevailing culture had no meaning. For him, God was not "the highest being" or "out there" but the depth of men's personal relationship with other men, the depth of all experience, but "interpreted by love." Sin was the separation

of man from his "ground of being," as Tillich called it (or, in old-fashioned terms, "grace"). "The man who stands on many boundaries," he wrote in terms of twentieth-century men, "experiences the unrest, insecurity, and inner limitation of existence in many forms." Yet without an awareness of the transcendent, Tillich believed, life becomes superficial.

Since every human institution is conditional, he argued, no human institution can speak for an unconditional divinity. He asked men to look for life's realities, not outside the world but in the depths that lie within it. He also insisted that Christianity be open to the religions of other cultures. "A Christian theology which is not able to enter into a creative dialogue with the theological thought of other religions," he wrote, "misses a world-historical occasion and remains provincial." As a philosopher-theologian, Paul Tillich was able to look into what might seem to some the negativity of the world. In that very negativity he found meaning. In it also, he found what seemed to be the meaning of life—or, as he put it, "the courage to be"—even in the midst of the ever more limiting conformity and collectivism surrounding twentieth-century man. "It is not astonishing," he once wrote, "that those who are unshaken in their courage to be ... are disturbed by the expressions of the existentialist courage of despair. They are unable to understand what is happening in our period. . . . They attack as morbid longing for negativity what in reality is courageous acceptance of the negative. They call decay what in reality is the creative expression of decay. They reject as meaningless the meaningful attempt to reveal the meaninglessness of our situation. . . . [The Christian] should realize that the courage to be as oneself is the necessary corrective to the courage to be as [a conformist or a collectivist]."

God, said theologian Paul Tillich, who died in the U.S. in 1965, is bigger than man thinks. Though his language was frequently obscure, it often appealed to twentieth-century man, who was frequently inclined to shrug his shoulders or throw up his hands about present-day theologians. Man, said Tillich, who believed in a nonpersonal force as a God, must, like men in all ages, learn to accept "the infinite tension between Yes and No"—a courage which, he said, is "possible because there is a Yes above the Yes and No of Life and of Truth." "But," he added, "it is a Yes which is not ours."

Acknowledgments

The complete design of this book, together with all pictorial layouts, was created and executed by Mr. Al Corchia, Jr., of The Corchia Group, Inc., New York City. Without his genuine talent, understanding, patience—and hard work —the completion of the book itself would not remotely have been possible.

I wish to express my gratitude to Professor Jaroslav Pelikan, Titus Street Professor of Ecclesiastical History at Yale University Divinity School, and to Professor Robert T. Handy, of Union Theological Seminary, for their careful reading of the manuscript in order that accuracy might be assured. I am equally deeply indebted to Professor Roland Bainton of Yale, not only for permission to quote from his superb biography of Martin Luther entitled *Here I Stand,* published by the Abingdon Press, but also for facts and interpretations of the life of Luther on which I have relied heavily in the early pages of this book. As a biography of a Protestant reformer, Professor Bainton's work ranks in a class by itself and should be recommended to all serious students of Protestantism.

I am also particularly grateful to Martin W. Robertson, son of Archie Robertson, author of "The King and Us," which first appeared in *Horizon* Magazine, for permission to freely use material about the missionary Dan Beach Bradley in Siam from that article.

William Glover of The Granger Collection, New York City, has, as a glance at the listing of picture credits will attest, supplied numerous illustrations for the book. I am also indebted for illustrations to Culver Pictures, Inc., of New York, and especially to the patience of Mr. Richard Meyer of that agency; to Dr. Otto Bettmann of the Bettmann Archive, Inc., New York, whose understanding of the length of time necessary for completing the project has helped materially to make the work possible; and to Miss Fern Magonet of Time, Inc.

Miss Catherine Oleson of Holt, Rinehart and Winston has, in addition to the normal laborious chores of copy editing, painstakingly checked details throughout the manuscript over a period of several months—and far above and beyond the call of duty; and I wish also to express my gratitude to Mr. David Zable of the Holt, Rinehart and Winston production department for his care and patience in the production details of the book.

The institutions and persons that have kindly provided research information would fill more than the space allotted, but I wish especially to thank the Rev. Dr. Ralph Stoody, former national Director of Press Relations of the Methodist Church; Mr. William B. Miller of the Presbyterian Historical Society; Miss Dorothy G. Harris, Associate Director of Friends Historical Library of Swarthmore College; Mr. John Taylor of the World Council of Churches in Geneva, Switzerland; the staff of the library of the Protestant Episcopal Church Center, New York; the Rev. E. H. Swavely of the Museum of the Moravian Historical Society, Nazareth, Pennsylvania; and the staffs of the Lutheran Theological Seminary Library, Germantown, Pennsylvania, and of the New York Public Library Picture Collection.

Without the help and encouragement of Mr. Edward Greif, Mr. Raymond Walters, Jr., and Mr. Arthur Cohen, this book could never have been begun. I am indebted also for aid, advice, encouragement—and, perhaps most of all, for forbearance—to the Rev. Dr. Everett C. Parker, Director of the Office of Communication of the United Church of Christ; to Mr. Allen Churchill, Miss Rochelle Girson, Miss Ethel M. Fair, Mr. Joseph Cunneen, Miss Marion Lazos, Mr. Parker Connors, Mrs. Ethel Walker, and Mr. Geoffrey Sowers; and, by no means least, to members of the staff of the Stewardship Council of the United Church of Christ, most especially the Rev. Dr. Sheldon E. Mackey and the Rev. Theodore S. Horvath, the Rev. Dr. Nelson C. Dreier, Miss Mary Lou Pettit, Mrs. Elizabeth Riddiough, Miss Dorothy Swedberg, Mrs. Mary Ella Brown, the Rev. David H. Sandstrom, the Rev. Albert C. Ronander, the Rev. William E. Wimer, and the Rev. Charles W. Cooper, Jr.

Picture Credits

Unless otherwise noted, the following abbreviations have been used:

Bettmann: The Bettmann Archive, Inc., New York City.
Brown: Brown Brothers, New York City.
Culver: Culver Pictures, Inc., New York City.
Granger: The Granger Collection, New York City.
N.Y.P.L.: The New York Public Library Picture Collection.

Frontispiece, Culver.

Introduction, Culver.

2. The British Museum, London.

3. Fratelli Alinari, Florence, Italy.

5. Edizioni Brogi, Sienna, Italy.

6. Archives photographiques, Paris, from miniature of Syriac gospel now in British Museum.

7. Granger.

8. Biblioteca Nacional, Madrid.

9. Granger.

10. *Left,* Granger; *right,* Brown.

11. *Upper left,* N.Y.P.L.; *center,* Granger; *right,* Brown; *bottom,* Culver.

12. Granger.

13. N.Y.P.L.

14. Culver.

15. Granger; *except for lower right,* Culver.

16. *Left,* Granger; *center and right,* Bettmann.

17. Granger; *except for upper left,* Culver.

19. Granger.

20. Granger.

21. Granger.

23. Culver.

25. Culver.

26. *Upper left,* Bettmann; *bottom,* Granger.

27. Granger; *except for upper right,* Culver.

28. Granger.

29. *Top,* Culver; *lower left,* N.Y.P.L.; *lower right,* Bettmann.

30. Brown.

31. *Upper left and right,* N.Y.P.L.; *lower left and right,* Granger.

32. Bettmann.

33. Granger.

34. N.Y.P.L.

36. Granger.

37. Granger.

38. Granger.

39. *Top,* Granger; *bottom,* Bettmann.

40. Culver.

42. N.Y.P.L., courtesy Theodore S. Horvath.

43. Culver.

44. N.Y.P.L.

46. N.Y.P.L.

47. N.Y.P.L.; *except for bottom center,* Culver.

48. Granger.

49. *Top,* Bettmann; *bottom,* Granger.

50. Culver.

51. *Top,* Granger; *bottom,* Culver.

52. Culver.

53. Culver.

54. *Top,* Granger; *bottom,* Culver.

55. Granger.

56. *Upper left,* Granger; *upper right,* Brown; *lower left,* Granger; *lower right,* N.Y.P.L.

57. Granger.

59. Granger.

60. Granger.

61. *Top,* Culver; *bottom,* Granger.

62. *Left,* Granger; *right,* Culver.

63. Granger; *except for extreme right, bottom row,* Culver.

64. Granger.

65. *Top and lower left,* Bettmann; *lower right,* Culver.

66. Granger.

67. Granger.

68. Granger.

69. Culver.

70. Granger.

71. American Bible Society.

72. N.Y.P.L.

73. Granger.

74. N.Y.P.L.

75. *Top and center,* Granger; *bottom,* Bettmann.

76. *Top,* reproduced by gracious permission of Her Majesty Queen Elizabeth, The Queen Mother; *bottom,* Granger.

77. Granger; *except for top right,* N.Y.P.L.

78. Granger

79. Granger.

81. Culver.

82. N.Y.P.L.

83. Granger; *except for lower right,* Culver.

84. Granger.

85. Culver; *except for top left,* Granger.

86. Lutheran Theological Seminary Library, Germantown, Pa.

87. Granger.

88. Brown.

89. Granger.

91. *Top,* Culver; *bottom,* Granger.

92. Culver.

93. Culver.

94. Culver.

95. Culver.

96. Culver.

97. *Top,* Brown; *lower left,* Granger; *lower right,* Bettmann.

98. Brown.

99. Friends Historical Library of Swarthmore College, Swarthmore, Pa.

100. Culver.

101. Culver.

102. N.Y.P.L.

104. N.Y.P.L.

105. N.Y.P.L.

106. Culver.

107. Framed *Fraktur,* by Heinrich Otto, Pennsylvania Dutch, 1760–1770. Collection of the Philadelphia Museum of Art: Titus C. Geesey Collection.

108. The Presbyterian Historical Society.

109. *Top,* N.Y.P.L.; *bottom,* Granger.

110. Granger.

111. Culver.

112. Granger.

113. Granger.

114. Association of Methodist Historical Societies.

115. Granger.

116. Culver.

117. *Top,* Culver; *lower left,* The William L. Clements Library, University of Michigan, Ann Arbor, Mich.; *lower right,* The Museum of the Moravian Historical Society, Nazareth, Pa.

118. Granger.

119. Granger.

120. Granger.

121. Granger; *except for top,* Culver.

122. Granger.

124. Granger.

125. Granger.

127. Congregational Library, American Congregational Association.

128. Granger.

129. *Top,* Granger; *bottom,* N.Y.P.L.

130. Granger.

131. Granger; *except for top,* Bettmann.

132. *Top,* N.Y.P.L.; *center,* Granger; *bottom,* Culver.

133. *Top,* Presbyterian Historical Society; *bottom,* Granger.

134. Culver.

135. *Upper left,* Granger; *upper center and right,* Culver; *bottom,* N.Y.P.L.

136. The Historical Society of the Eastern Conference of the Evangelical United Brethren Church.

137. The Lewis Miller drawing is furnished courtesy of The Historical Society of York County, Pa., from its book entitled *Lewis Miller, 1796–1882: Sketches and Chronicles,* published 1966; by permission of Robert P. Turner, President; photo by Henry M. Blatner, York, Pa.

138. From *Manuscript,* Illuminated *Fraktur* work, American, Pennsylvania German, G. S. Peters, early 19th century; Collection of the Philadelphia Museum of Art.

139. Granger.

141. Granger.

142. Granger.

143. *Top,* Granger; *bottom,* Culver.

144. Inspirational drawing, American, Shaker Collection of the Philadelphia Museum of Art.

145. *Top,* N.Y.P.L.; *bottom,* Culver.

146–147. Old Dartmouth Historical Society and Whaling Museum, New Bedford, Mass.

148. *Left,* Bettmann; *right,* Culver.

149. *Top,* Granger; *bottom,* Culver.

150. *Left,* Granger; *right,* Culver.

151. Granger; *except for upper left,* Culver, *and upper right,* N.Y.P.L.

152. Granger.

153. Granger.

154. N.Y.P.L.

156. Congregational Library, American Congregational Association.

157. Congregational Library, American Congregational Association; *except for upper right,* Granger.

159. N.Y.P.L.

161. Granger.

162. Congregational Library, American Congregational Association.

163. Culver.

164. The Bradley Family Album, courtesy William L. Bradley.

165. Donald H. Rochelin.

166. Granger.

167. *Top,* Granger; *bottom,* Culver.

168. Eden Theological Seminary Archives, Webster Groves, Mo., courtesy Dr. Carl E. Schneider.

169. Bettmann.

171. Courtesy Chao-Ying Fang, East Asian Institute, Columbia University

172. Bettmann.

173. *Upper left,* Culver; *upper and lower right,* Granger; *lower left,* Bettmann.

174. Culver.

175. *Top,* Library of Congress; *bottom,* Culver.

176. Granger.

177. Granger.

179. Granger.

180. Granger.

181. *Top,* Granger, *bottom,* N.Y.P.L.

182. Granger.

183. Granger.

184. Eden Theological Seminary Archives, Webster Groves, Mo., courtesy Dr. Carl E. Schneider.

185. Culver.

186. *Top,* Culver; *bottom,* N.Y.P.L.

187. Granger.

188. Culver.

189. Granger; *except for center,* N.Y.P.L.

191. Victoria and Albert Museum, London.

192. *Top,* reproduced by permission © 1952 The Christian Science Publishing Society. All rights reserved. *Bottom,* Culver.

193. Granger; *except for lower left,* Culver.

194. Culver.

195. Culver; *except for right center,* Bettmann; *and right bottom,* Granger.

196. Friends Historical Library of Swarthmore College, Swarthmore, Pa.

197. *Top,* Friends Historical Library of Swarthmore College, Swarthmore, Pa.; *bottom,* Old Dartmouth Historical and Whaling Museum, New Bedford, Mass.

198. Culver.

199. Culver.

200. *Left,* Granger; *right,* Culver.

201. Granger.

202. Granger.

203. Culver, *except bottom,* Granger.

204. N.Y.P.L.

205. *Top,* Granger; *center and bottom,* Brown.

206. Granger.

207. Granger.

209. Granger.

210. *Top,* Granger; *bottom,* N.Y.P.L.

211. *Top,* Culver; *lower left,* Brown; *lower right,* Granger.

212. Brown.

213. *Top,* Granger; *lower left,* Culver; *lower right,* Brown.

214. Presbyterian Historical Society.

215. *Top,* Culver; *bottom,* Congregational Library, American Congregational Association.

216. Congregational Library, American Congregational Association.

217. The Hoover Institution, Stanford University, Stanford, Calif.

219. Culver.

221. *Left,* Granger; *right,* Author.

223. *Top,* Harris & Ewing, courtesy Gilloon Photo Agency, New York; *bottom,* W. Eugene Smith, *Life* Magazine © Time, Inc.

225. *Top,* Culver; *bottom,* from a woodcut by Helen Siegel, in possession of Christ Church, Philadelphia.

226. Granger.

227. Granger; *except for upper left,* Associated Press.

229. Robert Newman.

230. Culver.

231. Culver.

233. Magnum Photos, Inc., by Cornell Capa.

234. Wide World Photos.

235. *Top and lower left,* Walter Sanders, *Life* Magazine © Time, Inc.; *lower right,* courtesy *United Church Herald.*

236. Magnum Photos, Inc., by Henri Cartier-Bresson.

237. Magnum Photos, Inc., by Henri Cartier-Bresson.

239. Larry Burrows, *Life* Magazine © Time, Inc.

240. World Council of Churches, Geneva, Switzerland.

241. Mark Kauffman, *Life* Magazine © Time, Inc.; *except for lower left,* Association of Methodist Historical Societies.

243. Illustration by Milton Glaser originally appeared as the jacket design for *Pen-ultimates: The Follies, Ploys, and Ironies of Contemporary Religion* as recorded by Martin E. Marty and Dean Peerman, published by Holt, Rinehart and Winston, Inc., 1963; reproduced by permission of Milton Glaser.

244. Leon V. Kofod.

245. Leon V. Kofod.

246. Charles R. Joy, Beacon Press, Boston, Mass.

247. *Top left,* Makarere (East Africa) College Art School, Rhodesia; Mr. K. M. Trowell's Collection, Photo by Evita-Jacoba, edita, Lausanne, Switzerland; *lower left,* Leon V. Kofod; *lower right,* Congregational Library, American Congregational Association.

248. Kenneth Thompson.

249. Kenneth Thompson.

250. Religious News Service.

251. Associated Press; *except for upper right,* ANSA.

253. Courtesy *Time* magazine, © 1966, Time, Inc.

254. Wide World Photos.

255. *Left,* David Rubinger, *Life* Magazine, © Time, Inc.; *right,* Philippe Halsman, copyright by Philippe Halsman.

256. Doris Rosenfeld, *DU* Magazine, Zurich.

257. Archie Lieberman.

Index

264

A Simplified Chart of Protestantism

Early Church   Roman Catholicism

1415
Hussites
John Hus

GERMAN-SCANDINAVIAN REFORMATION

1054*
Eastern Orthodoxy

Gnostics

1517
Lutheranism
Martin Luther

German Lutherans

452
Coptic Church

1523
Scandinavian Lutherans
Christian II

1173
Waldensians
Peter Waldo

GERMAN-SWISS REFORMATION

1521
Anabaptism

Ca. 1536
Mennonites
Menno Simons

Amish
Jacob Ammon

1647
Quakers
George Fox

Ca. 1606
English Baptists
John Smyth

1560
Congregationalism
Puritans

Ca. 1379
Lollards
John Wycliffe

ENGLISH REFORMATION

1534
Anglicanism
Henry VIII

GERMAN-SWISS-NETHERLANDS-SCOTTISH-FRENCH-HUNGARIAN REFORMATION

1523
Zwinglianism
Huldreich Zwingli

German, Dutch, and Hungarian Reformed Churches

1536
Calvinism
John Calvin

French Calvinists [Huguenots]

*Dates indicate approximate year of final divisions, without reference to the long prehistory of such divisions.

Ca. 1560
Scottish Presbyterians
John Knox

MESSIANISM   HELLENISTIC LOGIC   ARISTOTELIANISM   RENAISSANCE   HUMANISM   NATIONALISM   COVENANT THEOLOGY   PIETISM

18TH CENTURY | **19TH CENTURY** | **20TH CENTURY**

Ca. 1722
Moravians
Count Nikolaus Ludwig von Zinzendorf

1789
Swedenborgians
Emmanuel Swedenborg

1776
Shakers
Ann Lee

Ca. 1828
Hicksites
Elias Hicks

1863
Seventh-Day Adventists
William Miller

1879
Christian Science
Mary Baker Eddy

1819
Unitarianism
U. S.: William Ellery Channing

1785
Protestant Episcopal Church

1833
Anglo-Catholicism

1739
Methodism
John Wesley

1865
Salvation Army
William Booth

1807
Evangelical Association
Jacob Albright

1800
United Brethren in Christ
Philip Otterbein

MOST UNIONS AND TALKS OF UNIONS ARE TAKING PLACE IN THIS AREA PLUS A FEW GROUPS OF LUTHERAN ORIGIN

1831
Disciples of Christ
Thomas Campbell

1827
Christian Churches
Barton W. Stone

DEISM
MILLENNARIANISM
ROMANTICISM
GERMAN IDEALISM
ORIENTAL RELIGIONS
PANTHEISM
TRANSCENDENTALISM
MARXISM
DARWINISM
EXISTENTIALISM